FUNCTIONAL GERMAN

FUNCTIONAL GERMAN

MAX S. KIRCH
University of Delaware

HEINZ MOENKEMEYER
University of Pennsylvania

AMERICAN BOOK COMPANY   NEW YORK

PREFACE

Functional German stresses, as the title implies, a practical and realistic approach to language learning. The authors have depended systematically and consistently on the principle that oral control is best achieved through development of automatic response acquired by frequent repetition of speech patterns. It is their belief, based on classroom experiment, that the competent teacher, within the limits of a traditional three- or four-hour-per-week course, can achieve important and satisfying results by the application of this principle as set forth in this text. It should be noted, however, that the authors have included description of grammar, as well as abundant material for writing practice, as necessary elements in a thorough presentation. Both instructors and students, therefore, are invited to read carefully the following explanation of the authors' method and their recommendations with regard to classroom and study practices.

The text is so constructed that the student may do any given section of any lesson by working with the material of that section, provided that the material of the previous sections has been mastered to the point where memory and use are efficient. This facilitates the problem of dividing the lessons to fit available classroom time, for the day's work may be started or ended at any point in the lesson unit, provided, of course, that the sections are studied consecutively. Thus, though each section presents new material, as well as making use of previously learned subject matter, it does not require reference to subsequent sections.

Each lesson unit contains the following sections:

A. Units of Speech and Vocabulary. The phrases, word combinations, and words included in the A I section are the basic elements which are used to build up sentences and more complicated thought patterns. In mastering these minimum units, the student should try to approximate through imitation the pronunciation and intonation of the instructor, who, it is expected, will read them aloud to the class prior to assigning the lessons. In any event, the student should express the units aloud from the beginning.

The student should then study and read aloud the A I section outside of class until he is reasonably familiar with meaning and has developed some facility of articulation. The A II section provides for oral repetitive drill in various patterns of the A I units of speech, together with similar previously learned material. When the material is subsequently recited in class, it is suggested that the books be closed and that the instructor give the English version. *The student, however, should not be encouraged to think that he is translating the material thus presented, but rather that a language situation is being set up to which he is to respond as automatically as possible and by means of recall of learned material.* Much of the success of the method will be in proportion to the skill with which the instructor is able to develop an atmosphere of ready and natural response.

B. Model Sentences. After the minimum units of speech, the sentence pattern is presented as the next natural step in achieving language control. The authors have attempted to make the sentences functional—that is, sentences that are likely to be encountered in everyday speech. The model sentences contained in the thirty lesson units present all the essential grammatical and syntactical elements ordinarily included in beginning texts. The mastery and ready recall of these sentences thus provides the student with a pattern for the expression of any construction he is likely to need in normal everyday speech. The student should strive, therefore, to master these sentences in his outside study through oral expression, and the instructor is encouraged to call for their frequent classroom repetition. In the B II sections, the model sentences are varied by substitutions of units of speech already learned for purposes of further drill and control of the grammatical principle involved. Thus the variations of each model sentence serve to integrate the new element of learning with previously established language patterns.

C. Grammar. The grammar (with the exception of inflected forms) may be considered primarily as a description of the linguistic practices involved in the material *already learned and used.* In assigning the presentation of the grammar this position in the lesson unit, the authors indicate their belief that language control is a repetitively and imitatively conditioned response to a given linguistic situation far more than it is a mathematical application of linguistic theorems and corollaries. The authors recognize that the student who studies and uses this material will inevitably be assisted in improving and refining his usage.

D. Exercises. The D sentences are further variations of model sentences or new combinations of them. Since these sentences imply a knowledge of C, particularly with respect to inflected forms, they require more careful thought than is involved in the drill practice afforded by previous sections. It is suggested that the D sentences be written to establish the relationships implied between oral and written controls and to provide the written practice which is necessary for progress toward language mastery. It will be noted, however, that although the D sentences are to be written outside class, the directions call for their oral use in class.

E. Reading and Speaking. The primary purpose of the reading section is to illustrate the language control achieved at a given point. Since the E I passages thus represent the logical synthesis of material learned up to that point, they properly belong at the end of the lesson unit. This is consistent with the assumption that language skill develops naturally from unit of speech to sentence to connected paragraph. It is the authors' practice to have their students read the passages aloud as an individual recitation or as dialogue in order to give opportunity for the achievement of rhythm and intonation such as can come only through connected passages. Additional opportunity for oral use of these passages is provided by the E II questions, which allow the instructor to check comprehension of the entire passage and enable the student to practice what he has already learned, as well as to experiment with variety of expression. To this end, the E I passages are of such a nature that they may be used as the starting point for further dialogue or oral accounts of subject matter related to the students' daily living.

The materials embodied in this text have been tested over a period of three years. In classes meeting three times a week, the authors have found it possible to cover the A, B, and C sections in one class hour and the remainder in a second hour for the first half of the text. For the second half, each unit requires two and a half class hours. With this division of time, ample opportunity for supplementary reading is provided. In addition, the text has been used over the same three-year period in classes to which a language laboratory was available. The A and B sections were presented to the students in the laboratory, where they were able to learn and drill the Units of Speech and Vocabulary, as well as the Model Sentences. The materials were found admirably suited for laboratory work.

These suggestions are meant to be a guide to instructors using the text, rather than a categorical exposition of classroom method. The instructor will always find interesting and individual variations in technique. It has been the experience of the authors, however, that the learner who follows closely the spirit of the directions at the head of each section is the one who most rapidly achieves a satisfactory and stimulating oral control.

The authors wish to express their gratitude to Professors Wilmarth H. Starr, Alfred G. Pellegrino, and Henri A. Casavant, of the University of Maine, whose *Functional French* and *Functional Spanish* (both published by American Book Company) inspired them to develop this book, and who elaborated the basic description of the *Functional* method presented above.

CONTENTS

Im Hafen von Hamburg

Der Kölner Dom

Das Bundeshaus in Bonn

Am Rhein: die Lorelei

Frankfurt am Main: Eschenheimer Turm

Frankfurt am Main: Blick über den Main—rechts der Dom, links die Paulskirche

Am Rhein: die Burg Pfalz bei Kaub

Heidelberg: Schloß, Stadt und Neckar

Mainz: Gutenberg-Denkmal

In einem schwäbischen Gasthof

Schneebedeckte Berge in Oberbayern

Historisches Fest in Kaufbeuren (Bayern)

München: Frauenkirche und Rathaus bei Nacht

Wien: Tor zur Hofburg

Wien: Stephansdom

Die Schulkinder scheinen sich glänzend zu amüsieren

Hannover: auf den Messegeländen

An der Nordsee

☞ UNIT 1

A. UNITS OF SPEECH AND VOCABULARY

I. STUDY AND READ ALOUD.

Guten Morgen.	Good morning.
Wie geht es Ihnen?	How are you?
Es geht mir gut. Und Ihnen?	I'm fine. (I'm well.) And you?
Auch gut.	(I'm) fine, too. (I'm well, too.)
Danke.	Thanks. (Thank you.)
Auf Wiedersehen.	Good-by.

hat	has, is having, does have	**die Aufgabe**	the lesson
		eine Aufgabe	a lesson
haben	have, are having, do have	**das Buch**	the book
		ein Buch	a book
ist	is	**Frau**	Mrs.
sind	are	**Fräulein**	Miss
sagt	says, is saying, does say	**Herr**	Mr.
		das Kind	the child
sagen	say, are saying, do say	**der Lehrer**	the teacher
		ein Lehrer	a teacher
schreibt	writes, is writing, does write	**der Student**	the student
		die Studentin	the student, coed
schreiben	write, are writing, do write	**eine Studentin**	a student, coed

1

der Tisch	the table		**auch**	also, too
er	he, it		**dort**	there
sie	she, it, they		**hier**	here
es	it, he, she		**ja**	yes
was?	what?		**nein**	no
wer?	who?		**und**	and
wo?	where?			

II. DRILL. EXPRESS ORALLY IN GERMAN. REPEAT UNTIL IT IS NO LONGER
NECESSARY TO REFER TO SECTION I.

a. 1. Good morning. 2. Good morning, Mr. Schmidt. 3. Good morning, Mrs. Braun. 4. Good morning, Miss Meyer.

b. 1. How are you? 2. How are you, Mr. Braun? 3. How are you, Miss Schmidt? 4. How are you, Mrs. Meyer?

c. 1. I'm fine. 2. I'm fine. And you? 3. Thank you, I'm fine. 4. Thank you, I'm well. And you? 5. Thank you, I'm well. How are you? 6. I'm fine, too. 7. Thank you, I'm fine, too.

d. 1. . . . says . . . 2. The teacher says . . . 3. The teacher says "Good-by." 4. The child is saying "Good-by." 5. They are saying "Good-by." 6. They say "Good-by."

e. 1. . . . is writing . . . 2 The student (*f.*) is writing . . . 3. The student (*f.*) is writing the lesson. 4. The student writes the lesson. 5. The teacher and the student (*f.*) write. 6. They write. 7. They write the lesson. 8. They are writing the lesson.

f. 1. . . . has . . . 2. He has . . . 3. He has the book. 4. She has the book. 5. She has a book. 6. He has a book. 7. They have a book. 8. The student and the coed have the book.

g. 1. What . . . ? 2. What is . . . ? 3. What is here? 4. What is there? 5. What has . . . ? 6. What has she? 7. What have . . . ? 8. What have they?

h. 1. Who . . . ? 2. Who is the teacher? 3. Who is the student? 4. Who is the child? 5. Who is the student (*f.*)?

i. 1. Where . . . ? 2. Where is . . . ? 3. Where is the table? 4. Where are . . . ? 5. Where are the teacher and the child? 6. Where are they?

j. 1. . . . here 2. Is the table here? 3. Yes, the table is here. 4. Is the book there? 5. Yes, the book is there. 6. Is the table there? 7. No, the table is here. 8. Are the book and the table here? 9. No, they are there.

B. MODEL SENTENCES

I. STUDY UNTIL EACH SENTENCE CAN BE GIVEN CORRECTLY FROM THE ENGLISH.

1. Guten Morgen, Herr Schmidt. Wie geht es Ihnen?
2. Danke, es geht mir gut. Und Ihnen, Fräulein Braun?
3. Schreibt der Student die Aufgabe?—Ja, er schreibt sie.
4. Wo ist der Tisch?—Er ist hier.
5. Hat die Studentin ein Buch?—Ja, sie hat ein Buch.
6. Was schreibt das Kind?—Es schreibt eine Aufgabe.
7. Wer hat das Buch?—Der Lehrer hat es.

1. Good morning, Mr. Schmidt. How are you?
2. I'm fine, thanks. And you, Miss Braun?
3. Is the student writing the lesson?—Yes, he is writing it.
4. Where is the table?—It's here.
5. Does the student (*f.*) have a book?—Yes, she has a book.
6. What is the child writing?—He (she) is writing a lesson.
7. Who has the book?—The teacher has it.

II. DRILL. EXPRESS ORALLY IN GERMAN.

a. 1. Good morning, Mr. Schmidt. How are you? 2. Good morning, Miss Braun. How are you? 3. Good morning, Mrs. Meyer. How are you? 4. Good morning, Mr. and Mrs. Schmidt. How are you?

b. 1. I'm fine, thanks. And you, Miss Braun? 2. I'm fine, thanks. And you, Mrs. Schmidt? 3. I'm fine, thanks. And you, Mr. and Mrs. Meyer? 4. I'm fine, thanks. How are you? 5. I'm fine, too. 6. I'm fine, too, thanks.

c. 1. Is the student writing the lesson?—Yes, he is writing it. 2. Is the teacher writing the lesson?—Yes, he is writing it. 3. Is Mr. Schmidt writing the lesson?—Yes, he is writing it. 4. Is Mr. Meyer writing the lesson?—Yes, he is writing it.

d. 1. Where is the table?—It's here. 2. Where is the table?—It's there. 3. Is the table there?—Yes, it's there. 4. Is the table here?—No, it's there.

e. 1. Does the student (*f.*) have a book?—Yes, she has a book.
2. Does the student (*f.*) have the book?—Yes, she has the book.
3. Does the student (*f.*) have the lesson?—Yes, she has the lesson.
4. Does the student (*f.*) have a lesson?—Yes, she has a lesson.

f. 1. What is the child writing?—He (she) is writing a lesson.   2. What is the child writing?—He (she) is writing the lesson.   3. What is the child saying?—He (she) is saying "Good-by."   4. What is the child saying?—He (she) is saying "Good morning."

g. 1. Who has the book?—The teacher has it.   2. Who has the book?—The student has it.   3. Who has the book?—The child has it. 4. Who has the book?—The student (*f.*) has it.

C. GRAMMAR

1. German nouns are masculine, feminine, and neuter.

a. Masculine nouns use **der** as the subject form of the definite article. Nouns denoting male beings are usually in this category.

der Lehrer	the teacher
der Student	the student

But many names of inanimate things are also masculine.

der Tisch	the table

b. Feminine nouns use **die** as the subject (and direct object) form of the definite article. Nouns denoting female beings are usually in this category.

die Studentin	the student (*f.*), coed

The names of some inanimate things are also feminine.

die Aufgabe	the lesson

c. Neuter nouns use **das** as the subject (and direct object) form of the definite article. Neuter nouns include mostly inanimate objects.

das Buch	the book

The names of some animate beings are also neuter.

das Kind	the child

Note: All nouns in German are capitalized.

2. Masculine nouns use **ein** (a, an) for the subject form of the indefinite article.

ein Lehrer	a teacher

ein Student	a student
ein Tisch	a table

Feminine nouns use **eine** (a, an) for the subject (and direct object) form of the indefinite article.

eine Aufgabe	a lesson
eine Studentin	a student (*f.*), coed

Neuter nouns use **ein** (a, an) for the subject (and direct object) form of the indefinite article.

ein Buch	a book
ein Kind	a child

3. The pronoun used to replace the subject form of any masculine noun, regardless of whether it is animate or inanimate, is **er.** Either **der Student** or **der Tisch** is replaced by **er.**

   a. **Schreibt der Student die Aufgabe?—Ja, er schreibt die Aufgabe.**
   Is the student writing the lesson?—Yes, he is writing the lesson.

   b. **Wo ist der Tisch?—Er ist hier.**
   Where is the table?—It is here.

   Any feminine noun (subject and object forms) is replaced by **sie.**

   a. **Hat die Studentin ein Buch?—Ja, sie hat ein Buch.**
   Does the student (*f.*) have a book?—Yes, she has a book.

   b. **Schreibt der Student die Aufgabe?—Ja, er schreibt sie.**
   Is the student writing the lesson?—Yes, he is writing it.

   Any neuter noun (subject and object forms) is replaced by **es.**

   a. **Was schreibt das Kind?—Es schreibt eine Aufgabe.**
   What is the child writing?—He (she) is writing a lesson.

   b. **Wer hat das Buch?—Der Lehrer hat es.**
   Who has the book?—The teacher has it.

4. The German verb has only a single form for which English has three equivalent forms. For example, German **schreibt** may mean "writes," "is writing," "does write."

   Es schreibt eine Aufgabe.
   He (she) writes a lesson.
   He (she) is writing a lesson.
   He (she) does write a lesson.

5. Interrogative sentences usually begin, as in English, with an interrogative element.

   a. **Wo ist der Tisch?**
   Where is the table?

   b. **Was schreibt das Kind?**
      What is the child writing?
   c. **Wer hat das Buch?**
      Who has the book?
  Or, if there is no interrogative element, with the verb.
   d. **Schreibt der Student die Aufgabe?**
      Is the student writing the lesson?
   e. **Hat die Studentin ein Buch?**
      Does the student (*f.*) have a book?

D. EXERCISES

WRITE THE FOLLOWING SENTENCES IN GERMAN AND BE ABLE TO EXPRESS
THEM ORALLY IN CLASS.

1. Who has the book?—A child has the book.
2. Miss Meyer says "Good-by."
3. What is the teacher writing?
4. He is writing the lesson.
5. Here is a table. It's here.
6. Mr. and Mrs. Braun have a book.
7. A student and a coed are here.
8. Are they there?
9. What is the child saying?—He is saying "Good morning."
10. Is the child here?—No, she is there.
11. Does the student (*f.*) have the book?—Yes, she has it.
12. Does the student have the lesson here?—Yes, he has it here.
13. Where are they writing?
14. Where is Mr. Meyer?—He is there.
15. A teacher is writing the lesson.
16. They say "Good morning."

E. READING AND SPEAKING

I. READ THE FOLLOWING ALOUD UNTIL YOU ARE THOROUGHLY FAMILIAR
WITH IT.

Der Anfang[1]

Der Lehrer sagt: „Guten Morgen. Wie geht es Ihnen, Fräulein Braun?"

Die Studentin sagt: „Danke, es geht mir gut. Und Ihnen?"

„Danke, auch gut."

Die Studentin hat ein Buch und sie schreibt eine Aufgabe. Ein Student ist auch dort. Er schreibt auch die Aufgabe.

Der Lehrer sagt: „Auf Wiedersehen."

Der Student und die Studentin sagen: „Auf Wiedersehen."

II. ANSWER THE FOLLOWING QUESTIONS IN GERMAN.

1. Was sagt der Lehrer?
2. Was sagt die Studentin?
3. Was schreibt sie?
4. Wer schreibt auch die Aufgabe?
5. Wer sagt: „Auf Wiedersehen"?

[1] **Der Anfang**   The Beginning.

☞ UNIT 2

A. UNITS OF SPEECH AND VOCABULARY

I. STUDY AND READ ALOUD.

Wie heißen Sie?	What is your name?
Ich heiße Hans.	My name is Hans.
Wie heißt er?	What is his name?
Er heißt Robert.	His name is Robert.
Wie heißt sie?	What is her name?
Sie heißt Marie.	Her name is Marie.
in das Zimmer	into the room
an das Fenster	to the window
um zu lernen	in order to learn
um zu schreiben	in order to write

begrüßen	to greet, are greeting	**lernen**	to learn, to study, are learning, are studying
fragen	to ask, are asking		
gehen	to go, are going	**der Brief**	the letter
heißen	to be called, are called	**der Bruder**	the brother
		der Vater	the father
kommen	to come, are coming	**die Mutter**	the mother
		die Schwester	the sister
		die Tür	the door

8

der Onkel	the uncle		**die Eltern**	the parents
die Onkel	the uncles		**die Lehrer**	the teachers
das Fenster	the window		**ich**	I
die Fenster	the windows		**mich**	me
das Gebäude	the building		**wir**	we
die Gebäude	the buildings		**uns**	us
das Mädchen	the girl		**Sie**	you
die Mädchen	the girls		**ihn**	him, it
das Zimmer	the room		**sie**	her, it, them
die Zimmer	the rooms			

II. DRILL. EXPRESS ORALLY IN GERMAN. REPEAT UNTIL IT IS NO LONGER NECESSARY TO REFER TO SECTION I.

a. 1. What is your name? 2. My name is Hans. 3. What is your name? 4. My name is Marie. 5. What is his name? 6. His name is Robert. 7. What is her name? 8. Her name is Gretchen.

b. 1. . . . into the room. 2. They are coming into the room. 3. The girls are coming into the room. 4. The teachers are coming into the room. 5. The teachers are coming into the building. 6. The teachers are coming into the buildings. 7. The girls are coming into the rooms.

c. 1. . . . to the window. 2. They are going to the window. 3. The parents are going to the window. 4. The parents are going to the windows. 5. The parents go to the door. 6. The girls go to the door. 7. The teachers go to the door.

d. 1. . . . in order to learn. 2. . . . in order to write. 3. . . . in order to go. 4. . . . in order to study.

e. 1. . . . are greeting . . . 2. The father and the mother are greeting . . . 3. The father and the mother are greeting the sister. 4. The uncles are greeting the sister. 5. The brother and the sister are greeting the uncles. 6. The brother and the sister are greeting her. 7. The brother and the sister are greeting us. 8. The uncles are greeting us. 9. The uncles are greeting them.

f. 1. . . . are asking . . . 2. We are asking. 3. We are asking her. 4. We are asking him. 5. We are asking you. 6. You are asking me. 7. You are asking him. 8. He and she are asking me. 9. They are asking us. 10. The girls are asking them.

g. 1. ... the letter.   2. Where is the letter?   3. The letter is here.
4. The letter is there.

B. MODEL SENTENCES

I. STUDY UNTIL EACH SENTENCE CAN BE GIVEN CORRECTLY FROM THE
ENGLISH.

8. **Wie heißen Sie?**
9. **Ich heiße Hans.**
10. **Der Lehrer schreibt den Brief. Er schreibt ihn.**
11. **Die Eltern begrüßen einen Lehrer.**
12. **Die Lehrer gehen an die Tür.**
13. **Er schreibt um zu lernen.**

8. What is your name?
9. My name is Hans.
10. The teacher is writing the letter. He is writing it.
11. The parents are greeting a teacher.
12. The teachers are going to the door.
13. He writes in order to learn.

II. DRILL. EXPRESS ORALLY IN GERMAN.

a. 1. What is your name?   2. What is your name, miss?
b. 1. My name is Hans.   2. My name is Mr. Braun.   3. My name is
Marie.   4. My name is Miss Meyer.   5. My name is Mrs. Schmidt.
c. 1. The teacher is writing the letter. He is writing it.   2. The uncle
is writing the letter. He is writing it.   3. The uncles are writing the
letter. They are writing it.   4. The teachers are writing the letter.
They are writing it.   5. The uncle and the brother are writing the
letter. They are writing it.
d. 1. The parents are greeting a teacher.   2. The father and the mother
are greeting a teacher.   3. The brother and the sister are greeting
a teacher.   4. The girls are greeting a teacher.
e. 1. The teachers are going to the door.   2. The parents are going to
the door.   3. The father and the mother are going to the door.

4. The girl and the mother are going to the door.   5. The brother and the sister are going to the door.   6. The father and the mother are going to the door.

f. 1. He writes in order to learn.   2. She writes in order to learn. 3. The sister writes in order to learn.   4. The brother writes in order to learn.   5. The brother and the sister write in order to learn.   6. They write in order to learn.

C. GRAMMAR

1. Present indicative of the regular verb **sagen** (to say).

ich sag e	I say, am saying, do say
[du sag st	you say, are saying, do say]
er, sie, es sag t	he, she, it says, is saying, does say
wir sag en	we say, are saying, do say
[ihr sag t	you say, are saying, do say]
sie sag en	they say, are saying, do say
Sie sag en	you say, are saying, do say

Note 1: The present indicative of regular verbs is formed by dropping the **-en** of the infinitive and adding the endings shown above to the verb stem (**sag-**).

Note 2: The familiar forms **du** and **ihr** are used when addressing relatives, children, and close friends. Those who are beginning to learn German may well avoid these forms in favor of the polite form **Sie.** For practice the familiar forms will be used in E passages where appropriate, beginning with Unit 3. The direct-object form corresponding to **du** is **dich,** to **ihr** it is **euch.**

2. Present indicative of **sein** (to be).

ich bin	I am
[du bist	you are]
er, sie, es ist	he, she, it is
wir sind	we are
[ihr seid	you are]
sie sind	they are
Sie sind	you are

3. Present indicative of **haben** (to have).

ich habe	I have, am having, do have
[du hast	you have, are having, do have]

er, sie, es hat	he, she, it has, is having, does have
wir haben	we have, are having, do have
[ihr habt	you have, are having, do have]
sie haben	they have, are having, do have
Sie haben	you have, are having, do have

4. Many masculine and neuter nouns have the same form in the plural as in the singular. The plural form of the definite article for all genders is **die**.

der Lehrer	the teacher	**die Lehrer**	the teachers
der Onkel	the uncle	**die Onkel**	the uncles
das Fenster	the window	**die Fenster**	the windows
das Gebäude	the building	**die Gebäude**	the buildings
das Mädchen	the girl	**die Mädchen**	the girls

5. The subject of the verb is in the nominative case and the direct object is in the accusative case. The form of the noun is usually the same in both cases. The definite article has one form for both cases, except in the masculine singular, where the nominative form is **der**, the accusative **den**.

    a. **Wo ist der Brief?**
       Where is the letter?
       Der Lehrer schreibt den Brief.
       The teacher is writing the letter.

    b. **Hier ist die Aufgabe.**
       Here is the lesson.
       Schreibt der Student die Aufgabe?
       Is the student writing the lesson?

    c. **Das Buch ist dort.**
       The book is there.
       Wer hat das Buch?
       Who has the book?

6. The indefinite article also has only one form for both the nominative and accusative cases, except in the masculine singular, where the nominative form is **ein**, the accusative **einen**.

    a. **Ein Lehrer und ein Student kommen in das Zimmer.**
       A teacher and a student are coming into the room.
       Die Eltern begrüßen einen Lehrer.
       The parents are greeting a teacher.

b. **Hier ist eine Aufgabe?**
Here is a lesson.
Das Kind schreibt eine Aufgabe.
The child is writing a lesson.
c. **Dort ist ein Buch.**
There is a book.
Hat die Studentin ein Buch?
Does the student (*f.*) have a book?

7. Certain prepositions, such as **in** (into) and **an** (to), frequently require the accusative form of the following noun.
a. **Sie kommen in das Zimmer.**
They are coming into the room.
b. **Die Lehrer gehen an die Tür.**
The teachers are going to the door.
c. **Die Studentin geht an den Tisch.**
The student (*f.*) is going to the table.

8. The nominative and accusative forms of the personal pronouns **sie** and **es,** respectively, are the same.
a. **Die Studentin hat das Buch. Sie hat es.**
The student (*f.*) has the book. She has it.
b. **Das Kind schreibt die Aufgabe. Es schreibt sie.**
The child is writing the lesson. He (she) is writing it.

For the masculine, however, the nominative form is **er,** the accusative **ihn.**
a. **Wo ist der Tisch? Er ist hier.**
Where is the table? It is here.
b. **Der Lehrer schreibt den Brief. Er schreibt ihn.**
The teacher is writing the letter. He is writing it.
c. **Die Eltern begrüßen einen Lehrer. Sie begrüßen ihn.**
The parents are greeting a teacher. They are greeting him.

D. EXERCISES

WRITE THE FOLLOWING SENTENCES IN GERMAN AND BE ABLE TO EXPRESS THEM ORALLY IN CLASS.

1. She has a letter here.

2. The parents are coming to the table.
3. The teacher and the student are studying the lesson here.
4. Is he writing the lesson in order to learn?
5. I'm saying "Good-by."
6. Are you greeting me?
7. Do the girls have a table?
8. The uncles' names are Hans and Robert.
9. Do you have the book?—Yes, I have it here.
10. Where are you, Mr. Schmidt?
11. He is coming and she is going.
12. We are greeting the father and the brother.
13. Are you writing the letter?—Yes, I'm writing it.
14. We are here and you are there.
15. Are they saying "Good morning"?
16. We have the book here in order to study.
17. The brother is going to the door.
18. I am asking the father and the uncle.
19. Are the mother and the sister coming into the building?
20. His name is Hans and my name is Robert.
21. What do you have there, Mrs. Braun?
22. Who is greeting the father?—The teacher is greeting him.
23. Are you studying the lesson?—Yes, we are studying it.
24. Are the parents there?

E. READING AND SPEAKING

I. READ THE FOLLOWING ALOUD UNTIL YOU ARE THOROUGHLY FAMILIAR
WITH IT.

Im Klassenzimmer[1]

   **Der Student und die Studentin sind im Klassenzimmer. Der Student
fragt: „Wie heißt der Lehrer?"**
   „Er heißt Herr Schmidt", sagt das Mädchen. „Und wie heißen
5 **Sie?"**
   „Ich heiße Hans Braun. Und wie heißen Sie?"

---

[1] **Im Klassenzimmer**   In the classroom.

„Ich heiße Marie Meyer."

Die Studentin schreibt in das Buch. Der Student fragt: „Was schreiben Sie?"

„Ich schreibe die Aufgabe. Ich schreibe um zu lernen." 10

Der Lehrer kommt in das Zimmer und geht an den Tisch. Er begrüßt die Studenten (students). Sie begrüßen ihn auch.

II. ANSWER THE FOLLOWING QUESTIONS IN GERMAN.

1. Wo sind die Studenten?
2. Ist der Lehrer dort?
3. Wie heißt er?
4. Wie heißt der Student?
5. Was schreibt das Mädchen?
6. Begrüßen die Studenten den Lehrer?

A. UNITS OF SPEECH AND VOCABULARY

I. STUDY AND READ ALOUD.

Er lernt gerne.	He likes to learn (study).
Sie spielen gerne.	They like to play.
Schreibt sie gerne?	Does she like to write?
Sie schreiben der Mutter; sie schreiben ihr.	They are writing to the mother; they are writing to her.
Sie schreibt dem Vater; sie schreibt ihm.	She is writing to the father; she is writing to him.
Er schreibt dem Mädchen; er schreibt ihm.	He is writing to the girl; he is writing to her.
aus dem Hause	out of the house
bei Frau Meyer; bei ihr	at Mrs. Meyer's (house); at her house
bei mir	at my house
bei ihm	at his house
bei uns	at our house
bei ihnen	at their house
mit der Tochter; mit ihr	with the daughter; with her
nach Hause	home(ward)
zu Hause	at home

16

die **Brüder**	the brothers	**wohnen**	to dwell, to live
die **Frau**	the woman	**mir**	(to) me
das **Haus**	the house	**ihm**	(to) him, ~~(to) her~~,
der **Junge**	the boy		(to) it
der **Mann**	the man	**ihr**	(to) her, (to) it
die **Mütter**	the mothers	**uns**	(to) us
der **Sohn**	the son	**ihnen**	(to) them
die **Tochter**	the daughter	**Ihnen**	(to) you
die **Töchter**	the daughters	**gerne**	gladly
die **Väter**	the fathers	**aus**	from, out of
geben	to give	**bei**	at the house of
spielen	to play	**mit**	with

II. DRILL. EXPRESS ORALLY IN GERMAN. REPEAT UNTIL IT IS NO LONGER
NECESSARY TO REFER TO SECTION I.

a. 1. He likes to learn.   2. The student likes to learn.   3. The boy
likes to learn.   4. The son likes to study.   5. The man likes to study.

b. 1. They like to play.   2. The daughters like to play.   3. The brothers
like to play.   4. The son and the daughter like to play.

c. 1. Does she like to write?   2. Does the woman like to write?
3. Does the daughter like to write?   4. Does the student (*f.*) like
to write?

d. 1. They are writing to the mother.   2. The daughters are writing to
the mother.   3. The brothers are writing to the mother.   4. The
son and the daughter are writing to the mother.   5. They are
writing to her.   6. The brothers are writing to her.   7. The man
and the boy are writing to her.

e. 1. She is writing to the father.   2. The daughter is writing to the
father.   3. The boy is writing to the father.   4. He is writing to
him.   5. The woman is writing to him.   6. She is writing to him.

f. 1. He is writing to the girl.   2. He is writing to her.   3. The woman
is writing to the girl. She is writing to her.   4. The daughters are
writing to the girl. They are writing to her.

g. 1. . . . out of the house.   2. They are going out of the house.
3. The mothers are going out of the house.   4. The fathers are
going out of the house.   5. The fathers and the mothers are going
out of the house.

h. 1. . . . at Mrs. Meyer's.   2. I live at Mrs. Meyer's.   3. He lives at Mrs. Meyer's.   3. The boy lives at Mrs. Meyer's.   4. The man and the woman live at her house.   5. They live at her house.

i. 1. at my house   2. at his house   3. at our house   4. at their house

j. 1. . . . with the daughter.   2. The mother is coming with the daughter.   3. The woman is coming with the daughter.   4. The woman plays with the daughter.   5. The woman plays with her. 6. She is playing with her.

k. 1. . . . are going home.   2. The fathers are going home.   3. The mothers are going home.   4. The father and the son are going home.

l. 1. . . . at home.   2. The brothers are at home.   3. The mothers are at home.   4. The daughters are at home.   5. The fathers are at home.

m. 1. . . . are giving. . .   2. They are giving it to me.   3. They are giving it to you.   4. They are giving it to us.   5. We are giving it to them. 6. You are giving it to me.   7. You are giving it to them.   8. You are giving it to us.   9. We are giving it to you.

n. 1. . . . to you.   2. Who is writing to you?   3. Who is writing to us? 4. Who is writing to them?   5. Who is writing to me?

B. MODEL SENTENCES

I. STUDY UNTIL EACH SENTENCE CAN BE GIVEN CORRECTLY FROM THE ENGLISH.

14. **Das Kind spielt gerne.**
15. **Der Student schreibt der Mutter einen Brief.**
16. **Die Frau schreibt einer Tochter.**
17. **Die Brüder geben es dem Kind.**
18. **Sie geben es ihm.**
19. **Die Mütter kommen aus dem Hause.**
20. **Der Junge wohnt bei einem Onkel.**
21. **Die Mutter spielt mit den Töchtern.**

14. The child likes to play.
15. The student is writing the mother a letter.
16. The woman is writing to a daughter.
17. The brothers are giving it to the child.

18. They are giving it to him.
19. The mothers are coming out of the house.
20. The boy lives at an uncle's (house).
21. The mother is playing with the daughters.

II. DRILL. EXPRESS ORALLY IN GERMAN.

a. 1. The child likes to play. 2. The child likes to write. 3. The child likes to learn. 4. The girls like to learn. 5. The girls like to write. 6. The girls like to play.
b. 1. The student is writing the mother a letter. 2. The boy is writing the mother a letter. 3. The child is writing the mother a letter. 4. The girl is writing the mother a letter. 5. The daughter is writing the mother a letter.
c. 1. The woman is writing to a daughter. 2. She is writing to a daughter. 3. Mrs. Meyer is writing to a daughter. 4. The father is writing to a daughter. 5. Mr. Schmidt is writing to a daughter.
d. 1. The brothers are giving it to the child. 2. The brother and the sister are giving it to the child. 3. The boy and the girl are giving it to the child. 4. They are giving it to the child.
e. 1. They are giving it to him. 2. The brothers are giving it to him. 3. The girls are giving it to him. 4. The parents are giving it to him.
f. 1. The mothers are coming out of the house. 2. The brothers are coming out of the house. 3. The fathers are coming out of the house. 4. The woman and the boy are going out of the house.
g. 1. The boy lives at an uncle's (house). 2. The man lives at an uncle's (house).   3. The brothers live at an uncle's (house). 4. The sister and the brother live at an uncle's (house). 5. The woman lives at an uncle's (house).
h. 1. The mother is playing with the daughters. 2. The father is playing with the daughters. 3. The fathers are coming with the daughters. 4. The mothers are coming with the daughters. 5. The father and the mother are coming with the daughters.

C. GRAMMAR

1. The plural of some nouns is formed by changing the stem vowel to an umlaut vowel. This change occurs primarily in masculine nouns of more than one syllable and in the two feminine nouns **Mutter** and **Tochter.**

der Vater	the father	**die Väter**	the fathers
der Bruder	the brother	**die Brüder**	the brothers
die Mutter	the mother	**die Mütter**	the mothers
die Tochter	the daughter	**die Töchter**	the daughters

Note: Umlaut affects only **a, o, u,** or **au** and is indicated by two dots above the letter. For the pronunciation of **ä, ö, ü,** and **äu,** follow your instructor or see the Pronunciation Guide.

2. The indirect object of the verb is in the dative case. (In English the indirect object of a verb may be preceded by a preposition; in German, this almost never occurs.) The dative singular form of the definite article is **dem** for the masculine and neuter, **der** for the feminine. The dative plural form is **den** for all genders.

   a. **Der Student schreibt dem Vater.**
      The student is writing to the father.
   b. **Der Student schreibt der Mutter.**
      The student is writing to the mother.
   c. **Der Student schreibt dem Mädchen.**
      The student is writing to the girl.
   d. **Die Mutter schreibt den Töchtern.**
      The mother is writing to the daughters.

   Note: Nouns which do not end in **-n** in the nominative plural add **-n** in the dative plural.

3. The dative forms of the indefinite article are **einem** for the masculine and neuter, **einer** for the feminine.

   a. **Die Frau schreibt einem Sohn.**
      The woman is writing to a son.
   b. **Die Frau schreibt einer Tochter.**
      The woman is writing to a daughter.
   c. **Die Frau schreibt einem Kind.**
      The woman is writing to a child.

4. The dative forms of the personal pronoun.

mir	(to) me	**uns**	(to) us
[**dir**	(to) you]	[**euch**	(to) you]
ihm	(to) him, (to) it	**ihnen**	(to) them
ihr	(to) her, (to) it	**Ihnen**	(to) you

Note 1: **Dir** and **euch** are the dative forms of **du** and **ihr,** respectively.

The same observations which apply to **du** and **ihr** apply to **dir** and **euch** also. (See Note 2, page 11.)

Note 2: **Ihm** is the dative form of both **er** and **es.**

5. If there is a direct object noun and an indirect object noun or pronoun in the same clause, the indirect object precedes the direct object.

    a. **Der Student schreibt der Mutter einen Brief.**
       The student is writing a letter to the mother.

    b. **Der Student schreibt ihr einen Brief.**
       The student is writing her a letter.

If the direct object is a pronoun, it always precedes the indirect object.

    c. **Die Brüder geben es dem Kind.**
       The brothers are giving it to the child.

    d. **Sie geben es ihm.**
       They are giving it to him (her).

6. The dative form is required following certain prepositions. Common among these are

    aus   from, out of   **bei**   at the house of   **mit**   with

    a. **Die Mütter kommen aus dem Hause.**
       The mothers are coming out of the house.

    b. **Der Junge wohnt bei einem Onkel.**
       The boy lives at an uncle's house.

    c. **Die Mutter spielt mit den Töchtern.**
       The mother is playing with the daughters.

Note: One-syllable masculine and neuter nouns may add **-e** in the dative singular. The ending is regularly used in the phrases **zu Hause** and **nach Hause.**

D. EXERCISES

WRITE THE FOLLOWING SENTENCES IN GERMAN AND BE ABLE TO EXPRESS THEM ORALLY IN CLASS.

1. The daughters are writing a letter to the father.
2. Does the sister write to the brothers?
3. They are giving the student (*f.*) the lesson.
4. She is playing with a girl.
5. They are writing me a letter. They are writing it to me.

6. The brother and a sister are playing at our house.
7. Are you going home?
8. The boy and the girl are saying it to the teachers.
9. Who is living at your house?
10. The girl is playing with a sister.
11. Does the child like to study?
12. The brothers are coming with her.
13. I am giving the child a book.
14. Are the fathers at home?
15. A student is coming out of a building.
16. What are the mothers' names?
17. Their names are Mrs. Schmidt and Mrs. Braun.
18. Do you like to write?
19. We are giving a woman the book.
20. Who is going with them?
21. The mother and a son are at my house.
22. They are coming out of the rooms.
23. The son and the daughter live at the parents' house.
24. Is he living at home?

E. READING AND SPEAKING

I. READ THE FOLLOWING ALOUD UNTIL YOU ARE THOROUGHLY FAMILIAR
    WITH IT.

Zu Hause

Der Vater heißt Robert Braun. Er ist nicht (not) zu Hause. Die Mutter heißt Grete Braun. Sie ist zu Hause und spielt mit dem Sohn und den Töchtern.

5 **Der Junge heißt Willi und die Mädchen heißen Trude und Lotte. Der Junge und die Mädchen spielen gerne. Sie haben noch einen (another) Bruder. Er heißt Hans und ist Student. Er ist noch nicht (not yet) zu Hause.**

Der Onkel kommt in das Wohnzimmer (living room). Er heißt
10 **Karl Schmidt. „Guten Morgen", sagt er.**

„Guten Morgen, Onkel Karl", sagen sie. „Wie geht es dir?"
„Danke, es geht mir gut. Und euch?"
„Danke, auch gut."

Die Mutter geht mit Trude aus dem Zimmer. Der Onkel spielt mit Willi und Lotte. Er spielt gerne mit ihnen und sie spielen gerne mit ihm. 15
Hans kommt nach Hause. Er kommt in das Wohnzimmer und begrüßt den Onkel, den Bruder und die Schwester. Er geht an den Tisch und schreibt einen Brief.

II. ANSWER THE FOLLOWING QUESTIONS IN GERMAN.

1. Wie heißt der Vater?
2. Wo ist die Mutter?
3. Wer ist auch dort?
4. Wer kommt in das Wohnzimmer?
5. Wer geht aus dem Wohnzimmer?
6. Was schreibt Hans?

UNIT 4

A. UNITS OF SPEECH AND VOCABULARY

I. STUDY AND READ ALOUD.

Wieviel Uhr ist es?	What time is it?
Es ist ein Uhr.	It's one o'clock.
Um wieviel Uhr . . . ?	At what time . . . ?
um zwei Uhr	at two o'clock
in die Schule	to school
anstatt des Mannes	instead of the man
während des Tages	during the day
wegen des Wetters	on account of the weather

die Arbeit	the work	**lehren**	to teach
die Familie	the family	**machen**	to do, to make
der Freund	the friend	**jetzt**	now
die Freundin	the (girl) friend	**ein**	one
der Morgen	the morning	**zwei**	two
die Schule	the school	**drei**	three
der Tag	the day	**vier**	four
das Wetter	the weather	**fünf**	five
Deutsch	German	**dieser**	this, that
beginnen	to begin, to start	**jeder**	each, every
besuchen	to visit	**mancher**	many a
essen	to eat	**manche**	some

24

welcher? which?   **wegen** because of,
anstatt instead of   on account of
während during

II. DRILL. EXPRESS ORALLY IN GERMAN. REPEAT UNTIL IT IS NO LONGER
NECESSARY TO REFER TO SECTION I.

a. 1. What time is it? 2. What time is it, Mr. Braun? 3. It's one
o'clock. 4. It's two o'clock. 5. It's three o'clock. 6. It's four
o'clock. 7. It's five o'clock.

b. 1. At what time . . . ? 2. At what time is he coming? 3. At what
time is the friend coming? 4. At what time is the girl friend coming?
5. At what time does the work start?

c. 1. . . . at two o'clock. 2. They eat at two o'clock. 3. They eat at
five o'clock. 4. We eat at one o'clock. 5. We eat at four o'clock.
6. We eat at three o'clock.

d. 1. . . . to school. 2. She is going to school. 3. The girl friend is
going to school. 4. The friend is going to school.

e. 1. . . . instead of the man. 2. Is the boy going instead of the man?
3. Is the girl going instead of the man? 4. Is the woman going
instead of the man?

f. 1. . . . during the day. 2. They visit him during the day. 3. They
visit her during the day. 4. He visits them during the day. 5. He
teaches during the day. 6. We teach during the day.

g. 1. . . . on account of the weather. 2. She is going on account of
the weather. 3. He is going on account of the weather. 4. They
are going on account of the weather.

h. 1. . . . the work. 2. The family is doing the work. 3. A girl friend
is doing the work. 4. A friend is beginning the work. 5. The
family is beginning the work.

i. 1. this day 2. every day 3. many a morning 4. each morning
5. Which morning?

j. 1. some teachers 2. some girls 3. some fathers 4. some mothers

B. MODEL SENTENCES

I. STUDY UNTIL EACH SENTENCE CAN BE GIVEN CORRECTLY FROM THE
ENGLISH.

22. **Die Frau des Bruders heißt Lotte.**
23. **Der Sohn der Frau besucht einen Freund.**
24. **Die Familie des Kindes ist hier.**
25. **Der Bruder der Mädchen kommt mit ihnen.**
26. **Diese Studentin ist Maries Freundin.**
27. **Anstatt des Mannes kommt das Mädchen.**
28. **Während des Tages machen wir die Arbeit.**
29. **Jetzt lehrt sie Deutsch.**
30. **Geht er um ein Uhr in die Schule?**

22. The brother's wife is called Lotte.
23. The woman's son is visiting a friend.
24. The child's family is here.
25. The brother of the girls is coming with them.
26. This student (*f.*) is Marie's friend.
27. The girl is coming instead of the man.
28. We do the work during the day.
29. She is teaching German now.
30. Does he go to school at one o'clock?

II. DRILL. EXPRESS ORALLY IN GERMAN.

a. 1. The brother's wife is called Lotte. 2. The brother's daughter is called Gretchen. 3. The brother's son is called Hans. 4. The brother's friend is called Walter. 5. The brother's uncle is called Robert.

b. 1. The woman's son is visiting a friend. 2. The woman's daughter is visiting a friend. 3. The woman's child is visiting a friend. 4. The woman's son is visiting the family. 5. The woman's uncle is visiting the family.

c. 1. The child's family is here. 2. The child's mother is here. 3. The child's sister is here. 4. The child's father is here. 5. The child's brother is here.

d. 1. The brother of the girls is coming with them. 2. The father of the girls is coming with them. 3. The mother of the girls is coming with them. 4. The friend (*f.*) of the girls is coming with them.

e. 1. This student (*f.*) is Marie's friend. 2. This student (*f.*) is Marie's sister. 3. This student (*f.*) is Marie's daughter.

f. 1. The girl is coming instead of the man. 2. The son is coming instead of the man. 3. The daughter is coming instead of the man. 4. The woman is coming instead of the man.

g. 1. We do the work during the day. 2. We study the lesson during the day. 3. We begin the work during the day. 4. We learn German during the day. 5. She teaches German during the day.

h. 1. She is teaching German now. 2. He is teaching German now. 3. He is learning German now. 4. We are studying German now. 5. You are studying German now.

i. 1. Does he go to school at one o'clock? 2. Does she go to school at three o'clock? 3. Do they come to school at four o'clock? 4. Do you come to school at two o'clock? 5. Do they go to school at five o'clock?

C. GRAMMAR

1. Possession is indicated by the genitive case.
   a. **Die Frau des Bruders heißt Lotte.**
      The brother's wife is called Lotte.
   b. **Der Sohn der Frau besucht einen Freund.**
      The woman's son is visiting a friend.
   c. **Die Familie des Kindes ist hier.**
      The child's family is here.
   d. **Der Bruder der Mädchen kommt mit ihnen.**
      The brother of the girls is coming with them.

   Note: **Die Frau des Bruders** may mean "the brother's wife" or "the wife of the brother." Likewise, **der Sohn der Frau** may mean "the woman's son" or "the son of the woman"; **die Familie des Kindes,** "the child's family" or "the family of the child"; **der Bruder der Mädchen,** "the girls' brother" or "the brother of the girls."

   Most masculine and neuter nouns of one syllable add **-es** as the genitive singular ending: **des Mannes, des Kindes.** Those of two or more syllables usually add **-s: des Vaters, des Mädchens.**

   Nothing is added to the genitive singular of the feminine or to the genitive plural of any gender: **der Frau, der Mädchen.**

   The genitive forms of the definite article are **des** for the masculine and neuter singulars, **der** for the feminine singular and all plurals.

The genitive forms of the indefinite article are **eines** for the masculine and neuter, **einer** for the feminine.

2. The full inflection of the definite and indefinite articles.

	MASCULINE		FEMININE		NEUTER		PLURAL
NOM.	**der**	**ein**	**die**	**eine**	**das**	**ein**	**die**
GEN.	**des**	**eines**	**der**	**einer**	**des**	**eines**	**der**
DAT.	**dem**	**einem**	**der**	**einer**	**dem**	**einem**	**den**
ACC.	**den**	**einen**	**die**	**eine**	**das**	**ein**	**die**

3. Similarly inflected is **dieser** (this, that).

	MASCULINE	FEMININE	NEUTER	PLURAL
NOM.	**dies er**	**dies e**	**dies es**	**dies e**
GEN.	**dies es**	**dies er**	**dies es**	**dies er**
DAT.	**dies em**	**dies er**	**dies em**	**dies en**
ACC.	**dies en**	**dies e**	**dies es**	**dies e**

The same endings are used for
jeder each, every   **mancher** many a   **welcher?** which?
Note: Because they have endings similar to those of the definite article, these words are called **der**-words.

4. The genitive of proper names, regardless of gender, is formed by adding **-s.**

>   **Diese Studentin ist Maries Freundin.**
>   This student (*f.*) is Marie's friend.

Note: Proper names ending in **-s, -z,** or **-sch** do not add **-s** and indicate this omission by an apostrophe.

>   **Hans' Freundin heißt Fräulein Meyer.**
>   Hans's girl friend's name is Miss Meyer.

5. Some prepositions require the genitive form of the noun they govern.   TROTZDEM –INSPITE OF

anstatt instead of   **während** during   **wegen** because of, on account of

>   **anstatt des Mannes**   instead of the man
>   **während des Tages**   during the day
>   **wegen des Wetters**   because of, on account of, the weather

6. Ordinarily the subject precedes the verb in a statement. However, if the clause begins with any emphatic element, such as an adverb or a prepositional phrase, the subject must follow the verb.

   a. **Anstatt des Mannes kommt das Mädchen.**
      The girl is coming instead of the man.

b. **Während des Tages machen wir die Arbeit.**
We do the work during the day.

c. **Jetzt lehrt sie Deutsch.**
She is teaching German now.

7. In statements, adverbs and phrases of time are often used in initial position. (See examples *b* and *c* in the preceding paragraph.) If not in initial position, or if in questions, expressions of time precede other adverbial expressions and noun objects.

a. **Er geht um ein Uhr in die Schule.**
He goes to school at one o'clock.
Geht er um ein Uhr in die Schule?
Does he go to school at one o'clock?

b. **Sie lehrt jetzt hier.**
She is teaching here now.
Lehrt sie jetzt hier?
Is she teaching here now?

c. **Sie lehrt jetzt Deutsch.**
She is teaching German now.
Lehrt sie jetzt Deutsch?
Is she teaching German now?

D. EXERCISES

WRITE THE FOLLOWING SENTENCES IN GERMAN AND BE ABLE TO EXPRESS THEM ORALLY IN CLASS.

1. At what time does he begin?
2. Are the parents coming because of the son?
3. The son of a friend is teaching German here.
4. He is greeting the sister's two daughters.
5. Which family is doing the work?
6. Some girls like to study.
7. The child's brothers go to school at one o'clock.
8. That boy is Hans's son.
9. The son is visiting a friend instead of the father.
10. Is he learning German now?
11. The teacher has a student's (*f.*) book.
12. Which teachers are here now?

13. These two uncles come during the day.
14. Every daughter of that man is here.
15. Robert's mother's name is Trude.
16. The parents of the girls are visiting the teacher.
17. Into which building are the mothers going?
18. Many a child likes to play during the day.
19. We begin at four o'clock.
20. Instead of a woman a girl is coming.
21. Which boy is writing this letter?
22. Every student (*f.*) comes into the room during the morning.
23. Now they are beginning the lesson.
24. Do you go home at three o'clock?
25. The parents are giving the three brothers a house.

E. READING AND SPEAKING

I. READ THE FOLLOWING ALOUD UNTIL YOU ARE THOROUGHLY FAMILIAR WITH IT.

Die Familie

Robert Braun ist der Vater der Familie. Um vier Uhr kommt er nach Hause. Er kommt in das Wohnzimmer und begrüßt Frau Brauns Bruder.

5 **„Guten Tag, Karl", sagt er. „Wie geht es dir?"**
„Danke, es geht mir gut. Und dir?"
„Danke, auch gut." Jetzt fragt er die Mutter: „Ist Hans hier?"
„Noch nicht", sagt sie.
Es klingelt.[1] „Das muß Hans sein",[2] sagt die Mutter und geht an
10 **die Tür.**
Anstatt des Sohnes kommt Hans' Freundin, Käthe Meyer, in das Zimmer und begrüßt die Familie. Frau Braun stellt sie dem Onkel vor.[3]
Käthe sagt: „Hans kommt erst um fünf Uhr[4] nach Hause. Er ist noch (still) in der Schule."
15 **Onkel Karl fragt: „Gehen Sie in dieselbe (the same) Schule wie (as) Hans, Fräulein Meyer?"**

[1] **Es klingelt** The bell rings.   [2] **Das muß Hans sein** That must be Hans.
[3] **stellt sie dem Onkel vor** introduces her to the uncle.   [4] **erst um fünf Uhr** not until five o'clock.

„Ja, wir sind in derselben (the same) Klasse."
„Was lernen Sie jetzt?"
„Jetzt lerne ich Deutsch. Ich lerne gerne Deutsch."
Jetzt ist es fünf Uhr. Es klingelt. Käthe geht an die Tür und begrüßt 20
Hans.

II. ANSWER THE FOLLOWING QUESTIONS IN GERMAN.

1. Um wieviel Uhr kommt der Vater nach Hause?
2. In welches Zimmer kommt er?
3. Wer ist Onkel Karl?
4. Wie heißt Hans' Freundin?
5. Wer kommt um fünf Uhr nach Hause?

☞ UNIT 5

A. UNITS OF SPEECH AND VOCABULARY

I. STUDY AND READ ALOUD.

Er kommt nicht.	He isn't coming.
Die Söhne gehen nicht.	The sons aren't going.
Schreibt das Mädchen nicht?	Isn't the girl writing? Doesn't the girl write?
Lernen sie nicht?	Aren't they studying? Don't they study?
Wir essen zu Mittag.	We are eating lunch.
Sie essen zu Abend.	They are eating supper.
(schon) seit einem Jahr	for one year
(schon) seit zwei Jahren	for two years
zu Bett	to bed

die Briefe	the letters	**die Kinder**	the children
das Brot	the bread	**die Männer**	the men
die Bücher	the books	**die Söhne**	the sons
die Freunde	the friends	**die Tage**	the days
die Hand	the hand	**die Tische**	the tables
die Hände	the hands	**alt**	old
die Häuser	the houses	**schön**	beautiful, nice
das Jahr	the year	**nicht**	not
die Jahre	the years	**schon**	already

32

kein	no, not any	**sieben**	seven
mein	my	**acht**	eight
[**dein**	your]	**neun**	nine
sein	his, its *m.*	**zehn**	ten
ihr	her, its *f.*, their	**elf**	eleven
unser	our	**zwölf**	twelve
[**euer**	your]	**wann?**	when? at what
Ihr	your		time?
sechs	six	**seit** + *dat.*	since

II. DRILL. EXPRESS ORALLY IN GERMAN. REPEAT UNTIL IT IS NO LONGER NECESSARY TO REFER TO SECTION I.

a. 1. He isn't coming. 2. My son isn't coming. 3. Her son isn't coming. 4. Our boy isn't coming. 5. Your boy is not coming. 6. His boy is not coming.

b. 1. The sons aren't going. 2. The children aren't going. 3. The men are not going. 4. The friends are not going.

c. 1. Isn't the girl writing? 2. Isn't their child writing? 3. Isn't our brother writing? 4. Doesn't your brother write? 5. Doesn't his father write? 6. Doesn't my uncle write?

d. 1. Aren't they studying? 2. Aren't the men studying? 3. Aren't the friends studying? 4. Don't the sons study? 5. Don't the children study?

e. 1. We are eating lunch. 2. The men are eating lunch. 3. The children are eating lunch. 4. The sons are eating lunch. 5. The friends are eating lunch.

f. 1. They are eating supper. 2. The friends are eating supper. 3. The men are eating supper. 4. The children are eating supper. 5. The sons are eating supper.

g. 1. for one year 2. for two years 3. for three years 4. for six years 5. for seven years 6. for ten years

h. 1. to bed 2. Is your son going to bed? 3. Is our boy going to bed? 4. Is their child going to bed? 5. His child is going to bed. 6. My child is going to bed. 7. Her child is going to bed.

i. 1. He is writing six letters. 2. She is writing seven letters. 3. We are writing eight letters.

j. 1. She has nine books here.   2. He has ten tables here.   3. They
have eleven children.   4. They have twelve houses.   5. We have
two hands.

k. 1. nice   2. The days are nice.   3. The houses are nice.   4. The
tables are beautiful.   5. The books are beautiful.

l. 1. old   2. The tables are old.   3. The books are old.   4. The houses
are old.   5. The letters are old.   6. The bread is old.

m. 1. no bread   2. no table   3. no man   4. no house   5. no child

n. 1. When . . . ?   2. When do you eat?   3. When do you eat lunch?
4. At what time do they eat supper?   5. At what time do they go
to bed?

B. MODEL SENTENCES

I. STUDY UNTIL EACH SENTENCE CAN BE GIVEN CORRECTLY FROM THE
ENGLISH.

31. **Meine Freunde sind seit neun Tagen hier.**
32. **Ihr Bruder lernt schon seit drei Jahren Deutsch.**
33. **Essen Ihre Söhne kein Brot?**
34. **Seine Schwester schreibt ihm nicht.**
35. **Sie spielt jetzt nicht, sie lernt.**
36. **Unsere Kinder lernen nicht gerne.**
37. **Die Männer gehen nicht in die Häuser.**
38. **Dieser Mann ist nicht mein Onkel.**

31. My friends have been here for nine days.
32. Her brother has been studying German for three years.
33. Don't your sons eat any bread?
34. His sister is not writing to him.
35. She isn't playing now; she is studying.
36. Our children don't like to study.
37. The men are not going into the houses.
38. This man is not my uncle.

II. DRILL. EXPRESS ORALLY IN GERMAN.

a. 1. My friends have been here for nine days.   2. My friends have been here for ten days. 3. My books have been here for eleven days. 4. My sons have been here for twelve days.

b. 1. Her brother has been studying German for three years. 2. Her son has been studying German for three years. 3. Her father has been studying German for eight years. 4. Her child has been studying German for two years.

c. 1. Don't your sons eat any bread? 2. Don't your children eat any bread? 3. Don't your friends eat any bread? 4. Don't your daughters eat any bread? 5. Don't your brothers eat any bread?

d. 1. His sister is not writing to him. 2. His mother is not writing to him. 3. His daughter is not writing to him. 4. His family is not writing to him.

e. 1. She isn't playing now; she is studying. 2. He isn't playing now; he is studying. 3. We aren't playing now; we are studying. 4. They aren't playing now; they are studying.

f. 1. Our children don't like to study. 2. Our daughters don't like to study. 3. Our sons don't like to study. 4. Our brothers don't like to study.

g. 1. The men are not going into the houses. 2. The fathers are not going into the houses. 3. The mothers are not going into the houses. 4. The children are not going into the houses.

h. 1. This man is not my uncle. 2. This man is not my brother. 3. That man is not my father. 4. That man is not my friend.

C. GRAMMAR

1. An action which began in the past and continues into the present is expressed in the present tense. The duration of time is indicated by **seit** + the dative case.

> **Meine Freunde sind seit neun Tagen hier.**
> My friends have been here for nine days.

To emphasize duration, **schon** (already) may be added before **seit.**

> **Ihr Bruder lernt schon seit drei Jahren Deutsch.**
> Her brother has been studying German for three years.

2. Most German nouns form their plurals by adding a letter or a syllable. Many nouns add **-e.** The masculine nouns in this group frequently take umlaut, the feminine nouns usually, the neuter nouns never.

der Sohn	the son	**die Söhne**	the sons
der Tag	the day	**die Tage**	the days
die Hand	the hand	**die Hände**	the hands

3. Some nouns add **-er** to form the plural.

der Mann	the man	**die Männer**	the men
das Kind	the child	**die Kinder**	the children
das Buch	the book	**die Bücher**	the books

There are no feminine nouns in this group. The masculine and neuter nouns take umlaut wherever possible.

4. One cannot tell by simply looking at a noun what plural ending, if any, it will take. It is therefore best to memorize the principal parts of each noun learned. The principal parts are the nominative singular, genitive singular, and nominative plural.

NOM. SING.	GEN. SING.	NOM. PLURAL
der Lehrer	**des Lehrers**	**die Lehrer**
die Hand	**der Hand**	**die Hände**
das Haus	**des Hauses**	**die Häuser**

Note 1: In feminine nouns, the nominative singular and genitive singular always have identical forms.

Note 2: In vocabularies and word lists, the principal parts are usually indicated as follows.

der Lehrer, -s, -
die Hand, -, ̈e
das Haus, -es, ̈er

5. The negative indefinite article **kein** (no, not any) is declined in the singular like the indefinite article **ein** (a, an), in the plural like the **der**-words.

	Singular			Plural
	MASCULINE	FEMININE	NEUTER	ALL GENDERS
NOM.	kein	kein e	kein	kein e
GEN.	kein es	kein er	kein es	kein er
DAT.	kein em	kein er	kein em	kein en
ACC.	kein en	kein e	kein	kein e

Note 1: The case endings of **der**-words and **ein**-words are identical in all forms except these three: nominative masculine singular, nominative and accusative neuter singular, for which **ein**-words lack case endings.

Note 2: The sentence **Essen Ihre Söhne kein Brot?** means either "Don't your sons eat any bread?" or "Do your sons eat no bread?"

6. The possessive adjectives are as follows.

mein	my	**unser**	our
[**dein**	your]	[**euer**	your]
sein	his, its *m.*	**ihr**	their
ihr	her, its *f.*	**Ihr**	your

mein is the possessive adjective for **ich**
dein is the possessive adjective for **du**
sein is the possessive adjective for **er** and **es**
unser is the possessive adjective for **wir**
euer is the possessive adjective for **ihr**
ihr is the possessive adjective for **sie**
Ihr (always capitalized) is the possessive adjective for **Sie**

Note: Possessive adjectives are declined like **ein** and **kein**. Because **kein** and the possessive adjectives have endings similar to the indefinite article, they are called **ein**-words.

7. The negative word **nicht** (not) usually *follows* the verb plus its objects and adverbs of time.

a. **Seine Schwester schreibt ihm nicht.**
His sister is not writing to him.

b. **Sie spielt jetzt nicht, sie lernt.**
She is not playing now; she is studying.

Nicht usually *precedes* adverbs of manner or place.

c. **Unsere Kinder lernen nicht gerne.**
Our children don't like to study.

Nicht usually *precedes* prepositional phrases.

d. **Die Männer gehen nicht in die Häuser.**
The men are not going into the houses.

Nicht usually *precedes* predicate nouns and adjectives.

e. **Dieser Mann ist nicht mein Onkel.**
This man is not my uncle.

f. **Dieser Mann ist nicht alt.**
This man is not old.

D. EXERCISES

WRITE THE FOLLOWING SENTENCES IN GERMAN AND BE ABLE TO EXPRESS THEM ORALLY IN CLASS.

1. These books are beautiful.
2. My son's children are not here.
3. Do your father and your mother eat at six o'clock?
4. My brother is not going into his room.
5. Aren't her sister's hands beautiful?
6. They are giving the books to my friends.
7. When do her children go to bed?
8. These men have been living here for a year.
9. No student (*f.*) is there now.
10. That girl is not their sister.
11. Some houses have eight rooms.
12. This girl has been going to school for four years.
13. Their child is ten days old.
14. The men don't have any bread.
15. He is writing his son seven letters.
16. Our houses are not old.
17. Their friends have been at their house for twelve days.
18. His children eat at nine o'clock.
19. These rooms have no tables.
20. They are not going on account of the weather.
21. He is doing the work with one hand.
22. Isn't your son going to bed now?
23. He has been writing this letter for three days.
24. Has the student no book?
25. The boy and the girl do not eat any bread.

E. READING AND SPEAKING

I. READ THE FOLLOWING ALOUD UNTIL YOU ARE THOROUGHLY FAMILIAR
   WITH IT.

Zu Besuch[1]

 Hans und Käthe haben zwei Freunde. Sie heißen Richard und Klara.
**Richard und Klara haben ein Haus. Das Haus ist nicht neu (new), es
ist alt. Sie haben zwei Kinder. Der Junge heißt Thomas, das Mädchen**
5 **heißt Luise.**

---

[1] **Zu Besuch** Visiting.

Hans und Käthe besuchen ihre Freunde. Sie kommen in das Haus und gehen in das Wohnzimmer. Richard und Klara begrüßen ihre Freunde.

Klaras zwei Kinder spielen draußen (outside). Jetzt kommen die Kinder in das Wohnzimmer. 10

Käthe sagt: „Sind sie nicht nett (nice)!"

„Wie (how) alt ist Thomas jetzt?" fragt Hans.

„Er ist noch nicht zwei", sagt Klara.

„Und wie alt ist Luise?"

„Sie ist drei." 15

Käthe spielt mit den Kindern, denn sie hat Kinder sehr gerne.[2]

Richard kommt in das Zimmer und begrüßt Hans und Käthe. Um sieben Uhr essen sie zu Abend. Die zwei Kinder gehen zu Bett und die Eltern reden (talk) mit ihren Freunden. Um zehn Uhr gehen Hans und Käthe nach Hause. 20

II. ANSWER THE FOLLOWING QUESTIONS IN GERMAN.

1. Wer sind Richard und Klara?
2. Wo spielen die Kinder?
3. Wie alt ist der Junge?
4. Wann essen sie zu Abend?
5. Wer geht zu Bett?
6. Wann gehen Hans und Käthe nach Hause?

[2] **denn sie hat Kinder sehr gerne**   for she is very fond of children.

☞ UNIT 6

A. UNITS OF SPEECH AND VOCABULARY

I. STUDY AND READ ALOUD.

Er legt es auf den Tisch.	He is putting it on the table.
im Zimmer	in the room
ins Zimmer	into the room
am Fenster	at the window
ans Fenster	to the window

die Aufgaben	the lessons	**sitzen**	to sit
die Familien	the families	**stehen**	to stand
die Frauen	the women	**verstehen**	to understand
der Herr	the gentleman	**groß**	big, large, tall
die Herren	the gentlemen	**gut**	good
die Jungen	the boys	**jung**	young
die Schulen	the schools	**klein**	small, little
die Schwestern	the sisters	**an**	at, to
die Studenten	the students	**auf**	on
die Studentinnen	the students *f.*, coeds	**hinter**	behind
		in	in, into
beschreiben	to describe	**neben**	next to, near
finden	to find	**über**	above, over
legen	to lay, to put	**unter**	under
liegen	to lie, to be (situated)	**vor**	in front of
		zwischen	between, among

II. DRILL. EXPRESS ORALLY IN GERMAN. REPEAT UNTIL IT IS NO LONGER NECESSARY TO REFER TO SECTION I.

a. 1. He is putting it on the table. 2. She is putting it on the table. 3. They are laying it on the table. 4. We are laying it on the table.

b. 1. . . . in the room. 2. The students are standing in the room. 3. The students (*f.*) are standing in the room. 4. The sisters are sitting in the room. 5. The women are sitting in the room.

c. 1. . . . into the room. 2. The boys are coming into the room. 3. The families are coming into the room. 4. The women are going into the room. 5. The students (*f.*) are going into the room.

d. 1. . . . at the window. 2. He is sitting at the window. 3. She is sitting at the window. 4. They are standing at the window. 5. I am standing at the window.

e. 1. . . . to the window. 2. They are going to the window. 3. He is going to the window. 4. I am going to the window. 5. We are going to the window.

f. 1. . . . big. 2. The boys are big. 3. The students are big. 4. The families are large. 5. The sisters are tall. 6. The women are tall. 7. The schools are good. 8. The lessons are good.

g. 1. . . . young. 2. The students (*f.*) are young. 3. The gentlemen are young. 4. The families are small. 5. The schools are small. 6. The sisters are little. 7. The women are little.

h. 1. . . . are describing. 2. The women are describing the families. 3. The students (*f.*) are describing the schools. 4. The gentlemen are describing the students. 5. The students are describing their families. 6. The boys are describing their families. 7. The brothers are describing their lessons.

i. 1. They find . . . 2. The boys find their sisters. 3. The women find their families. 4. The students find their friends. 5. The students (*f.*) find their lessons.

j. 1. . . . are lying. 2. The lessons are lying here. 3. The books are lying here. 4. They are lying here. 5. The book is lying there. 6. It is lying there.

k. 1. They understand. 2. The gentlemen understand. 3. We understand the gentlemen. 4. They understand the gentlemen. 5. The gentlemen understand you.

B. MODEL SENTENCES

I. STUDY UNTIL EACH SENTENCE CAN BE GIVEN CORRECTLY FROM THE ENGLISH.

39. **Beschreiben Sie die Schulen!**
40. **Die Schwestern des Studenten sind klein.**
41. **Die Studentinnen verstehen den Herrn.**
42. **Herrn Brauns Jungen sind groß.**
43. **Die Frauen gehen ans Fenster.**
44. **Die Frau steht am Fenster.**
45. **Die Familie sitzt im Zimmer.**
46. **Die Studenten legen die Aufgaben auf den Tisch.**
47. **Die Aufgaben liegen auf dem Tisch.**

39. Describe the schools.
40. The student's sisters are small.
41. The students (*f.*) understand the gentleman.
42. Mr. Braun's boys are big.
43. The women are going to the window.
44. The woman is standing at the window.
45. The family is sitting in the room.
46. The students are putting the lessons on the table.
47. The lessons are lying on the table.

II. DRILL. EXPRESS ORALLY IN GERMAN.

a. 1. Describe the schools. 2. Describe the boys. 3. Describe the students. 4. Find the students. 5. Find the boys. 6. Find the friends.
b. 1. The student's sisters are small. 2. The student's brothers are small. 3. The student's father is tall. 4. The student's mother is young.
c. 1. The students (*f.*) understand the gentleman. 2. The coeds understand the student. 3. The students (*f.*) understand the woman. 4. The students (*f.*) understand the lessons. 5. The boys understand the lessons.
d. 1. Mr. Braun's boys are big. 2. Mr. Braun's sisters are tall. 3. Mr. Braun's students are young. 4. Mr. Braun's sons are little.

5. Mr. Braun's letters are good.   6. Mr. Braun's lessons are good.
e. 1. The women are going to the window.   2. The men are going to the window.   3. The students (*f.*) are going to the window.   4. The woman is going to the window.   5. The man is going to the window.
f. 1. The woman is standing at the window.   2. The gentleman is standing at the window.   3. The women are standing at the window. 4. The gentlemen are standing at the window.
g. 1. The family is sitting in the room.   2. The boy is sitting in the room.   3. The girl is sitting in the room.   4. The woman is sitting in the room.   5. The boys are sitting in the room.   6. The gentlemen are sitting in the room.
h. 1. The students are putting the lessons on the table.   2. The students (*f.*) are putting the lessons on the table.   3. The gentlemen are putting the lessons on the table.   4. The sisters are putting the lessons on the table.   5. He is putting them on the table.   6. I am putting them on the table.
i. 1. The lessons are lying on the table.   2. The books are lying on the table.   3. They are lying on the table.   4. The book is lying on the table. It is lying on the table.   5. The letter is lying on the table. It is lying on the table.

C. GRAMMAR

1. Direct formal commands are expressed by putting the pronoun **Sie** after the verb.

Beschreiben Sie die Schulen!
Describe the schools.

Such sentences usually end with an exclamation mark.

2. Most feminine nouns form their plurals by adding **-n** or **-en.** Those of more than one syllable ending in **-e, -l,** or **-r** take the plural ending **-n;** others take **-en.**

die Aufgabe	the lesson	**die Aufgaben**	the lessons
die Schwester	the sister	**die Schwestern**	the sisters
die Frau	the woman	**die Frauen**	the women

3. Feminine nouns ending in **-in** add **-nen.**
die Studentin the student (*f.*)   **die Studentinnen** the students (*f.*)

4. Masculine nouns ending in **-e** form their plural by adding **-n.**
der Junge   the boy   **die Jungen**   the boys

Some other masculine nouns, especially those of more than one syllable with the accent on the last syllable, form their plural by adding **-en.**

der Student   the student   **die Studenten**   the students

These nouns usually add the same endings for the genitive, dative, and accusative singulars. Thus, there are two forms: the nominative singular and a form ending in **-n** or **-en** for all other cases.

	SINGULAR		PLURAL	
NOM.	**der Junge**	**der Student**	**die Jungen**	**die Studenten**
GEN.	**des Jungen**	**des Studenten**	**der Jungen**	**der Studenten**
DAT.	**dem Jungen**	**dem Studenten**	**den Jungen**	**den Studenten**
ACC.	**den Jungen**	**den Studenten**	**die Jungen**	**die Studenten**

Note 1: The principal parts of **der Junge** and **der Student** are **der Junge, -n, -n** and **der Student, -en, -en.**

Note 2: **Der Herr** (the gentleman) adds **-n** for singular genitive, dative, and accusative, but **-en** for *all* plural case forms. The principal parts are **der Herr, -n, -en.** The title **Herr** (Mr.) also adds **-n** in the singular forms, except the nominative.

5. Certain prepositions may combine with the definite article to form contracted forms. Though the use of these contractions is optional, they are preferred in colloquial German.

$$an + dem = am \qquad an + das = ans$$
$$in + dem = im \qquad in + das = ins$$
$$auf + das = aufs$$

6. Certain prepositions govern the accusative case when *motion* toward the object of the preposition is indicated, the dative case when *position* is indicated.

   a. **Die Frauen gehen ans Fenster.**   (motion)
      The women are going to the window.

   b. **Die Frau steht am Fenster.**   (position)
      The woman is standing at the window.

   c. **Der Student kommt ins Zimmer.**   (motion)
      The student is coming into the room.

   d. **Die Familie sitzt im Zimmer.**   (position)
      The family is sitting in the room.

   e. **Die Studenten legen die Aufgaben auf den Tisch.**   (motion)
      The students are putting the lessons on the table.

f. **Die Aufgaben liegen auf dem Tisch.** (position)
The lessons are lying on the table.
Included in this category are the following prepositions.

an	at, to	**über**	above, over
auf	on	**unter**	under
hinter	behind	**vor**	in front of, before
in	in, into	**zwischen**	between, among
neben	near, next to		

D. EXERCISES

WRITE THE FOLLOWING SENTENCES IN GERMAN AND BE ABLE TO EXPRESS
THEM ORALLY IN CLASS.

1. They are putting the boys' books under these tables.
2. His sisters are sitting behind my mother.
3. The fathers of the children are going into the teacher's house.
4. They are at the teacher's house now.
5. His sisters write letters to the student.
6. The gentlemen are sitting at the windows.
7. Do you understand Mr. Meyer?
8. Is the girl standing in front of the boys?
9. Describe the student.
10. Is the school next to these buildings?
11. Are your families sitting at the table now?
12. Mr. Braun's lessons are good.
13. Find the books, Miss Schmidt.
14. The women are standing in front of the building.
15. These schools begin at eight o'clock.
16. Every boy's mother is here.
17. Is the teacher coming to the door?
18. Don't put the letters on the books.
19. Their brothers' families are small.
20. Above the table is a window.
21. Begin the lesson now.
22. The students are coming with Mr. Schmidt.
23. The students (*f.*) are putting the lessons between the books.
24. The women are not old. They are young.
25. We are giving the boy the book.
26. She likes to stand at the window.

E. READING AND SPEAKING

I. READ THE FOLLOWING ALOUD UNTIL YOU ARE THOROUGHLY FAMILIAR
    WITH IT.

In der Schule

Es ist noch nicht neun Uhr. Die Studenten und die Studentinnen
gehen jetzt in die Schule. Manche stehen vor dem Gebäude und reden
miteinander[1].

5   Jetzt kommt Hans in die Schule. Sein Freund Günther steht an der
Tür des Gebäudes. Hans begrüßt ihn und sie gehen zusammen (to-
gether) ins Gebäude. Sie gehen in ein Zimmer. Im Zimmer sind fünf
Tische. Manche Studenten sitzen schon an den Tischen und ihre
Bücher liegen unter den Tischen.

10 Hans und Günther legen ihre Bücher unter einen der Tische. Günther
legt seine Aufgaben auf den Tisch und fragt: „Wo sind deine Aufgaben, Hans?"

„Ich habe sie nicht, denn (for) jetzt besuchen uns mein Onkel und
seine Familie, und ich muß den ganzen Tag mit den Kindern spielen[2]."

15 „Spielst du gerne mit Kindern?"

„Ich spiele nicht gerne mit ihnen, aber ich muß der Mutter helfen[3].
In zwei Tagen gehen sie nach Hause. Dann mache ich (I'll do) meine
Aufgaben."

Jetzt ist es neun Uhr und die Schule beginnt. Der Lehrer kommt
20 ins Zimmer und begrüßt die Studenten.

II. ANSWER THE FOLLOWING QUESTIONS IN GERMAN.

1. Wer steht vor der Schule?
2. Wo sitzen die Studenten im Zimmer?
3. Wo liegen die Bücher?
4. Hat Hans seine Aufgaben?
5. Wer besucht Hans' Familie?
6. Wann gehen sie nach Hause?

---

[1] **reden miteinander** talk to one another.   [2] **ich muß den ganzen Tag . . .
spielen** I have to play all day long.   [3] **ich muß der Mutter helfen** I must help
my mother.

☞ UNIT 7

A. UNITS OF SPEECH AND VOCABULARY

I. STUDY AND READ ALOUD.

wir müssen essen	we must eat, we have to eat
so groß wie	as big as
in die Stadt	to town, downtown
in der Stadt	in town
noch ein Glas	another glass
noch eine Tante	another aunt
wenig Geld	little money

das Geld, -es, -er	the money	**kalt**	cold
das Glas, -es, ̈er	the glass	**neu**	new
die Kusine, -, -n	the cousin *f.*	**reich**	rich
der Vetter, -s, -n	the cousin	**viel**	much
die Tante, -, -n	the aunt	**viele**	many
die Stadt, -, ̈e	the town, city	**warm**	warm
das Wasser, -s, -	the water	**wenig**	little (*in number*)
bringen	to bring	**wenige**	few
müssen	must, to have to	**dreizehn**	thirteen
trinken	to drink	**vierzehn**	fourteen
wessen?	whose?	**noch**	still, yet
wem?	(to) whom?	**aber**	but
wen?	whom?	**denn**	for, because, since
arm	poor		

II. DRILL. EXPRESS ORALLY IN GERMAN. REPEAT UNTIL IT IS NO LONGER
NECESSARY TO REFER TO SECTION I.

a. 1. we must eat   2. we must drink   3. we have to eat and drink
   4. you have to learn   5. they have to come

b. 1. as big as   2. as poor as   3. as rich as   4. as cold as   5. as
   warm as   6. as much as   7. as little as

c. 1. . . . to town.   2. He is going to town.   3. My cousin is going
   to town.   4. His aunt is going downtown.   5. Her cousin (*f.*) is
   going downtown.   6. They are going downtown.

d. 1. . . . in town.   2. Whose aunt lives in town?   3. Whose cousin
   (*f.*) lives in town?   4. Whose uncle lives in town?   5. Whose
   brother lives in town?

e. 1. another glass   2. another child   3. another cousin   4. another
   brother

f. 1. another aunt   2. another cousin (*f.*)   3. another city   4. another
   lesson

g. 1. . . . little money.   2. He has little money.   3. She has little
   money.   4. They have little money.

h. 1. the water   2. much water   3. little water   4. I am drinking the
   water.   5. The water is still cold.   6. The water is still warm.
   7. The water is in the glass.

i. 1. . . . are you bringing . . . ?   2. To whom are you bringing the
   water?   3. To whom are you bringing the money?   4. To whom
   are you bringing the glass?

j. 1. Whom . . . ?   2. Whom is he teaching?   3. Whom is she greeting?   4. Whom are they visiting?

k. 1. . . . new.   2. The glass is new.   3. The school is new.   4. The
   books are new.   5. The glasses are new.

l. 1. . . . thirteen cities.   2. They are visiting thirteen cities.   3. He
   has thirteen cousins and fourteen aunts.   4. I have fourteen
   cousins (*f.*).

m. 1. . . . but . . .   2. poor but young   3. rich but old   4. poor but
   nice   5. rich but not nice

n. 1. because . . .   2. He has no money, because he is poor.   3. She
   has much money, because she is rich.   4. I am drinking the water
   because it is cold.   5. I am not drinking the water because it is warm.
   6. We are visiting our aunt, since she is in town.   7. They are
   bringing little money, for they are not rich.

B. MODEL SENTENCES

I. STUDY UNTIL EACH SENTENCE CAN BE GIVEN CORRECTLY FROM THE ENGLISH.

48. **Hier ist mein Brief. Wo ist Ihrer?**
49. **Er hat zwei Bücher und ich habe ein(e)s.**
50. **Sein Onkel hat wenig Geld, aber viele Freunde.**
51. **Alte Häuser sind nicht so gut wie neue Häuser.**
52. **Ihr alter Vater wohnt bei ihnen.**
53. **Sein altes Haus ist so groß wie mein neues Haus.**
54. **Mein Vetter Franz und meine Kusine Anna müssen nach Hause gehen.**
55. **Er schreibt gerne Briefe.**

48. Here is my letter. Where is yours?
49. He has two books and I have one.
50. His uncle has little money, but many friends.
51. Old houses are not as good as new houses.
52. Their old father lives at their house.
53. His old house is as big as my new house.
54. My cousin Franz and my cousin Anna must go home.
55. He likes to write letters.

II. DRILL. EXPRESS ORALLY IN GERMAN.

a. 1. Here is my letter. Where is yours? 2. Here is my son. Where is yours? 3. Here is my table. Where is yours? 4. Here is my cousin. Where is yours? 5. Here is my father. Where is yours?

b. 1. He has two books and I have one. 2. He has two glasses and I have one. 3. She has two children and her cousin (*f.*) has one. 4. My aunt has two girls and I have one.

c. 1. His uncle has little money, but many friends. 2. His cousin has little money, but many friends. 3. His cousin (*f.*) has little money, but many friends. 4. His aunt has little money, but many friends.

d. 1. Old houses are not as good as new houses. 2. Old buildings are not as good as new buildings. 3. Old glasses are not as good as new glasses.

e. 1. Their old father lives at their house. 2. Our old father lives at our house. 3. My old uncle lives at my house. 4. His old uncle lives at his house.

f. 1. His old house is as big as my new house. 2. My old house is as big as her new house. 3. Your old house is as big as his new house. 4. Our old house is as big as their new house.

g. 1. My cousin Franz and my cousin Anna must go home. 2. Our children must go home. 3. They have to go home. 4. Do you have to go home?

h. 1. He likes to write letters. 2. I like to write letters. 3. She likes to drink water. 4. They like to study German.

C. GRAMMAR

1. The interrogative pronoun **wer?** (who?) is inflected as follows.

NOMINATIVE	**wer?**	who?
GENITIVE	**wessen?**	whose?
DATIVE	**wem?**	(to) whom?
ACCUSATIVE	**wen?**	whom?

2. An **ein**-word used as a pronoun has the same endings as a **der**-word. In the nominative singular masculine, the pronoun ends in **-er,** whereas the adjective has no ending.

   a. **Hier ist mein Brief. Wo ist Ihrer?**
       Here is my letter. Where is yours?

   In the nominative and accusative singulars of the neuter, the pronoun ends in **-(e)s;** the adjective has no ending.

   b. **Ein Kind ist dort und ein(e)s ist hier.**
       One child is there and one is here.

   c. **Er hat zwei Bücher und ich habe ein(e)s.**
       He has two books and I have one.

   In all other cases, the **ein**-word pronoun has the same form as the adjective.

   d. **Sie hat ihre Aufgabe und ich habe meine.**
       She has her lesson and I have mine.

   Note: Articles, **ein**-words, **der**-words, and cardinal numbers are called *limiting adjectives*, because they limit the number, position, or ownership of things. Adjectives which describe some quality of a noun are called *descriptive adjectives*.

3. **Viel** and **wenig** are limiting adjectives which usually have no endings in the singular, but which are inflected like **der**-words in the plural.

Sein Onkel hat wenig Geld, aber viele Freunde.
His uncle has little money, but many friends.
4. A descriptive adjective which modifies and precedes a noun must
be inflected. If the descriptive adjective is not preceded by a definite
article, a **der**-word, or an **ein**-word *with an ending*, the descriptive
adjective has "strong" endings. The strong endings are for the most
part identical with the **der**-word endings.
   a. **Alte Häuser sind nicht so gut wie neue Häuser.**
      Old houses are not as good as new houses.
   b. **Ihr alter Vater wohnt bei ihnen.**
      Their old father lives at their house.
   c. **Sein altes Haus ist so groß wie mein neues Haus.**
      His old house is as big as my new house.
5. In comparisons, **so . . . wie** is equivalent to English "as . . . as."
   (See examples 4a and 4c above.)
6. Present indicative of the irregular verb **müssen** (must, to have to).

ich muß	I must, have to
[**du mußt**	you must, have to]
er, sie, es muß	he, she, it must, has to
wir müssen	we must, have to
[**ihr müßt**	you must, have to]
sie müssen	they must, have to
Sie müssen	you must, have to

7. In a main clause, the infinitive stands last.
   Mein Vetter Franz und meine Kusine Anna müssen nach Hause gehen.
   My cousin Franz and my cousin Anna must go home.
8. **Gerne** (gladly) precedes noun objects.
   Er schreibt gerne Briefe.
   He likes to write letters.

D. EXERCISES

WRITE THE FOLLOWING SENTENCES IN GERMAN AND BE ABLE TO EXPRESS
THEM ORALLY IN CLASS.

1. Whose child is there?—Yours.
2. To whom do I have to bring water?
3. Your old uncle has rich daughters.

4. Her friend (*f.*) has little money, because she is poor.
5. My cousin (*f.*) is as old as your cousin (*f.*).
6. Whom is our old friend visiting?
7. They live in old houses.
8. That girl likes to live in town.
9. Is their house as warm as ours?
10. Good books are good friends.
11. Small boys do not like to play with small girls.
12. Two books are lying on the table, and I have one here.
13. Does your school have many rooms?—No, it has few.
14. Does he have a new house?
15. Are you learning much German?
16. Our cousin (*f.*) is coming home, for she has to study.
17. You must bring another glass.
18. Does the student (*f.*) like to study her lesson?
19. His rich uncle has thirteen houses, but he has none.
20. One young student is still living here.
21. My friends have to eat now.
22. My brother is not as big as his.
23. Is your old teacher still teaching German?
24. The parents of many students are there.
25. The student must study the lesson.

E. READING AND SPEAKING

I. READ THE FOLLOWING ALOUD UNTIL YOU ARE THOROUGHLY FAMILIAR
WITH IT.

Tante Johanna

Tante Johanna kommt mit ihren Kindern zu Besuch. Hans' junger
Vetter heißt Hermann and die Kusine heißt Hilde. Er ist dreizehn
Jahre alt und sie ist vierzehn, aber er ist so groß wie sie.

5   Hermann sagt: ,,Hans, ich muß ein Glas Wasser[1] haben, denn ich
habe Durst.''[2]

Hans bringt dem Vetter ein Glas Wasser.

Hermann sagt ,,Danke'' und trinkt das Glas Wasser, aber er hat
noch Durst. Hans muß noch eins bringen.

---

[1] **ein Glas Wasser**   a glass of water.   [2] **ich habe Durst**   I am thirsty.

Die Tante sagt: „Jetzt müssen wir in die Stadt gehen. Bitte, komm' 10
mit (come along), Hans. Wir haben unser Auto hier."

„Gut", sagt Hans, „ich komme gerne, denn ich muß etwas (something) kaufen (buy)."

Um zwölf Uhr gehen sie in die Stadt. Sie essen in der Stadt zu Mittag, und um fünf Uhr gehen sie nach Hause. 15

II. ANSWER THE FOLLOWING QUESTIONS IN GERMAN.

1. Wie heißt Hans' Tante?
2. Wie alt ist der Vetter?
3. Ist er so alt wie seine Schwester?
4. Wer hat Durst?
5. Wer kommt mit in die Stadt?
6. Wo essen sie zu Mittag?

☞ UNIT 8

A. UNITS OF SPEECH AND VOCABULARY

I. STUDY AND READ ALOUD.

Ich habe Hunger.	I am hungry.
Er hat Durst.	He is thirsty.
Sie hat recht.	She is right.
Sie haben unrecht.	They are wrong.
Heute geht er.	He is going today.
Morgen kommt sie.	She is coming tomorrow.
ein anderer Hut	a different hat
eine andere Aufgabe	a different lesson
ein anderes Kino	a different movie theater

das Auto, -s, -s	the car	**die Verkäuferin,**	
der Hut, -es, ⸗e	the hat	**-, -nen**	the salesgirl
das Kino, -s, -s	the movie, movie theater	**antworten**	to answer
		kaufen	to buy
der Laden, -s, ⸗	the store	**reden**	to talk
die Leute *pl.*	the people (*in a crowd*)	**werden**	to become, to get
		anderer, andere,	
das Restaurant,		**anderes**	other, different
-s, -s	the restaurant	**fünfzehn**	fifteen
die Straße, -, -n	the street	**sechzehn**	sixteen
der Verkäufer,		**siebzehn**	seventeen
-s, -	the salesman		

54

achtzehn	eighteen	**heute**	today
neunzehn	nineteen	**morgen**	tomorrow

II. DRILL. EXPRESS ORALLY IN GERMAN. REPEAT UNTIL IT IS NO LONGER NECESSARY TO REFER TO SECTION I.

a. 1. I am hungry.   2. He is hungry.   3. We are hungry.   4. They are hungry.

b. 1. He is thirsty.   2. She is thirsty.   3. You are thirsty.   4. The people are thirsty.   5. They are thirsty.

c. 1. She is right.   2. They are right.   3. The people are right.   4. The salesman is right.   5. He is right.

d. 1. They are wrong.   2. The people are wrong.   3. You are wrong.   4. The salesgirl is wrong.   5. She is wrong.

e. 1. He is going today.   2. He is going to the restaurant today.   3. She is going to the restaurant today.   4. Fifteen people are going to the restaurant today.

f. 1. She is coming tomorrow.   2. We are coming tomorrow.   3. You are coming tomorrow.   4. Sixteen people are coming tomorrow.   5. The people are coming to the store tomorrow.   6. They are going to the movies tomorrow.

g. 1. a different hat   2. a different store   3. a different salesman   4. a different teacher

h. 1. a different lesson   2. a different student (*f.*)   3. a different woman   4. a different salesgirl

i. 1. a different movie theater   2. a different restaurant   3. a different girl   4. a different child   5. a different car

j. 1. The street . . .   2. The street is big.   3. The street is small.   4. The street is old.   5. The street is new.   6. The car is new.

k. 1. . . . are answering.   2. They are answering.   3. The people are answering.   4. The salesman and the salesgirl are answering.   5. Seventeen students are answering.

l. 1. . . . are buying.   2. They are buying hats.   3. Eighteen people are buying hats.   4. They are buying nineteen hats.   5. They are buying the store.   6. They are buying the movie theater.   7. They are buying two cars.

m. 1. . . . are talking.   2. They are talking much.   3. The salesman and the salesgirl are talking much.   4. The salesman and the salesgirl are talking little.

n. 1. . . . are getting . . .   2. We are getting old.   3. They are getting old.   4. The salesmen are getting old.   5. The salesgirls are getting old.

B. MODEL SENTENCES

I. STUDY UNTIL EACH SENTENCE CAN BE GIVEN CORRECTLY FROM THE ENGLISH.

56. Die andere Tochter besucht die neue Schule.
57. Das junge Mädchen lehrt das kleine Kind.
58. Der arme Vater hat einen reichen Sohn.
59. Der Onkel des jungen Mannes ist reich.
60. Die jungen Leute essen in den guten Restaurants.
61. Das Kind schreibt gut.
62. Gehen wir ins Kino!
63. Morgen kauft er ein neues Auto.

56. The other daughter attends the new school.
57. The young girl is teaching the little child.
58. The poor father has a rich son.
59. The young man's uncle is rich.
60. The young people are eating in the good restaurants.
61. The child writes well.
62. Let's go to the movies.
63. He will buy a new car tomorrow.

II. DRILL. EXPRESS ORALLY IN GERMAN.

a. 1. The other daughter attends the new school.   2. The other sister attends the new school.   3. The other cousin (*f.*) attends the new school.   4. The other girl friend attends the new school.
b. 1. The young girl is teaching the little child.   2. The young girl is greeting the little child.   3. The little child is greeting the young girl.   4. The little child is visiting the young girl.
c. 1. The poor father has a rich son.   2. The poor man has a rich son. 3. The poor man has a rich father.   4. The poor son has a rich father.

d. 1. The young man's uncle is rich. 2. The young man's father is rich. 3. The young man's aunt is rich. 4. The young man's cousin (*f.*) is rich.

e. 1. The young people are eating in the good restaurants. 2. The young men are eating in the good restaurants. 3. The young women are eating in the good restaurants. 4. The young students (*f.*) are eating in the good restaurants.

f. 1. The child writes well. 2. The girl writes well. 3. The boy writes well. 4. The student writes well. 5. The student (*f.*) writes well.

g. 1. Let's go to the movies. 2. Let's go to the restaurant. 3. Let's go into the store. 4. Let's go to school. 4. Let's go home.

h. 1. He will buy a new car tomorrow. 2. We will buy a new car tomorrow. 3. She will buy a new car tomorrow. 4. I will buy a new car tomorrow. 5. They will buy a new car tomorrow.

C. GRAMMAR

1. When a descriptive adjective is preceded by an article, a **der**-word, or an **ein**-word with ending, the descriptive adjective has "weak" endings.

   The "weak" ending is **-e** in the nominative singular of all genders and in the accusative singular of the feminine and neuter.

   a. **Die andere Tochter besucht die neue Schule.**
      The other daughter attends the new school.

   b. **Das junge Mädchen lehrt das kleine Kind.**
      The young girl is teaching the little child.

   c. **Der arme Vater hat einen reichen Sohn.**
      The poor father has a rich son.

   In all other cases, the "weak" ending is **-en**: the masculine singular accusative (*c*, above); the genitive and dative singulars of all genders; all cases in the plural.

   d. **Der Onkel des jungen Mannes ist reich.**
      The young man's uncle is rich.

   e. **Die jungen Leute essen in den guten Restaurants.**
      The young people are eating in the good restaurants.

2. Most descriptive adjectives are used without endings as adverbs.
                         Das Kind schreibt gut.
                         The child writes well.

3. A few masculine and neuter nouns form their plural by adding -s.

das Auto, -s, -s   the car
das Kino, -s, -s   the movies
das Restaurant, -s, -s   the restaurant

Note: These nouns do *not* add **-n** to the dative plural.

Die jungen Leute essen in den guten Restaurants.
The young people eat in the good restaurants.

4. The command form of the first person plural is the same as the indicative form, with the verb preceding the subject.

Gehen wir ins Kino!
Let's go to the movies.

5. The present tense is frequently used with future meaning, especially when the future idea is made clear by an adverb.

Morgen kauft er ein neues Auto.
He will buy a new car tomorrow.

6. Verbs whose stems end in **-d** or **-t** add **-e** before the endings **-st** and **-t**. The present tense of **reden** and **antworten** follows.

ich rede	I talk, am talking, do talk
[du redest	you talk, are talking, do talk]
er, sie, es redet	he, she, it talks, is talking, does talk
wir reden	we talk, are talking, do talk
[ihr redet	you talk, are talking, do talk]
sie reden	they talk, are talking, do talk
Sie reden	you talk, are talking, do talk

ich antworte	I answer, am answering, do answer
[du antwortest	you answer, are answering, do answer]
er, sie, es antwortet	he, she, it answers, is answering, does answer
wir antworten	we answer, are answering, do answer
[ihr antwortet	you answer, are answering, do answer]
sie antworten	they answer, are answering, do answer
Sie antworten	you answer, are answering, do answer

7. The present indicative of **werden** (to become, get).

ich werde	I become, am becoming, do become; get, am getting, do get
[du wirst	you become, are becoming, do become; get, are getting, do get]

er, sie, es wird	he, she, it becomes, is becoming, does become; gets, is getting, does get
wir werden	we become, are becoming, do become; get, are getting, do get
[ihr werdet	you become, are becoming, do become; get, are getting, do get]
sie werden	they become, are becoming, do become; get, are getting, do get
Sie werden	you become, are becoming, do become; get, are getting, do get

D. EXERCISES

WRITE THE FOLLOWING SENTENCES IN GERMAN AND BE ABLE TO EXPRESS THEM ORALLY IN CLASS.

1. The beautiful hat is in the other store.
2. Fifteen boys are answering.
3. These old restaurants are good.
4. Let's go into the new restaurant.
5. The salesman is talking with an old woman.
6. The little child understands German well.
7. His other daughter will become sixteen tomorrow.
8. Let's drink water.
9. The young girl's hat is new.
10. The students are visiting two movie theaters.
11. She'll talk with us tomorrow.
12. The young woman's son does not answer.
13. We are getting old.
14. My mother teaches in the new school.
15. Is she buying the new hat?
16. The other schools are small.
17. He is bringing me the cold water.
18. Let's eat now.
19. The students of the new teacher talk well.
20. Do you understand the little girl?
21. Nineteen people will come tomorrow.
22. His children are getting big.

23. He is talking with his old friends.
24. Let's go home.

E. READING AND SPEAKING

I. READ THE FOLLOWING ALOUD UNTIL YOU ARE THOROUGHLY FAMILIAR
   WITH IT.

In der Stadt

Tante Johanna, Hilde, Hermann und Hans sind in der Stadt. Viele
Leute gehen und stehen auf der Straße. Hilde muß einen neuen Hut
kaufen. Sie gehen in einen Laden. Ein Verkäufer kommt und fragt:
5 „Womit kann ich dienen?"[1]
   Hilde antwortet: „Ich möchte (would like) einen neuen Hut kaufen."
   „Gut", antwortet der Verkäufer. „Wir haben schöne Hüte im
Laden."
   Hilde probiert sechzehn Hüte an[2] und kauft keinen. Sie gehen in
10 einen anderen Laden. Hilde probiert dort siebzehn Hüte an. Schließlich
(Finally) kauft sie einen schönen Hut. Auch die Mutter muß einen Hut
kaufen. Sie probiert nur (only) fünfzehn an. Auch sie kauft schließlich
einen Hut.
   Hans probiert nur drei Hüte an und kauft einen. Er gibt dem Ver-
15 käufer das Geld und alle gehen aus dem Laden. Sie essen in einem
guten Restaurant zu Abend. Um sieben Uhr kommen sie nach Hause.

II. ANSWER THE FOLLOWING QUESTIONS IN GERMAN.

1. **Warum (Why) geht Hilde in einen Laden?**
2. **Wer fragt: „Womit kann ich dienen?"**
3. **Wie viele Hüte probiert Hilde an?**
4. **Was gibt Hans dem Verkäufer?**
5. **Wo essen sie zu Abend?**
6. **Wann kommen sie nach Hause?**

---

[1] **Womit kann ich dienen?**   What can I do for you?   [2] **Hilde probiert sechzehn
Hüte an**   Hilde tries on sixteen hats.

☛ UNIT 9

A. UNITS OF SPEECH AND VOCABULARY

I. STUDY AND READ ALOUD.

er dankt mir	he thanks me
ich helfe ihm	I help him
Sie macht eine Reise.	She is taking a trip.
nach Deutschland	to Germany
nach Frankreich	to France
nach Italien	to Italy
nach Spanien	to Spain
nach den Vereinigten Staaten	to the United States
in die Schweiz	to Switzerland
älter als	older than
ein älterer Mann	an elderly man

Berlin, -s[1]	Berlin	**Spanien, -s**	Spain
Deutschland, -s	Germany	**die Vereinigten**	the United
England, -s	England	**Staaten** *pl.*	States
Europa, -s	Europe	**die Reise, -, -n**	the trip
Frankreich, -s	France	**die Tasche, -, -n**	the pocket
Italien, -s	Italy	**danken** + *dat.*	to thank
Österreich, -s	Austria	**helfen** + *dat.*	to help
die Schweiz, -	Switzerland	**reisen**	to travel

[1] If only the genitive ending is indicated, the word usually has no plural.

stecken	to put, to stick	**als**	than
hoch	high	**zu**	too, excessively

II. DRILL. EXPRESS ORALLY IN GERMAN. REPEAT UNTIL IT IS NO LONGER NECESSARY TO REFER TO SECTION I.

a. 1. he thanks me   2. she thanks me   3. they thank me   4. you thank me

b. 1. I help him   2. we help him   3. they help him   4. the father and the mother help him   5. the brothers help him

c. 1. She is taking a trip.   2. He is taking a trip.   3. They are taking a trip.   4. We are taking a trip.   5. You are taking a trip.

d. 1. . . . to Germany.   2. We are traveling to Germany.   3. They are traveling to Germany.   4. They are traveling to France.   5. He is traveling to France.   6. She is traveling to France.   7. She is traveling to Italy.   8. He is traveling to Italy.   9. We are traveling to Italy.   10. We are traveling to Spain.   11. They are traveling to Spain.   12. He is traveling to Spain.   13. He is traveling to the United States.

e. 1. . . . to Switzerland.   2. Are you traveling to Switzerland?   3. Is he traveling to Switzerland?   4. Is she traveling to Switzerland?

f. 1. . . . older than . . .   2. He is older than she.   3. She is older than he.   4. We are older than they.   5. You are older than we.

g. 1. . . . an elderly man.   2. He is an elderly man.   3. Is he an elderly man?   4. Is Mr. Braun an elderly man?

h. 1. . . . Berlin.   2. She is in Berlin.   3. He is in Berlin.   4. He is in Europe.   5. She is in Europe.   6. They are in Europe.   7. They are in Austria.   8. He is in Austria.   9. She is in Austria.   10. She is in England.   11. He is in England.   12. They are in England.

i. 1. . . . the United States.   2. She is describing the United States.   3. They are describing the United States.   4. We are describing the United States.

j. 1. He is putting . . .   2. He is putting the letter . . .   3. He is putting the letter into the pocket.   4. She is putting the letter into the pocket.   5. She is putting the book into the pocket.

k. 1. . . . too . . .   2. . . . too high.   3. The house is too high.   4. The building is too high.   5. The buildings are too high.

B. MODEL SENTENCES

I. STUDY UNTIL EACH SENTENCE CAN BE GIVEN CORRECTLY FROM THE ENGLISH.

64. **Der Sohn dankt dem Vater.**
65. **Er reist nach Deutschland.**
66. **Sie reist in die Schweiz.**
67. **Der Mann ist älter als die Frau.**
68. **Sein Freund ist ein reicherer Mann als mein Freund.**
69. **Das Gebäude ist hoch.**
70. **Es ist ein schönes hohes Gebäude.**
71. **Der Student wird eine Reise machen.**
72. **Der Junge steckt die Hand in die Tasche.**

64. The son thanks his father.
65. He is traveling to Germany.
66. She is traveling to Switzerland.
67. The man is older than the woman.
68. His friend is a richer man than my friend.
69. The building is high.
70. It is a beautiful high building.
71. The student will take a trip.
72. The boy is putting his hand in his pocket.

II. DRILL. EXPRESS ORALLY IN GERMAN.

a. 1. The son thanks his father. 2. The boy thanks his father. 3. The child thanks his father. 4. The daughter thanks her father.
b. 1. He is traveling to Germany. 2. The student is traveling to Germany. 3. The student (*f.*) is traveling to Germany. 4. The parents are traveling to Germany. 5. The teachers are traveling to Germany.
c. 1. She is traveling to Switzerland. 2. The student (*f.*) is traveling to Switzerland. 3. The girl is traveling to Switzerland. 4. The man is traveling to Switzerland. 5. The men are traveling to Switzerland.
d. 1. The man is older than the woman. 2. The woman is older than the man. 3. The sister is older than the brother. 4. The brothers are older than the sisters. 5. The uncles are older than the aunts.
e. 1. His friend is a richer man than my friend. 2. His father is a

richer man than my father.   3. His brother is a richer man than my brother.   4. His uncle is a richer man than my uncle.

f.   1. The building is high.   2. The room is high.   3. The rooms are high.   4. The buildings are high.

g.   1. It is a beautiful high building.   2. The school is a beautiful high building.   3. The movie theater is a beautiful high building.   4. Is it a beautiful high building?

h.   1. The student will take a trip.   2. The student (*f.*) will take a trip.   3. The girl will take a trip.   4. The family will take a trip.

i.   1. The boy is putting his hand in his pocket.   2. The man is putting his hand in his pocket.   3. The student is putting his hand in his pocket.   4. The teacher is putting his hand in his pocket.

C. GRAMMAR

1. A few verbs, as **danken** (to thank), **helfen** (to help), **antworten** (to answer), require the object to be in the dative case.

   a. **Der Sohn dankt dem Vater.**
   The son thanks the father.

   b. **Ich helfe ihm.**
   I am helping him.

   c. **Er antwortet Ihnen.**
   He is answering you.

2. The names of cities, states, continents, and most countries are neuter nouns and are usually employed without the article, as in English.

(das) **Berlin, -s**	Berlin
(das) **Deutschland, -s**	Germany
(das) **England, -s**	England
(das) **Europa, -s**	Europe
(das) **Frankreich, -s**	France
(das) **Italien, -s**	Italy
(das) **Österreich, -s**	Austria
(das) **Spanien, -s**	Spain

3. Some names of countries are feminine nouns.

   die Schweiz, -   Switzerland

   Others are plural nouns.

   die Vereinigten Staaten   the United States

   Feminine and plural nouns always require the use of the definite article.

Note: **Die Vereinigten Staaten** is a grammatical plural and requires a plural verb when used as a subject.

4. **Nach** (to) indicates direction with neuter and plural geographical names.
   a. **Er reist nach Deutschland.**
      He is traveling to Germany.
   b. **Er reist nach den Vereinigten Staaten.**
      He is traveling to the United States.
   In plus the article is used with feminine geographical names.
   c. **Sie reist in die Schweiz.**
      She is traveling to Switzerland.

5. The comparative form of adjectives is formed by adding the suffix **-er** to the stem. If the adjective is a monosyllable whose stem vowel is **a, o,** or **u,** the vowel is umlauted.
      Der Mann ist älter als die Frau.
      The man is older than the woman.
      Sein neues Haus ist schöner als sein altes Haus.
      His new house is more beautiful than his old house.

6. The comparative form of the adjective is inflected when it precedes the noun it modifies.
      Sein Freund ist ein reicherer Mann als mein Freund.
      His friend is a richer man than my friend.
   Note: The comparative form of the adjective is often used absolutely, without reference to any other person or thing.
      ein älterer Mann   an elderly man, a rather old man

7. The adjective **hoch** has two forms. When a vowel follows, the stem is **hoh-,** otherwise the stem is **hoch-.**
   a. **Das Gebäude ist hoch.**
      The building is high.
   b. **Es ist ein schönes hohes Gebäude.**
      It is a beautiful high building.
   Note: When two or more descriptive adjectives precede a noun, both have the same ending.

8. The present tense of **werden** plus the infinitive of the main verb forms the future tense.
      Der Junge wird eine Reise machen.
      The boy will take a trip.
   The future of **machen** (to make, to do).

ich werde . . . machen	I will do, make
[**du wirst . . . machen**	you will do, make]
er, sie, es wird . . . machen	he, she, it will do, make
wir werden . . . machen	we will do, make
[**ihr werdet . . . machen**	you will do, make]
sie werden . . . machen	they will do, make
Sie werden . . . machen	you will do, make

9. The definite article rather than the possessive adjective is used for articles of clothing or parts of the body when ownership is clear from the context.

   Der Junge steckt die Hand in die Tasche.

   The boy is putting his hand in his pocket.

   Note: With nouns of relationship the definite article *may* be used in place of the possessive adjective.

   Der Sohn dankt dem Vater.

   The son thanks *his* father.

D. EXERCISES

WRITE THE FOLLOWING SENTENCES IN GERMAN AND BE ABLE TO EXPRESS THEM ORALLY IN CLASS.

1. The mother is thanking her daughters.
2. They will take a trip to Austria.
3. The girl is putting her hand in her pocket.
4. He has a newer car than I.
5. He is not coming to Germany.
6. Is your house as high as the school?
7. Berlin is a big city.
8. I am helping the teachers now.
9. The younger brother is poorer.
10. They are traveling to France but not to Switzerland.
11. The older children are helping the younger child.
12. This building is high, but the other building is higher.
13. Are you answering me?
14. We will begin the lesson.
15. Is the child playing in that big cold room?
16. The teachers are helping the students.
17. He will buy the books.

18. She is a rather young woman.
19. Are you taking a trip to Europe?
20. Don't thank me.
21. Switzerland is smaller than Spain.
22. She is answering her mother.
23. We will go home now.
24. My two sisters are taller than I.
25. The United States is big and beautiful.
26. Is he putting the letters in his pocket?

E. READING AND SPEAKING

I. READ THE FOLLOWING ALOUD UNTIL YOU ARE THOROUGHLY FAMILIAR WITH IT.

Die Reise

Hans kommt nach Hause und sagt zu seiner Mutter: „Mein Freund Walter reist nach Deutschland. Ich möchte auch nach Deutschland reisen."[1]

Die Mutter sagt: „Ich werde dir helfen. Ich werde mit deinem Vater reden." 5

Herr Braun kommt nach Hause und Frau Braun sagt zu ihm: „Unser Sohn möchte eine Reise nach Deutschland machen."

Der Vater steckt die Hände in die Taschen und geht im Zimmer auf und ab.[2] „Aber er ist zu jung", sagt er schließlich. 10

„Nein", antwortet seine Frau. „Er ist nicht zu jung. Sein Freund Walter reist nach Europa und Hans ist älter als er."

Hans kommt ins Wohnzimmer. Der Vater fragt ihn: „Wohin willst du reisen,[3] Hans?"

Hans antwortet: „Ich möchte nach Deutschland reisen und Berlin, 15 Hamburg und München (Munich) besuchen."

„Gut", sagt Herr Braun. „Ich glaube (believe), wir haben genug (enough) Geld. Du darfst die Reise machen."[4]

„Das ist wunderbar (wonderful). Jetzt muß ich Walter anrufen (call up)." 20

---

[1] Ich möchte . . . reisen I'd like to travel.   [2] auf und ab back and forth.
[3] Wohin willst du reisen? Where do you want to travel to?   [4] Du darfst die Reise machen You may take the trip.

II. ANSWER THE FOLLOWING QUESTIONS IN GERMAN.

1. **Wer wird eine Reise nach Deutschland machen?**
2. **Wer will auch reisen?**
3. **Ist Walter älter als Hans?**
4. **Wird Herr Braun seinem Sohn helfen?**
5. **Was macht Hans jetzt?**

☞ UNIT 10

A. UNITS OF SPEECH AND VOCABULARY

I. STUDY AND READ ALOUD.

Das tut mir leid.	I'm sorry.
Das tut ihm leid.	He's sorry.
Das tut ihr leid.	She's sorry.
Zuerst sehen wir Köln, dann sehen wir Heidelberg.	First we see Cologne; then we see Heidelberg.
Wohin gehen Sie?	Where are you going (to)?
an den Fluß	to the river
an den Rhein	to the Rhine
an den See	to the lake
an die See	to the ocean, to the sea(shore)
am Fluß	at the river, on the river
am Rhein	at the Rhine, on the Rhine
an der See	at the sea(shore)
aufs Land	to the country
auf dem Lande	in the country
für mich	for me
ohne ihn	without him

bleiben	to remain, to stay		**fährt**	drives, rides
			gibt	gives
fahren	to drive, to ride		**ißt**	eats

69

laufen	to run	der Rhein, -s	the Rhine
läuft	runs	der See, -s, -n	the lake
lesen	to read	die See, -, -n	the ocean, sea
liest	reads	die Universität,	
sehen	to see	-, -en	the university
sieht	sees	etwas	something
der Fluß,		durch + *acc.*	through
des Flusses,		für + *acc.*	for
die Flüsse	the river	ohne + *acc.*	without
das Land, -es, =er	the country	dann	then
Heidelberg, -s	Heidelberg	nur	only
Köln, -s	Cologne	oder	or
München, -s	Munich	zuerst	first
die Nordsee, -	the North Sea	wohin?	where (to)?
die Ostsee, -	the Baltic Sea		

II. DRILL. EXPRESS ORALLY IN GERMAN. REPEAT UNTIL IT IS NO LONGER
NECESSARY TO REFER TO SECTION I.

a. 1. I'm sorry. 2. He's sorry. 3. She's sorry. 4. They are sorry.
5. We are sorry.

b. 1. First we see Cologne, then we see Heidelberg. 2. First we see
Heidelberg, then we see Munich. 3. First we see Munich, then we
see Cologne. 4. First we see Munich, then we see Berlin.

c. 1. Where are you going (to)? 2. Where are we going (to)?
3. Where is he going (to)? 4. Where is she going (to)?

d. 1. . . . to the river. 2. They are running to the river. 3. We are
running to the river. 4. He is running to the river. 5. He is
running to the lake. 6. She is running to the lake. 7. The child
is running to the lake.

e. 1. . . . to the seashore. 2. They are driving to the seashore. 3. We
are driving to the seashore. 4. Are you driving to the ocean?
5. She is driving to the ocean. 6. The student (*f.*) is driving to
the North Sea. 7. The student is driving to the North Sea. 8. The
teacher is driving to the Baltic Sea. 9. The man is driving to the
Baltic Sea. 10. He is driving to the Rhine. 11. Are you driving
to the Rhine?

f. 1. . . . on the river. 2. The city lies on the river. 3. Our city lies on the river.   4. Cologne lies on the Rhine.   5. It lies on the Rhine. 6. The city lies on the Rhine.

g.   1. ... at the seashore.   2. Is he staying at the seashore?   3. Are you staying at the seashore?   4. Are you staying at the Baltic Sea? 5. Is she staying at the Baltic Sea?   6. Is she staying at the North Sea?   7. Are you staying at the North Sea?

h.   1. ... to the country.   2. We are driving to the country.   3. He is driving to the country.   4. She is going to the country.   5. They are going to the country.

i.   1. ... in the country.   2. He lives in the country.   3. She lives in the country.   4. They live in the country.   5. We live in the country.

j.   1. for me   2. for you   3. for her   4. for him   5. for them   6. only for them   7. only for him   8. only for me

k.   1. without him   2. without them   3. without us   4. without me 5. without her

l.   1. He sees ...   2. He sees the university.   3. The student (*f.*) sees the university.   4. She sees the university.   5. She sees Munich. 6. He sees Munich.

m.   1. ... something.   2. He is giving them something.   3. He is giving us something.   4. She is giving us something.   5. She is eating something.   6. He is eating something.   7. The child is eating something.   8. The woman is reading something.   9. She is reading something.   10. He is reading something.   11. He and she are reading something.   12. We are reading something. 13. They are reading something.

n.   1. through ...   2. through the country   3. through Munich 4. through Heidelberg   5. through Cologne

o.   1. ... or ...   2. the lake or the river   3. the river or the ocean 4. the city or the country

B. MODEL SENTENCES

I.   STUDY UNTIL EACH SENTENCE CAN BE GIVEN CORRECTLY FROM THE ENGLISH.

73. Wohin gehen Sie?
74. Seine Eltern fahren an den Rhein.

75. **Sie wohnen an der See.**
76. **Sie besucht die Stadt Köln und die Universität Heidelberg.**
77. **Er macht eine Reise ohne seinen Freund.**
78. **Ich reise durch das Land.**
79. **Hans ist der älteste Sohn.**
80. **Österreich ist schöner als England, aber Deutschland ist am schönsten.**
81. **Er schreibt besser als ich, aber sie schreibt am besten.**

73. Where are you going (to)?
74. His parents are driving to the Rhine.
75. They live at the seashore.
76. She is visiting the city of Cologne and the University of Heidelberg.
77. He is taking a trip without his friend.
78. I am traveling through the country.
79. Hans is the oldest son.
80. Austria is more beautiful than England, but Germany is most beautiful.
81. He writes better than I, but she writes best.

II. DRILL. EXPRESS ORALLY IN GERMAN.

a. 1. Where are you going (to)? 2. Where are you running (to)?
   3. Where is he running (to)? 4. Where is she traveling (to)?
   5. Where are they taking a trip (to)?
b. 1. His parents are driving to the Rhine. 2. Your parents are driving to the river. 3. Her friends are driving to the lake. 4. My brothers are driving to the seashore. 5. My sisters are driving to the North Sea. 6. Their uncles are driving to the Baltic Sea.
c. 1. They live at the seashore. 2. They live at the Baltic Sea. 3. He lives at the North Sea. 4. He lives at the lake. 5. He lives at the river. 6. She lives at the Rhine.
d. 1. She is visiting the city of Cologne and the University of Heidelberg. 2. She is visiting the city of Cologne and the University of Cologne. 3. She is visiting the city of Heidelberg and the University of Heidelberg. 4. She is visiting the city of Heidelberg and the University of Cologne.
e. 1. He is taking a trip without his friend. 2. He is taking a trip

without his father.   3. He is taking a trip without his brother.   4. He is taking a trip without his mother.   5. He is taking a trip without his sister.

f.   1. I am traveling through the country.   2. I am traveling through the city.   3. I am traveling through the cities.   4. I am traveling through the countries.

g.   1. Hans is the oldest son.   2. Hans is the oldest boy.   3. Hans is the oldest brother.   4. Hans is the oldest friend.

h.   1. Austria is more beautiful than England, but Germany is most beautiful.   2. Marie is more beautiful than Klara, but Grete is most beautiful.   3. Cologne is more beautiful than Berlin, but Heidelberg is most beautiful.   4. Our house is more beautiful than his house, but your house is most beautiful.

i.   1. He writes better than I, but she writes best.   2. She writes better than I, but he writes best.   3. She writes better than he, but I write best.

C. GRAMMAR

1. **Wohin?** (where? where to?) is used to inquire after a goal, **wo?** (where?) to determine a location.
   a. **Wohin gehen Sie?**
      Where are you going?
   b. **Wo sind Sie?**
      Where are you?

2. A geographical name stands immediately after a common noun and is not inflected.
   Sie besucht die Stadt Köln und die Universität Heidelberg.
   She is visiting the city of Cologne and the University of Heidelberg.

3. Some common prepositions *always* govern the accusative case. Among them are **durch** (through), **für** (for), **ohne** (without).
   a. **Er macht eine Reise ohne seinen Freund.**
      He is taking a trip without his friend.
   b. **Ich reise durch das Land.**
      I am traveling through the country.
   c. **Er schreibt es für mich.**
      He is writing it for me.

4. The superlative form of the descriptive adjective is obtained by adding to the positive form **-st** and the appropriate strong or weak endings. Superlatives are almost always inflected. If the comparative takes umlaut, the superlative also takes umlaut.

der junge Sohn	**der jüngere Sohn**	**der jüngste Sohn**
the young son	the younger son	the youngest son

If the stem of the adjective ends in **-d, -t,** or a vowel other than **-e,** then **-est** is added in the superlative.

sein alter Freund	**sein älterer Freund**	**sein ältester Freund**
his old friend	his older friend	his oldest friend
das neue Haus	**das neuere Haus**	**das neueste Haus**
the new house	the newer house	the newest house

5. Some adjectives have irregular comparative and superlative forms.

gut	**besser**	**der, die, das beste**
good	better	the best
groß	**größer**	**der, die, das größte**
big	bigger	the biggest
hoch	**höher**	**der, die, das höchste**
high	higher	the highest

6. The predicate form of the superlative adjective consists of **am** plus the superlative with the ending **-en.**

Österreich ist schöner als England, aber Deutschland ist am schönsten.

Austria is more beautiful than England, but Germany is most beautiful.

7. The comparative form of the adverb is identical with that of the adjective.

Er schreibt besser als ich.

He writes better than I.

The superlative form of the adverb corresponds to that of the *predicate* adjective (paragraph 6, above).

Sie schreibt am besten.

She writes best.

8. Many verbs have irregular forms in the second and third persons singular of the present tense.

Some verbs whose stem vowel is **e** change **e** to **i,** like **geben** (to give) and **essen** (to eat). The present tense of **geben.**

ich gebe	I give
[du gibst	you give]

er, sie, es gibt	he, she, it gives
wir geben	we give
[ihr gebt	you give]
sie geben	they give
Sie geben	you give

The present tense of **essen** (to eat).

ich esse	I eat
[du ißt	you eat]
er, sie, es ißt	he, she, it eats
wir essen	we eat
[ihr eßt	you eat]
sie essen	they eat
Sie essen	you eat

Other verbs change **e** to **ie**, like **lesen** (to read) and **sehen** (to see).
The present tense of **sehen**.

ich sehe	I see
[du siehst	you see]
er, sie, es sieht	he, she, it sees
wir sehen	we see
[ihr seht	you see]
sie sehen	they see
Sie sehen	you see

Some verbs whose stem vowel is **a** or **au** umlaut the stem vowel.
The present tense of **fahren** (to drive, ride).

ich fahre	I drive, ride
[du fährst	you drive, ride]
er, sie, es fährt	he, she, it drives, rides
wir fahren	we drive, ride
[ihr fahrt	you drive, ride]
sie fahren	they drive, ride
Sie fahren	you drive, ride

The present tense of **laufen** (to run).

ich laufe	I run
[du läufst	you run]
er, sie, es läuft	he, she, it runs
wir laufen	we run
[ihr lauft	you run]
sie laufen	they run
Sie laufen	you run

D. EXERCISES

WRITE THE FOLLOWING SENTENCES IN GERMAN AND BE ABLE TO EXPRESS
THEM ORALLY IN CLASS.

1. Where are your friends going?
2. My girl friend is taking a trip to the seashore.
3. The student is writing the lesson for the teacher.
4. Our cousin (*f.*) lives in the city of Berlin.
5. The oldest daughter is smallest.
6. His parents live in Cologne on the Rhine.
7. The Rhine is the biggest river in Germany.
8. He is eating without his sister.
9. Their son is traveling through the country.
10. Where is the boy running to?
11. He is the youngest child here.
12. Where are you putting the letter?
13. First we are driving to the Baltic Sea and then to the North Sea.
14. My uncle is coming without his children.
15. The newest car is not the best car.
16. This school is the highest building in town.
17. I will travel through Germany and Switzerland.
18. They are visiting friends at the lake.
19. The new student understands the teacher best.
20. Go without us.
21. Karl is young, Hermann is younger, but Hans is youngest.
22. His son is doing the work for me.
23. Are you visiting the University of Cologne?
24. Where is he bringing the money?
25. My best friend is giving me his books.

E. READING AND SPEAKING

I. READ THE FOLLOWING ALOUD UNTIL YOU ARE THOROUGHLY FAMILIAR
WITH IT.

Auf der Straße

Hans begegnet (meets) seiner Freundin Käthe Meyer auf der Straße.
,,Käthe", sagt er, ,,ich muß dir etwas sagen."

„Was ist es denn?"[1]

„Ich werde eine Reise nach Deutschland machen." 5

„Wirklich? (Really?) Wenn ich nur auch mitkommen könnte![2] Aber ich muß zu Hause bleiben, denn es geht meiner Mutter nicht gut. Du mußt ohne mich gehen."

„Das tut mir leid. Ich werde dich vermissen (miss)."

„Wohin wirst du fahren?" 10

„Ich fahre zuerst an den Rhein. Das Rheinland ist der schönste Teil (part) Deutschlands. Ich werde die Stadt Köln sehen, und ich muß die Universität Heidelberg besuchen."

„Das wird schön sein. Und dann?"

„Dann fahre ich an den Bodensee (Lake Constance)." 15

„Wirst du auch andere Länder besuchen, oder nur Deutschland?"

„Ich fahre in die Schweiz und nach Österreich. Dann reise ich an die Ostsee und an die Nordsee. Ich bleibe gerne an der See."

„Jetzt muß ich gehen. Auf Wiedersehen."

„Auf Wiedersehen." 20

II. ANSWER THE FOLLOWING QUESTIONS IN GERMAN.

1. Wer begegnet seiner Freundin auf der Straße?
2. Wohin wird er eine Reise machen?
3. Wer muß zu Hause bleiben?
4. Welcher Teil Deutschlands ist am schönsten?
5. Welche Universität muß er besuchen?
6. Durch welche Länder wird Hans fahren?

---

[1] **Was ist es denn?** Well, what is it?   [2] **Wenn ich nur auch mitkommen könnte!** If I could only come along too!

☞ UNIT 11

A. UNITS OF SPEECH AND VOCABULARY

I. STUDY AND READ ALOUD.

Sie können gehen	you can go, you are able to go
sie sollen lernen	they are (supposed) to learn
wir wollen laufen	we want to run
am Montag	on Monday
am nächsten Tag	(on) the next day
im Juli	in July
im Frühling	in spring
nächsten Monat	next month
den ganzen Nachmittag	the whole afternoon (long), all afternoon long
die ganze Nacht	the whole night (long), all night long
den ganzen Sommer	the whole summer (long), all summer long
ganz Deutschland	all of Germany

der Abend, -s, -e	the evening	der Nachmittag,		
die Nacht, -, ⸗e	the night	-s, -e	the afternoon	
der Vormittag,		Wien, -s	Vienna	
-s, -e	the morning	der Sonntag, -s	Sunday	

78

der Montag, -s	Monday	**der Oktober, -s**	October
der Dienstag, -s	Tuesday	**der November, -s**	November
der Mittwoch, -s	Wednesday	**der Dezember, -s**	December
der Donnerstag,		**der Frühling,**	
-s	Thursday	**-s, -e**	spring
der Freitag, -s	Friday	**der Sommer, -s, -**	summer
der Samstag, -s	Saturday	**der Herbst, -es, -e**	autumn, fall
der Sonnabend, -s	Saturday	**der Winter, -s, -**	winter
der Monat, -s, -e	the month	**können**	can, to be able (to)
der Januar, -s	January		
der Februar, -s	February	**sollen**	to be (to), to be supposed (to)
der März, -es	March		
der April, -s	April	**wollen**	to want (to)
der Mai, -s	May	**ganz**	entire, whole, all of
der Juni, -s	June		
der Juli, -s	July	**nächster, nächste,**	
der August, -s	August	**nächstes**	next
der September, -s	September		

II. DRILL. EXPRESS ORALLY IN GERMAN. REPEAT UNTIL IT IS NO LONGER NECESSARY TO REFER TO SECTION I.

a. 1. you can go   2. we can go   3. we are able to see   4. they are able to talk

b. 1. they are supposed to learn   2. we are supposed to read   3. we are to take a trip   4. we are to travel

c. 1. we want to run   2. we want to eat   3. they want to write   4. they want to talk

d. 1. on Monday   2. on Friday   3. on Wednesday   4. on Sunday   5. on Tuesday   6. on Saturday   7. on Thursday

e. 1. (on) the next day   2. (on) the next morning   3. (on) the next afternoon   4. (on) the next evening

f. 1. in July   2. in January   3. in February   4. in June   5. in March   6. in April   7. in September   8. in October   9. in May   10. in August   11. in November   12. in December

g. 1. in spring   2. in winter   3. in fall   4. in summer

h. 1. next month   2. next Tuesday   3. next Saturday   4. next Wednesday   5. next Sunday   6. next Monday   7. next Thursday   8. next Friday

i. 1. the whole summer (long) 2. the whole winter (long) 3. all
    spring long 4. all autumn long 5. the whole month (long) 6. all
    evening long 7. all day long 8. the whole morning (long) 9. all
    afternoon long 10. all night long
j. 1. all of Germany 2. all of Vienna 3. all of Europe 4. all of
    Austria

B. MODEL SENTENCES

I. STUDY UNTIL EACH SENTENCE CAN BE GIVEN CORRECTLY FROM THE
    ENGLISH.

82. Der Winter ist kalt.
83. Im Juni fahren wir nach Europa.
84. Am Freitag kommt mein Freund.
85. Nächsten Monat bin ich dort.
86. Sie bleiben den ganzen Sommer hier.
87. Er wird durch ganz Europa reisen.
88. Sie soll ihn morgen sehen.
89. Wollen Sie nach Hause?

82. Winter is cold.
83. We are going to Europe in June.
84. My friend is coming on Friday.
85. I'll be there next month.
86. They are staying here the whole summer.
87. He'll travel through all of Europe.
88. She is to see him tomorrow.
89. Do you want to go home?

II. DRILL. EXPRESS ORALLY IN GERMAN.

a. 1. Winter is cold. 2. Summer is warm. 3. Spring is nice.
    4. Autumn is nice.
b. 1. We are going to Europe in June. 2. We are going to Europe in
    August. 3. We are going to Europe in spring. 4. We are going
    to Europe in summer.

c. 1. My friend is coming on Friday. 2. My friend is coming on Sunday. 3. My friend is coming on Wednesday. 4. My friend is coming on Thursday. 5. My friend is coming on Tuesday. 6. My friend is coming on Saturday.

d. 1. I'll be there next month. 2. I'll be there next Tuesday. 3. I'll be there next Sunday. 4. I'll be there next Saturday. 5. I'll be there next Wednesday. 6. I'll be there next Thursday.

e. 1. They are staying here the whole summer. 2. They are staying here the whole winter. 3. They are staying here the whole afternoon 4. They are staying here the whole morning. 5. They are staying here the whole month.

f. 1. He'll travel through all of Europe. 2. He'll travel through all of Germany. 3. He'll travel through all of Austria. 4. They'll travel through all of Spain. 5. They'll travel through all of Italy.

g. 1. She is to see him tomorrow. 2. She is to visit us tomorrow. 3. He is to visit us tomorrow. 4. He is to ask them tomorrow.

h. 1. Do you want to go home? 2. Do we want to go home? 3. Do your friends want to go home? 4. Do your parents want to go home? 5. Do your cousins want to go home?

C. GRAMMAR

1. Nouns denoting seasons, months, days, or parts of days are usually used with the definite article.
   a. **Der Winter ist kalt.**
      Winter is cold.
   b. **Im Juni fahren wir nach Europa.**
      We are going to Europe in June.
   c. **Am Freitag kommt mein Freund.**
      My friend is coming on Friday.

2. Definite time is expressed by the accusative case.
   Nächsten Monat bin ich dort.
   I'll be there next month.

3. Duration of time is expressed by the accusative case.
   Sie bleiben den ganzen Sommer hier.
   They are staying here the whole summer.

4. The adjective **ganz** (all of, the whole of) is usually used uninflected before neuter geographical names.

Er wird durch ganz Europa reisen.
He will travel through all of Europe.

Otherwise it is inflected, as in the example in paragraph 3, above.

5. Present indicative of **können** (can, to be able).

ich kann	I can, am able
[du kannst	you can, are able]
er, sie, es kann	he, she, it can, is able
wir können	we can, are able
[ihr könnt	you can, are able]
sie können	they can, are able
Sie können	you can, are able

6. Present indicative of **sollen** (to be to, to be supposed to).

ich soll	I am to, am supposed to
[du sollst	you are to, are supposed to]
er, sie, es soll	he, she, it is to, is supposed to
wir sollen	we are to, are supposed to
[ihr sollt	you are to, are supposed to]
sie sollen	they are to, are supposed to
Sie sollen	you are to, are supposed to

7. Present indicative of **wollen** (to want [to]).

ich will	I want (to)
[du willst	you want (to)]
er, sie, es will	he, she, it wants (to)
wir wollen	we want (to)
[ihr wollt	you want (to)]
sie wollen	they want (to)
Sie wollen	you want (to)

8. **Können** (can, to be able), **müssen** (must, to have to), **sollen** (to be, to be supposed to), and **wollen** (to want [to]) are modal auxiliary verbs, which may be used without the infinitive of a verb of motion if the direction is indicated by an adverb or a prepositional phrase. The verb of motion is then understood.

   a. **Wollen Sie nach Hause (gehen)?**
      Do you want to go home?

   b. **Mein Vetter Franz und meine Kusine Lotte müssen nach Hause (gehen).**
      My cousin Franz and my cousin Lotte have to go home.

   Note: An infinitive dependent upon a modal auxiliary never uses the preposition **zu.**

  a. **Mein Vetter und meine Kusine müssen nach Hause gehen.**
  b. **Sie soll ihn morgen sehen.**
    She is to see him tomorrow.

D. EXERCISES

WRITE THE FOLLOWING SENTENCES IN GERMAN AND BE ABLE TO EXPRESS THEM ORALLY IN CLASS.

1. January is a cold month.
2. We want to go to the movies on Saturday.
3. They will be able to go in August.
4. He stays home on Sunday.
5. I am to visit my friends tomorrow.
6. On Thursday she teaches German.
7. All of Germany is beautiful in the summer.
8. The students will study the whole evening.
9. Autumn in the United States is beautiful.
10. The boy can read well.
11. The student (*f.*) is taking a trip next Saturday.
12. We learn German on Monday, Wednesday, and Friday.
13. My uncle wants to see all of Berlin.
14. Must you go home now?
15. They'll come to school next month.
16. They live at the seashore all winter long.
17. Vienna is supposed to be beautiful in the spring.
18. I can read all afternoon long.
19. We don't like to travel in December.
20. He works the whole morning.
21. Where are we to go now?
22. September is nice and warm.
23. My cousin wants to read that book.
24. Next year we'll travel through the whole country.

E. READING AND SPEAKING

I. READ THE FOLLOWING ALOUD UNTIL YOU ARE THOROUGHLY FAMILIAR WITH IT.

Reisepläne[1]

Hans begegnet (meets) seinem Freund und fragt: „Wie geht es dir, Walter?"

„Mir geht es nicht gut."

5   „Warum?"

„Wegen der Reise. Ich denke zuviel[2] und ich kann nicht schlafen (sleep)."

„Das sollst du nicht machen. Aber ich möchte etwas wissen (to know). Wann willst du deine Reise machen?"

10   „Im Juni. Im Frühling und im Sommer soll Deutschland schön sein."

„Wirst du den ganzen Sommer dort sein?"

„Nein. Nur im Juni und Juli. Im August fahre ich nach Österreich."

„Das ist gut. Wien soll eine der schönsten Städte Europas sein."

„Wann kommst du nach Hause?"

15   „Im September. Im Herbst muß ich in die Schule gehen."

„Ich möchte auch gehen. Mein Vater sagt, ich darf die Reise machen."

„Das freut mich sehr.[3] Ich fahre gerne mit dir. Aber es ist jetzt neun Uhr und ich muß in die Schule. Auf Wiedersehen."

20   „Auf Wiedersehen."

II. ANSWER THE FOLLOWING QUESTIONS IN GERMAN.

1. **Wie geht es Walter?**
2. **Warum?**
3. **Wann will Walter nach Deutschland fahren?**
4. **Wohin wird er im August reisen?**
5. **Welche Stadt in Österreich soll schön sein?**
6. **Fährt Walter gerne mit Hans?**

[1] **Reisepläne** Travel Plans.   [2] **Ich denke zuviel** I think too much.   [3] **Das freut mich sehr** I'm very glad.

☞ UNIT **12**

A. UNITS OF SPEECH AND VOCABULARY

I. STUDY AND READ ALOUD.

Wir hören Radio.	We are listening to the radio.
Was tut er?	What is he doing?
Dürfen wir es tun?	May we do it?
Ich habe keine Zeit.	I have no time.
in der Kirche	in church, at church
in die Kirche	to church
nach der Kirche	after church
nach der Schule	after school
vor einem Monat	a month ago
vor einer Stunde	an hour ago

der Arzt, -es, ⸗e	the physician, doctor	**die Stunde, -, -n**	the hour, class
		der Vogel, -s, ⸗	the bird
der Baum, -es, ⸗e	the tree	**die Woche, -, -n**	the week
die Kirche, -, -n	the church	**die Zeit, -, -en**	the time
die Lehrerin,		**dürfen**	may, to be permitted to
-, -nen	the teacher *f.*		
der Professor,		**hören**	to hear, to listen to
-s, -en	the professor		
das Radio, -s, -s	the radio	**mögen**	to like, to care (to)
der Stuhl, -es, ⸗e	the chair		

studieren	to study (*at a university*)	**schnell**	quick, quickly, fast
tun	to do	**spät**	late
tut	does, is doing	**gestern**	yesterday
war	was	**vorgestern**	the day before yesterday
waren	were		
interessant	interesting	**immer**	always
langsam	slow, slowly	**oft**	often
		sehr	very

II. DRILL. EXPRESS ORALLY IN GERMAN. REPEAT UNTIL IT IS NO LONGER NECESSARY TO REFER TO SECTION I.

a. 1. We are listening to the radio.   2. They are listening to the radio. 3. She is listening to the radio.   4. He is listening to the radio. 5. I am listening to the radio.

b. 1. What is he doing?   2. What is she doing?   3. What is your sister doing?   4. What is your brother doing?

c. 1. May we do it?   2. Are you permitted to do it?   3. Are they permitted to do it?   4. Are the children permitted to do it?

d. 1. I have no time.   2. We have no time.   3. She has no time. 4. They have no time.

e. 1. . . . in church.   2. The professor is in church.   3. The professor is often in church.   4. The teacher (*f.*) is often in church.   5. The physician is often at church.   6. The physician and the professor are often at church.

f. 1. . . . to church.   2. The teacher (*f.*) is going to church.   3. The doctor is going to church.   4. The professor is going to church.

g. 1. After church . . .   2. After church the doctor goes home. 3. After church the teacher (*f.*) goes home.   4. After church the professor goes home.

h. 1. After school . . .   2. After school the professors drive home. 3. After school the teachers (*f.*) and the students (*f.*) drive home. 4. After school the professors and the students drive home.

i. 1. a month ago   2. a year ago   3. an hour ago   4. a week ago

j. 1. The bird . . .   2. The bird is sitting on the tree.   3. The birds are sitting on the tree.   4. The birds are sitting on the trees.

k. 1. The class . . .   2. The class is interesting.   3. The class is always interesting.   4. The class is always very interesting.

l. 1. They like . . .   2. They like the chair.   3. We like this chair. 4. We like the chairs.

m. 1. . . . slow   2. . . . fast   3. Does he drive slowly?   4. Does he drive fast?   5. Does she drive fast?   6. Do they drive slowly? 7. Do you drive fast?

n. 1. . . . late.   2. He is coming late.   3. They are coming later. 4. We are going later.

o. 1. He is studying . . .   2. He is studying in Berlin.   3. He is studying in Heidelberg.   4. She is studying in Germany.   5. They are studying in Austria.

p. 1. Yesterday . . .   2. Yesterday was Monday.   3. Yesterday was Wednesday.   4. Yesterday was Sunday.

q. 1. The day before yesterday . . .   2. The day before yesterday was Sunday.   3. The day before yesterday was Tuesday.   4. The day before yesterday was Saturday.

B. MODEL SENTENCES

I. STUDY UNTIL EACH SENTENCE CAN BE GIVEN CORRECTLY FROM THE ENGLISH.

90. Er hat das Buch gelesen.
91. Ich habe in den Vereinigten Staaten studiert.
92. Vor einem Jahr ist sie durch Europa gereist.
93. Unsere Freunde sind alt geworden.
94. Heute mag der Junge nicht lernen.
95. Darf ich ins Kino gehen, Vater?—Ja, du darfst es.
96. Wir dürfen nicht reden.

90. He (has) read the book.
91. I (have) studied in the United States.
92. She traveled through Europe a year ago.
93. Our friends have become old.
94. The boy doesn't care to study today.
95. May I go to the movies, Father?—Yes, you may.
96. We mustn't talk.

II. DRILL. EXPRESS ORALLY IN GERMAN.

a. 1. He (has) read the book.   2. The professor (has) read the book.
3. The teacher (*f.*) read the book.   4. She has read the book.
5. The girl read the book.   6. The child read the book.

b. 1. I (have) studied in the United States.   2. I studied in Europe.
3. I studied in Vienna.   4. I have studied in Cologne.

c. 1. She traveled through Europe a year ago.   2. She traveled through
Austria a year ago.   3. The teacher (*f.*) traveled through Spain a
year ago.   4. The teacher (*f.*) traveled through Italy a year ago.
5. The doctor traveled through Germany a year ago.   6. He
traveled through Switzerland a year ago.

d. 1. Our friends have become old.   2. Your cousins have become old.
3. His parents have become old.   4. Her sisters have become old.

e. 1. The boy doesn't care to study today.   2. He doesn't care to study
today.   3. The girl doesn't care to study today.   4. The child
doesn't care to study today.   5. His daughter doesn't care to study
today.   6. Her son doesn't care to study today.

f. 1. May I go to the movies, Father?—Yes, you may.   2. May I go
to town, Father?—Yes, you may.   3. May I go to the restaurant,
Father?—Yes, you may.   4. May I go home, Father?—Yes, you
may.

g. 1. We mustn't talk.   2. We mustn't run.   3. They mustn't play.
4. They mustn't go.

C. GRAMMAR

1. The preposition **vor** plus the dative case of a noun of time expresses
the idea of "ago":

vor einem Jahr	a year ago
vor einer Stunde	an hour ago

2. The past participle of most regular (or "weak") verbs is formed by
prefixing **ge-** to the present stem and adding the suffix **-t.**

INFINITIVE		PAST PARTICIPLE	
sag en	to say	**ge sag t**	said
reis en	to travel	**ge reis t**	traveled

Haben forms its past participle similarly.

hab en   to have   **ge hab t**   had

The following regular verbs form their past participles like **sagen**.
danken (to thank), **fragen** (to ask), **hören** (to hear), **kaufen** (to buy),
legen (to lay, to put), **lehren** (to teach), **lernen** (to learn), **machen**
(to make), **reisen** (to travel), **sollen** (to be [supposed] to), **spielen**
(to play), **stecken** (to stick, to put), **wohnen** (to dwell, to live), **wollen**
(will, to want [to]).
Some verbs also change their stem vowel. Among these are the
following.

INFINITIVE		PAST PARTICIPLE	
bring en	to bring	**ge brach t**	brought
dürf en	may, to be permitted to	**ge durf t**	permitted
könn en	can, to be able	**ge konn t**	been able
mög en	like, care to	**ge moch t**	liked, cared to
müss en	must, to have to	**ge muß t**	had to

3. Verbs whose stems end in **-d** or **-t**, like **reden** (to talk) or **antworten**
(to answer), add **e** before the suffix **-t**.

INFINITIVE		PAST PARTICIPLE	
red en	to talk	**ge red et**	talked
antwort en	to answer	**ge antwort et**	answered

4. Verbs in **-ieren** form their past participle without the **ge-** prefix.
studier en   to study   **studier t**   studied
5. Irregular (or "strong") verbs form their past participles by prefixing
ge- to the past-participle stem and adding the suffix **-en**. The vowel
of the past participle is frequently different from that of the present
stem. A list of irregular past participles follows.

INFINITIVE		PAST PARTICIPLE	
bleib en	to remain	**ge blieb en**	remained
ess en	to eat	**ge gess en**	eaten
find en	to find	**ge fund en**	found
geb en	to give	**ge geb en**	given
geh en	to go	**ge gang en**	gone
heiß en	to be called	**ge heiß en**	called

INFINITIVE		PAST PARTICIPLE	
helf en	to help	**ge holf en**	.helped
komm en	to come	**ge komm en**	come
lauf en	to run	**ge lauf en**	run
les en	to read	**ge les en**	read
lieg en	to lie	**ge leg en**	lain
schreib en	to write	**ge schrieb en**	written
seh en	to see	**ge seh en**	seen
sein	to be	**ge wes en**	been
sitz en	to sit	**ge sess en**	sat
steh en	to stand	**ge stand en**	stood
trink en	to drink	**ge trunk en**	drunk
tu n	to do	**ge ta n**	done
werd en	to become	**ge word en**	become

6. The present perfect tense of most verbs is formed of the present tense of the auxiliary verb **haben** (to have) and the past participle. In a main clause, the past participle, like the infinitive, stands last.

   a. **Er hat das Buch gelesen.**

      He read the book.

      He has read the book.

   b. **Ich habe in den Vereinigten Staaten studiert.**

      I studied in the United States.

      I have studied in the United States.

   The present perfect tense is commonly used in conversation to denote past action. It is equivalent to both the simple past and the present perfect tense in English.

   Note: The above sentences could also have the following meanings.

   a. He did read the book.

   b. I did study in the United States.

7. Some intransitive verbs require **sein** (to be) as their auxiliary in the present perfect tense.

   a. **Vor einem Jahr ist sie durch Europa gereist.**

      She traveled through Europe a year ago.

   b. **Unsere Freunde sind alt geworden.**

      Our friends have become old.

   This group includes verbs of motion, such as **reisen** (to travel), **fahren** (to ride), **kommen** (to come), **gehen** (to go), **laufen** (to run); verbs of change of state or condition, such as **werden** (to become), **wachsen** (to grow); and **sein** (to be) and **bleiben** (to remain).

8. The present tense of the modal auxiliary **mögen** (to like, care to).

ich mag	I like, care (to)
[du mag st	you like, care (to)]
er, sie, es mag	he, she, it likes, cares (to)
wir mög en	we like, care (to)
[ihr mög t	you like, care (to)]
sie mög en	they like, care (to)
Sie mög en	you like, care (to)

9. The present tense of the modal auxiliary **dürfen** (may, to be permitted to).

ich darf	I may, am permitted to
[du darf st	you may, are permitted to]
er, sie, es darf	he, she, it may, is permitted to
wir dürf en	we may, are permitted to
[ihr dürf t	you may, are permitted to]
sie dürf en	they may, are permitted to
Sie dürf en	you may, are permitted to

Note: When **dürfen** is used in the negative, it may be translated "must not."

Wir dürfen nicht reden.
We mustn't talk.

Note that **nicht** (not) usually precedes the infinitive.

10. A modal auxiliary may be used without a dependent infinitive when it refers to a previous sentence in which the modal auxiliary has a dependent infinitive. When used without an infinitive, the modal auxiliary regularly has an indefinite neuter pronoun object, usually **es** (it) or **das** (that).

   a. **Darf ich ins Kino gehen, Vater?—Ja, du darfst es.**
   May I go to the movies, Father?—Yes, you may.
   b. **Muß er den Brief lesen?—Ja, das muß er.**
   Must he read the letter?—Yes, he must.

11. The present tense of **tun** (to do).

ich tu e	I do, am doing
[du tu st	you do, are doing]
er, sie, es tu t	he, she, it does, is doing
wir tu n	we do, are doing
[ihr tu t	you do, are doing]
sie tu n	they do, are doing
Sie tu n	you do, are doing

D. EXERCISES

WRITE THE FOLLOWING SENTENCES IN GERMAN AND BE ABLE TO EXPRESS THEM ORALLY IN CLASS.

1. They ask what I am doing.
2. Two months ago the professor took a trip to Europe.
3. The girl answered her mother.
4. The students (*f.*) are permitted to go home today.
5. I brought her the letter an hour ago.
6. You must not eat in this room.
7. Did you stay at my sister's house yesterday?
8. The children don't care to go to the movies now.
9. What did your brother eat?
10. Has my uncle been here?
11. What did the teacher (*f.*) want?
12. Did those men study in Europe?
13. Her father wrote the letter the day before yesterday.
14. Has your mother talked with the doctor?
15. May I read your book?—Yes, you may.
16. Where did you live five years ago?
17. Don't you care to go to school today?—No, I don't care to.
18. My father listened to the radio.
19. Are the children permitted to play here?
20. The boy ran into the house.
21. The students learned the lesson after school.
22. We must drink no cold water.
23. She did see her father a week ago.
24. My uncle has become old.

E. READING AND SPEAKING

I. READ THE FOLLOWING ALOUD UNTIL YOU ARE THOROUGHLY FAMILIAR WITH IT.

Ein Wochenende[1]

Hans sitzt im Klassenzimmer und ist sehr müde (tired).

[1] **Ein Wochenende**   A Week End.

Sein Freund Walter fragt: „Warum bist du so müde? Seit Freitag habe ich dich nicht mehr gesehen. Was hast du denn das ganze Wochenende getan?" 5

„Am Freitag bin ich mit Käthe zu einem Tanz (dance) gegangen. Den ganzen Abend haben wir getanzt (danced). Am Samstag habe ich meinem Vater im Laden geholfen. Dann bin ich am Abend mit meiner Freundin ins Kino gegangen. Nach dem Kino haben wir Hunger gehabt und sind in ein Restaurant gegangen. Nach dem Essen habe ich sie nach 10 Hause gebracht, aber es ist schon zwei Uhr gewesen."

„Aber das war am Samstag. Was hast du am Sonntag getan?"

„Um acht Uhr habe ich in die Kirche gemußt und den ganzen Tag habe ich zu Hause gearbeitet. Wir haben viel zu tun gehabt, denn die Mutter ist die ganze Woche krank (sick) gewesen." 15

„Das ist zuviel. Das solltest (should) du nicht mehr tun."

„Ich habe noch mehr getan. Am Abend habe ich meine Aufgaben gelernt und bin wieder (again) spät zu Bett gegangen. Verstehst du jetzt, warum ich so müde bin?"

„Ja, jetzt verstehe ich es." 20

II. ANSWER THE FOLLOWING QUESTIONS IN GERMAN.

1. Seit wann hat Walter seinen Freund nicht mehr gesehen?
2. Wer ist mit Hans zu einem Tanz gegangen?
3. Wohin sind sie am Samstag gegangen?
4. Um wieviel Uhr hat Hans in die Kirche gemußt?
5. Wer ist krank gewesen?
6. Warum ist Hans am Sonntag wieder spät zu Bett gegangen?

☞ UNIT **13**

A. UNITS OF SPEECH AND VOCABULARY

I. STUDY AND READ ALOUD.

Das ist mein Freund.	That's my friend.
Dies sind meine Nachbarn.	These are my neighbors.
Ich kann Deutsch.	I know German.
Wir kennen die Lehrerin.	We know the teacher *f*.
Wir haben die Lehrerin gekannt.	We knew the teacher *f*.
Er weiß es.	He knows it.
Haben Sie das gewußt?	Did you know that?
nicht wahr?	isn't it?, aren't they?, don't I? etc.
vor dem Frühstück	before breakfast
nach dem Mittagessen	after lunch
während des Abendessens	during supper

das Essen, -s	the meal, food	**das Wohnzimmer,**	
das Frühstück, -s	the breakfast	**-s, -**	the living room
das Mittagessen,	the lunch,	**die Küche, -, -n**	the kitchen
-s	dinner	**der Nachbar,**	
das Abendessen,	the supper,	**-s, -n**	the neighbor
-s	dinner	**die Hauptstadt,**	
das Eßzimmer,		**-, ⸗e**	the capital (city)
-s, -	the dining room	**Englisch**	English, the
das Schlafzimmer,			English
-s, -	the bedroom		language

94

das	that	**gewöhnlich**	usual ⌐Lᴎ⌐
dies	this	**hübsch**	pretty (⌐ᴊⁱᶻ)
kennen	to know	**kurz**	short
gekannt *past part.*	known	**lang**	long
schlafen	to sleep	**zwanzig**	twenty
schläft	sleeps	**einundzwanzig**	twenty-one
sprechen	to speak, to talk	**dreißig**	thirty
spricht	speaks, talks	**zweiunddreißig**	thirty-two
wissen	to know	**vierzig**	forty
gewußt *past part.*	known	**fünfzig**	fifty
zeigen	to show	**fast**	almost
erst	not until	**warum?**	why?
früh	early		

II. DRILL. EXPRESS ORALLY IN GERMAN. REPEAT UNTIL IT IS NO LONGER
NECESSARY TO REFER TO SECTION I.

a. 1. That's my friend.   2. That's my neighbor.   3. That's the capital.
    4. That's the kitchen.   5. That's the dining room.   6. That's the
    bedroom.   7. That's the living room.
b. 1. These are my neighbors.   2. These are my cousins.   3. These are
    my friends.   4. These are my teachers.
c. 1. I know German.   2. He knows German.   3. We know German.
    4. Do you know German?   5. Does she know English?   6. Does he
    know English?   7. Do they know English?
d. 1. We know the teacher (*f.*).   2. You know the teacher (*f.*).
    3. She knows the teacher (*f.*).   4. I know the teacher (*f.*).
e. 1. We knew the teacher (*f.*).   2. You knew the teacher (*f.*).   3. She
    knew the teacher (*f.*).   4. I knew the teacher (*f.*).
f. 1. He knows it.   2. She knows it.   3. They know it.   4. We know it.
g. 1. Did you know that?   2. Did she know that?   3. Did he know
    that?   4. Did they know that?
h. 1. . . . isn't it?   2. That's my friend, isn't it?   3. These are my
    neighbors, aren't they?   4. I know German, don't I?   5. We know
    the teacher (*f.*), don't we?   6. He knows it, doesn't he?
i. 1. before breakfast   2. before lunch   3. before supper
j. 1. after lunch   2. after breakfast   3. after supper
k. 1. during supper   2. during lunch   3. during breakfast

l. 1. . . . is sleeping.   2. He is sleeping.   3. The neighbor is sleeping.
4. The neighbors are sleeping.   5. They are sleeping.   6. Are you
sleeping?

m. 1. . . . is speaking.   2. He is speaking.   3. My neighbor is
speaking.   4. My neighbors are speaking.   5. They are speaking.
6. We are speaking.

n. 1. . . . is showing . . .   2. He is showing me the dining room.
3. He is showing me the kitchen.   4. He is showing me the bedroom.
5. He is showing me the living room.

o. 1. not until . . .   2. not until after breakfast   3. not until after
lunch   4. not until after supper

p. 1. Usually . . .   2. Usually she comes . . .   3. Usually she comes
early.   4. Usually he goes early.   5. Usually we go early.

q. 1. . . . pretty.   2. The girl is pretty.   3. The daughter is pretty.
4. The woman is pretty.

r. 1. . . . short.   2. Is the lesson short?   3. Are the lessons short?
4. Are the days short?

s. 1. . . . long.   2. Is the lesson long?   3. Are the lessons long?
4. Are the nights long?

t. 1. twenty neighbors   2. thirty neighbors   3. forty neighbors
4. fifty neighbors 5. twenty-one neighbors 6. thirty-two neighbors

u. 1. Why . . . ?   2. Why is he in the kitchen?   3. Why is she in the
dining room?   4. Why are you there?   5. Why are you in the city?
6. Why are they in the capital?   7. Why are your friends in the
capital?

B. MODEL SENTENCES

I. STUDY UNTIL EACH SENTENCE CAN BE GIVEN CORRECTLY FROM THE
ENGLISH.

97. **Es ist mein Vater.**
98. **Dies sind meine Brüder und das sind meine Nachbarn.**
99. **Kennen Sie meinen Vetter?**
100. **Meine Schwester kann Deutsch.**
101. **Wissen Sie, wann er kommt?—Ja, ich weiß es.**
102. **Der Junge heißt Hans, nicht wahr?**

97. It's my father.
98. These are my brothers and those are my neighbors.
99. Do you know my cousin?
100. My sister knows German.
101. Do you know when he is coming?—Yes, I know.
102. The boy's name is Hans, isn't it?

II. DRILL. EXPRESS ORALLY IN GERMAN.

a. 1. It's my father. 2. It's my mother. 3. It's your girl friend. 4. It's his child.
b. 1. These are my brothers and those are my neighbors. 2. These are my cousins and those are my uncles. 3. These are her parents and those are her sisters. 4. These are his uncles and those are his aunts.
c. 1. Do you know my cousin? 2. Do you know my cousin (*f.*)? 3. Do you know my neighbor? 4. Do you know my girl friend? 5. Do you know my aunt?
d. 1. My sister knows German. 2. My friend knows German. 3. The doctor knows English. 4. The students know English. 5. His parents know English.
e. 1. Do you know when he is coming?—Yes, I know. 2. Do you know why he is coming?—Yes, I know. 3. Do the girls know why he is coming?—Yes, they know. 4. Do the children know who is coming?—Yes, they know.
f. 1. The boy's name is Hans, isn't it? 2. The child's name is Hans, isn't it? 3. The man's name is Hans, isn't it? 4. The student's name is Hans, isn't it? 5. The neighbor's name is Hans, isn't it?

C. GRAMMAR

1. The neuter indefinite pronouns **es** (it), **dies** (this), and **das** (that) are used with the verb **sein** (to be) and predicate nouns in identifications.
   a. **Es ist mein Vater.**
      It's my father.
   b. **Dies sind meine Brüder und das sind meine Nachbarn.**
      These are my brothers and those are my neighbors.

Note: If the predicate noun is plural, a plural verb is used, but the pronoun remains singular. In such cases, **es** is equivalent to English "they," **dies** to "these," and **das** to "those."

2. **Kennen** means "to know" in the sense of "to be acquainted with" and is usually used with nouns or pronouns denoting persons.

>   **Kennen Sie meinen Vetter?**
>   Do you know my cousin?

3. **Können** means "to know" with nouns denoting subjects of study.
>   **Meine Schwester kann Deutsch.**
>   My sister knows German.

4. **Wissen** means "to know" in the sense of "to have knowledge of." It is usually followed by a clause or by a neuter indefinite pronoun object (**es, das**).

>   **Wissen Sie, wann er kommt?—Ja, ich weiß es.**
>   Do you know when he is coming?—Yes, I know.

5. The present tense of **wissen** (to know).

ich weiß	I know
[du weißt	you know]
er, sie, es weiß	he, she, it knows
wir wissen	we know
[ihr wißt	you know]
sie wissen	they know
Sie wissen	you know

6. The phrase **nicht wahr?** (is it not true?) makes a question out of a statement.

>   **Der Junge heißt Hans, nicht wahr?**
>   The boy's name is Hans, isn't it?

7. Two-digit numbers from 21 on are formed by putting the units digit first, followed by **und** and the tens digit, all written as one word.

einundzwanzig	21, twenty-one
zweiunddreißig	32, thirty-two

Note: Cardinal numbers, except **ein** (one), are not inflected.

8. Regular (or "weak") verbs form their past tense by adding the past endings to the stem (**sag-**):

ich sag te	I said, was saying, did say
[du sag test	you said, were saying, did say]
er, sie, es sag te	he, she, it said, was saying, did say

wir sag ten   we said, were saying, did say
[**ihr sag tet**   you said, were saying, did say]
sie sag ten   they said, were saying, did say
Sie sag ten   you said, were saying, did say

9. The following regular verbs form their past tense like **sagen**:

begrüßen	to greet	**lernen**	to learn, to study
besuchen	to visit	**machen**	to make, to do
danken	to thank	**reisen**	to travel
fragen	to ask	**sollen**	to be (supposed) to
hören	to hear, to listen to	**spielen**	to play
kaufen	to buy	**stecken**	to stick, to put
legen	to lay, to put	**wohnen**	to dwell, to live
lehren	to teach	**wollen**	will, to want

10. Verbs whose stems end in **-d** or **-t,** like **reden** (to talk) or **antworten** (to answer), add **e** before the past endings.

reden   to talk   **ich redete**   I talked, was talking, did talk

antworten   to answer   **ich antwortete**   I answered, was answering, did answer

11. Some verbs add the past endings and alter the stem.

bringen   to bring   **ich brachte** I brought, was bringing, did bring

dürfen	may, to be permitted to	**ich durfte**	I was permitted to
haben	to have	**ich hatte**	I had
können	can, to be able to	**ich konnte**	I could, was able to
mögen	to like, care to	**ich mochte**	I liked, cared to
müssen	must, to have to	**ich mußte**	I had to
wissen	to know	**ich wußte**	I knew

12. The past tense is used primarily in connected narrative. In this book, it will therefore be used principally in the narrative portions of the E sections. The student should use the conversational present perfect tense to represent past action, particularly in questions, answers, and other isolated statements. However, the past tense of **sein** and of modal auxiliaries is generally preferred even in conversation.

D. EXERCISES

WRITE THE FOLLOWING SENTENCES IN GERMAN AND BE ABLE TO EXPRESS
THEM ORALLY IN CLASS.

1. I know why he is going.
2. He gave his brother money, didn't he?
3. They found forty-one books there.
4. Those are her sisters.
5. Did he know Mr. Meyer?
6. Who is speaking with my mother?—It's your uncle.
7. Your mother has read this book, hasn't she?
8. She knows where we are.
9. This is my aunt.
10. Your cousins know English, don't they?
11. My father knows your teacher.
12. You have talked with the doctor, haven't you?
13. Did she know that?—Yes, she knew it.
14. Is that our new teacher (*f.*)?
15. Your brother has come home, hasn't he?
16. We know your neighbors.
17. Thirty-eight students are in this room.
18. His parents knew German.
19. The children played in the dining room, didn't they?
20. Do your friends know English?
21. After supper they went to church, didn't they?
22. Did you know her younger sister?
23. These are my best friends.
24. Did the students (*f.*) know the lesson?

E. READING AND SPEAKING

I. READ THE FOLLOWING ALOUD UNTIL YOU ARE THOROUGHLY FAMILIAR
WITH IT.

Der Aufsatz[1]

Trude Braun sitzt im Wohnzimmer und schreibt einen Aufsatz für

[1] **Der Aufsatz**   The Composition.

die Schule. Ihr Bruder Hans kommt ins Zimmer und fragt sie, was sie
schreibt.

„Einen Aufsatz für die Schule. Du kannst ihn lesen." 5

Hans liest: „Gestern begegnete (met) ich meiner alten Lehrerin auf
der Straße. Ich begrüßte sie und sie begrüßte mich. Wir redeten
miteinander. Vor zwei Jahren lehrte sie mich Deutsch. Ich lernte
viel in ihren Deutschstunden. Damals (At that time) wohnte sie bei
ihrem Sohn, aber vor einem Jahr machte er eine Reise nach Europa, 10
und sie mußte bei ihrer Tochter wohnen."

„Die Lehrerin sagte zu mir: ,Du spielst gerne mit deinem Freund
Karl, nicht wahr? Wie geht es Karl?' "

„Ich antwortete: ,Karl geht es gut.' "

„Die Lehrerin steckte die Hand in die Tasche und brachte ein kleines 15
Buch hervor (out). ,Hier ist etwas für dich.' "

„Es war (was) ein schönes Buch. Ich dankte ihr und wir sagten
,Auf Wiedersehen.' "

„Gut", sagt Hans und legt den Aufsatz auf den Tisch.

II. ANSWER THE FOLLOWING QUESTIONS IN GERMAN.

1. Was schreibt Trude?
2. Wen hat sie auf der Straße begrüßt?
3. Was hat sie gelehrt?
4. Wo hat sie vor zwei Jahren gewohnt?
5. Wann hat ihr Sohn eine Reise gemacht?
6. Wohin ist er gereist?

☞ UNIT 14

A. UNITS OF SPEECH AND VOCABULARY

I. STUDY AND READ ALOUD.

er ist ihr begegnet	he met her
gestern morgen	yesterday morning
gestern nachmittag	yesterday afternoon
gestern abend	yesterday evening
heute morgen	this morning
heute nachmittag	this afternoon
heute abend	this evening
morgen früh	tomorrow morning
morgen nachmittag	tomorrow afternoon
morgen abend	tomorrow evening
Freitag morgen	Friday morning
Sonntag nachmittag	Sunday afternoon
Dienstag abend	Tuesday evening
nicht mehr	no longer, no more, not . . . any more

der Apfel, -s, ⸚	the apple	**der Garten, -s, ⸚**	the garden
die Blume, -, -n	the flower	**das Gras, -es, ⸚er**	the grass
der Boden, -s, -	the ground, floor	**begegnen** + *dat.*	to meet (*by chance*)
das Ende, -s, -n	the end	**bekommen**	to get, to receive

102

fallen	to fall	**gelb**	yellow
fällt	falls	**grün**	green
nehmen	to take	**halb**	half
nimmt	takes	**reif**	ripe
schicken	to send	**rot**	red
tragen	to carry, to wear	**also**	therefore, con-
trägt	carries, wears		sequently
wachsen	to grow	**mehr**	more
wächst	grows	**wieder**	again

II. DRILL. EXPRESS ORALLY IN GERMAN. REPEAT UNTIL IT IS NO LONGER
NECESSARY TO REFER TO SECTION I.

a. 1. he met her   2. she met him   3. she met them   4. she met us
5. he met me   6. he met them

b. 1. yesterday morning   2. tomorrow evening   3. this afternoon
4. tomorrow morning   5. yesterday evening   6. this morning
7. yesterday afternoon   8. this evening   9. tomorrow afternoon

c. 1. Friday morning   2. Sunday afternoon   3. Tuesday evening
4. Wednesday afternoon   5. Thursday morning   6. Saturday
evening   7. Monday afternoon

d. 1. . . . no longer   2. The apple is no longer green.   3. The apple
is no longer yellow.   4. The garden is no longer green.   5. Aren't
you studying any more?   6. Aren't you teaching any more?

e. 1. . . . the end   2. That is the end.   3. That is the end of the hour.
4. That is the end of the book.

f. 1. . . . are getting   2. They are getting the apples.   3. We are
getting the flowers.   4. He is getting the flowers.   5. She is getting
the flowers.   6. You are getting the flowers.

g. 1. . . . are falling   2. The apples are falling.   3. The apples in
the garden are falling.   4. The apple is falling into the grass.
5. The apple is falling on the ground.   6. The ripe apples are
falling on the ground.

h. 1. . . . are taking   2. We are taking it.   3. They are taking it.
4. She is taking the apple.   5. He is taking the ripe apple.   6. He is
taking the ripe apples.

i. 1. . . . are sending   2. You are sending flowers.   3. You are
sending red flowers.   4. We are sending yellow flowers.

j. 1. ... are carrying   2. They are carrying the child.   3. They are wearing yellow hats.   4. He is wearing a hat.   5. She is wearing a green hat.   6. She is carrying the book.   7. He is carrying the books into the garden.

k. 1. Therefore ...   2. Therefore he is sending it.   3. Therefore he is carrying it.   4. Consequently she is wearing it.   5. Consequently she is doing it.

l. 1. ... again   2. He is coming again.   3. She is going again.   4. They are eating again.

B. MODEL SENTENCES

I. STUDY UNTIL EACH SENTENCE CAN BE GIVEN CORRECTLY FROM THE ENGLISH.

103. Welche Städte in Europa haben Sie gesehen?
104. Welches sind die größten Städte in Europa?
105. Mein Onkel ist nicht Lehrer. Er ist Arzt.
106. Zeige mir dein Buch, Hans!
107. Lernt euere Aufgaben, Kinder!
108. Hat der Junge in die Schule gehen können?
109. Nein, er hat es nicht gekonnt.

103. Which cities in Europe did you see?
104. Which are the biggest cities in Europe?
105. My uncle is not a teacher. He is a doctor.
106. Show me your book, Hans.
107. Learn your lessons, children.
108. Has the boy been able to go to school?
109. No, he has not been able to.

II. DRILL. EXPRESS ORALLY IN GERMAN.

a. 1. Which cities in Europe did you see?   2. Which countries in Europe did you see?   3. Which countries did you visit?   4. Which books did you read?

b. 1. Which are the biggest cities in Europe?   2. Which are the most

interesting cities in Europe? 3. Which are the best books?
4. Which are the newest cars? 5. Which are the ripest apples?

c. 1. My uncle is not a teacher. He is a doctor. 2. My cousin is not
a doctor. He is a teacher. 3. My brother is not a doctor. He is a
professor. 4. My father is not a professor. He is a physician.

d. 1. Show me your book, Hans. 2. Show me your flowers, Trude.
3. Show me your friend, Richard. 5. Show me your hat, Klara.

e. 1. Learn your lessons, children. 2. Learn German, children.
3. Learn English, Hans and Trude. 4. Learn English and German,
Klara and Richard.

f. 1. Has the boy been able to go to school? 2. Has the girl been
able to go to the movies? 3. Has the child been able to go to
church? 4. Has your mother been able to go to town? 5. Has
he been able to go home?

g. 1. No, he has not been able to. 2. No, the boy has not been able to.
3. No, the girl has not been able to. 4. No, the child has not been
able to.

C. GRAMMAR

1. When **Morgen** (morning), **Vormittag** (morning, forenoon), **Nachmittag** (afternoon), **Abend** (evening), or **Nacht** (night) is used in
adverbial combination with **gestern** (yesterday), **vorgestern** (the day
before yesterday), **heute** (today), **morgen** (tomorrow), or names of
days of the week, it is *not* capitalized.

gestern morgen	yesterday morning
heute nachmittag	this afternoon
morgen abend	tomorrow evening
Freitag morgen	Friday morning

2. **Welcher?** (which?), when used as an adjective, agrees in gender,
number, and case with the noun it modifies.

a. **Welche Städte in Europa haben Sie gesehen?**
Which cities in Europe did you see?

When the noun is in the predicate, the neuter indefinite pronoun
form **welches?** (which?) is used, regardless of the gender or number
of the noun.

b. **Welches sind die größten Städte in Europa?**
   Which are the biggest cities in Europe?

3. The indefinite article is not used before predicate nouns of vocation.
   Mein Onkel ist nicht Lehrer. Er ist Arzt.
   My uncle is not a teacher. He is a doctor.

4. The imperative (or command) forms of the familiar second person for regular verbs are obtained by adding **-e** to the present stem in the singular and **-t** to the present stem in the plural. The pronoun is omitted, as in English. Imperative sentences usually end with an exclamation mark.
   a. **Zeige mir dein Buch, Hans!**
      Show me your book, Hans.
   b. **Lernt euere Aufgaben, Kinder!**
      Learn your lessons, children.

5. When a perfect-tense form of a modal auxiliary is used with a dependent infinitive, the past participle of the auxiliary is replaced by the infinitive form.
   Hat der Junge in die Schule gehen können (in place of **gekonnt**)?
   Has the boy been able to go to school?
   This construction is known as the "double infinitive." Note that the modal auxiliary is last, with the dependent infinitive of the main verb preceding it.

6. When used without a dependent infinitive, modal auxiliary verbs use the regular past participle form beginning with **ge-** and ending in **-t.**
   Nein, er hat es nicht gekonnt.
   No, he has not been able to.
   Note: **Nicht** immediately precedes a past participle.

7. Most irregular (or "strong") verbs form their past tense by changing the stem vowel and then adding endings, as in the past tense of **kommen** (to come).

ich kam	I came, did come, was coming
[**du kam st**	you came, did come, were coming]
er, sie, es kam	he, she, it came, did come, was coming
wir kam en	we came, did come, were coming
[**ihr kam t**	you came, did come, were coming]
sie kam en	they came, did come, were coming
Sie kam en	you came, did come, were coming

8. The basic forms of irregular verbs, from which all other forms can be derived, are called the "principal parts." For most irregular verbs, three principal parts suffice: the infinitive, the third person singular of the past tense, and the past participle. Where the auxiliary verb of the present perfect tense is **sein**, that is also usually indicated.

Verbs with a different stem vowel in the (second and) third person(s) singular of the present indicative from that of the infinitive have the third person singular of the present indicative as a fourth principal part.

Since changes in stem vowels are irregular and hard to predict, it is best to *memorize* the principal parts of an irregular verb as it occurs.

Following are the principal parts of most of the irregular verbs of Units 1-14.

INFINITIVE		PAST TENSE	PAST PART.	3RD SG. PRESENT
bleiben	to remain	**blieb**	ist geblieben	
essen	to eat	**aß**	gegessen	**ißt**
fahren	to ride	**fuhr**	ist gefahren	**fährt**
fallen	to fall	**fiel**	ist gefallen	**fällt**
finden	to find	**fand**	gefunden	
geben	to give	**gab**	gegeben	**gibt**
gehen	to go	**ging**	ist gegangen	
heißen	to be called	**hieß**	geheißen	
helfen	to help	**half**	geholfen	**hilft**
kommen	to come	**kam**	ist gekommen	
laufen	to run	**lief**	ist gelaufen	**läuft**
lesen	to read	**las**	gelesen	**liest**
liegen	to lie	**lag**	gelegen	
nehmen	to take	**nahm**	genommen	**nimmt**
schlafen	to sleep	**schlief**	geschlafen	**schläft**
schreiben	to write	**schrieb**	geschrieben	
sehen	to see	**sah**	gesehen	**sieht**
sein	to be	**war**	ist gewesen	**ist**
sitzen	to sit	**saß**	gesessen	

	INFINITIVE	PAST TENSE	PAST PART.	3RD SG. PRESENT
sprechen	to speak	**sprach**	**gesprochen**	**spricht**
stehen	to stand	**stand**	**gestanden**	
tragen	to carry, to wear	**trug**	**getragen**	**trägt**
trinken	to drink	**trank**	**getrunken**	
wachsen	to grow	**wuchs**	ist **gewachsen**	**wächst**
werden	to become	**wurde**	ist **geworden**	**wird**

D. EXERCISES

WRITE THE FOLLOWING SENTENCES IN GERMAN AND BE ABLE TO EXPRESS THEM ORALLY IN CLASS.

1. What did your son eat this morning?
2. His sister is becoming a teacher.
3. Which are your friends?
4. Did she wear her new hat Monday evening?
5. Answer me, Klara.
6. Did your friends ride to town?
7. She has been able to go to church again.
8. The ripe apples have fallen on the ground.
9. Why did you go home yesterday afternoon?
10. Tell me what your names are, children.
11. My cousin took my books home Wednesday evening.
12. Which apples did you eat?
13. His mother has always wanted to visit us.
14. He'll visit us tomorrow afternoon.
15. Did your neighbor bring his wife flowers?
16. Play in the living room, Marie and Trude.
17. Which was their garden?
18. Send your mother flowers, Karl.
19. Did you sit on this chair?
20. Which lesson did you learn the day before yesterday?
21. Why did your sister have to stay at home?
22. Isn't your friend a professor?—No, he's a physician.
23. I spoke with him Thursday morning.
24. My cousin (*f.*) was permitted to take a trip to Europe.

E. READING AND SPEAKING

I. READ THE FOLLOWING ALOUD UNTIL YOU ARE THOROUGHLY FAMILIAR
WITH IT.

Nach dem Abendessen

Nach dem Abendessen kam Hans ins Wohnzimmer und fand fast die
ganze Familie dort. Der Vater saß am Tisch und las ein Buch. Der
Bruder lag auf dem Sofa und hörte Radio. Er aß etwas und trank aus
einem Glas. Die Schwester stand mit ihrer Freundin Luise am Fenster 5
und zeigte ihr einige Photographien (a few photographs).
   Die Freundin fragte: „Wer ist das?"
   „Das ist meine Tante und dies sind meine Freundinnen." Dann
zeigte sie ihr die anderen Photographien.
   Durch die Tür konnte Hans die Mutter in der Küche sehen. Sie 10
machte ihre Arbeit. Gewöhnlich half Trude der Mutter, aber heute
durfte sie im Wohnzimmer bleiben, denn ihre Freundin war da (there).
   Hans ging in die Küche und wollte der Mutter helfen, aber sie wollte
es nicht, denn sie konnte ihre Arbeit allein (alone) besser und schneller
machen. Hans blieb in der Küche und schrieb etwas. Dann ging er 15
wieder ins Wohnzimmer und sprach mit dem Vater.

II. ANSWER THE FOLLOWING QUESTIONS IN GERMAN.

1. Wann ist Hans ins Wohnzimmer gekommen?
2. Was hat der Bruder getan?
3. Wer war auch da?
4. Warum durfte Trude im Wohnzimmer bleiben?
5. Wer hat in der Küche gearbeitet?
6. Was hat Hans in der Küche getan?

☞ UNIT 15

A. UNITS OF SPEECH AND VOCABULARY

I. STUDY AND READ ALOUD.

sie wartet auf ihn (ACC)	she is waiting for him
ich esse lieber Kuchen	I prefer to eat cake
er ißt am liebsten Eis	he likes best to eat ice cream
immer besser	better and better
immer mehr	more and more
eine Flasche Milch	a bottle of milk
ein Glas Bier	a glass of beer
ein Stück Käse	a piece of cheese
eine Tasse Tee	a cup of tea
eine halbe Stunde	half an hour, a half hour
ein halbes Glas	half a glass
ein halber Apfel	half an apple

das Bier, -s, -e	the beer	die Milch, -	the milk
das Eis, -es	the ice, ice cream	das Stück, -s, -e	the piece
die Flasche, -, -n	the bottle	die Tasse, -, -n	the cup
das Fleisch, -es	the meat	der Tee, -s	the tea
das Gemüse, -s, -	the vegetable	der Wein, -s, -e	the wine
der Kaffee, -s	the coffee	glauben	to believe
der Käse, -s	the cheese	hoffen	to hope
der Kuchen, -s, -	the cake		

110

treffen, traf,		**siebzig**	seventy
getroffen, trifft	to meet	**achtzig**	eighty
warten	to wait	**neunzig**	ninety
sechzig	sixty		

II. DRILL. EXPRESS ORALLY IN GERMAN. REPEAT UNTIL IT IS NO LONGER NECESSARY TO REFER TO SECTION I.

a. 1. she is waiting for him   2. we are waiting for him   3. we are waiting for them   4. they are waiting for us   5. he is waiting for us 6. he is waiting for you

b. 1. I prefer to eat cake   2. I prefer to eat meat   3. I prefer to eat cheese   4. we prefer to eat cheese   5. we prefer to eat vegetables

c. 1. he likes best to eat ice cream   2. she likes best to eat ice cream 3. she likes best to eat cheese   4. they like best to eat meat   5. they like best to eat cake   6. I like best to eat vegetables

d. 1. better and better   2. more and more   3. bigger and bigger 4. older and older   5. smaller and smaller

e. 1. a bottle of milk   2. a bottle of wine   3. a bottle of beer

f. 1. a glass of beer   2. a glass of wine   3. a glass of milk

g. 1. a piece of cheese   2. a piece of meat   3. a piece of cake

h. 1. a cup of tea   2. a cup of coffee   3. a cup of milk   4. a cup of tea and a cup of coffee

i. 1. half an hour   2. half a bottle   3. half a cup   4. half a glass 5. half a year   6. half an apple   7. half a day

j. 1. I believe . . .   2. I believe he has ice cream.   3. I believe she has coffee.   4. I believe he has tea.   5. I believe we have wine.

k. 1. We hope . . .   2. We hope you are fine.   3. We hope he is fine. 4. We hope she is fine.   5. We hope they are fine.

l. 1. They are meeting . . .   2. They are meeting him.   3. He is meeting them.   4. She is meeting us.   5. She has met him.   6. He has met her.

m. 1. sixty bottles   2. seventy bottles   3. eighty cups   4. ninety cups

B. MODEL SENTENCES

I. STUDY UNTIL EACH SENTENCE CAN BE GIVEN CORRECTLY FROM THE ENGLISH.

110. **Gehe zu Bett und schlafe, mein Kind!**
111. **Gib ihr das Geld und laufe nach Hause, Hans!**
112. **Kommt ins Zimmer und lest euere Bücher, Richard und Klara!**
113. **Er hatte eine halbe Stunde auf mich gewartet.**
114. **Ich war in der Stadt geblieben.**
115. **Sie werden wohl ihren Freund getroffen haben.**
116. **Mein Vater wird wohl zu Hause sein.**
117. **Der Arzt trinkt gerne Milch, er trinkt lieber Tee, aber am liebsten trinkt er Kaffee.**
118. **Das Mädchen ißt ein Stück Kuchen und trinkt eine Tasse Tee.**

110. Go to bed and sleep, my child.
111. Give her the money and run home, Hans.
112. Come into the room and read your books, Richard and Klara.
113. He had waited half an hour for me.
114. I had stayed in town.
115. They probably met their friend.
116. My father is probably at home.
117. The doctor likes to drink milk, he prefers to drink tea, but he likes best to drink coffee.
118. The girl is eating a piece of cake and drinking a cup of tea.

II. DRILL. EXPRESS ORALLY IN GERMAN.

a. 1. Go to bed and sleep, my child. 2. Come to bed and sleep, my child. 3. Stay there and sleep, my child. 4. Stay there and write, my child.

b. 1. Give her the money and run home, Hans. 2. Give her the book and run home, Marie. 3. Give him the letter and run home, Klara. 4. Give him the apple and run home, Richard.

c. 1. Come into the room and read your books, Richard and Klara. 2. Come into the living room and read your books, Richard and Klara. 3. Come into the dining room and read your books, Richard and Klara. 4. Come into the kitchen and read your lessons, Richard and Klara.

d. 1. He had waited half an hour for me. 2. She had waited half an hour for him. 3. She had waited half an hour for us. 4. I had waited half an hour for them. 5. I had waited half an hour for him.

e. 1. I had stayed in town.   2. He had stayed in town.   3. My friend had stayed in town.   4. Her friend (*f.*) had stayed in town.   5. Our aunt had stayed in town.
f. 1. They probably met their friend.   2. They probably met their friends.   3. They probably met their parents.   4. They probably met their cousins.   5. They probably met their brothers.   6. They probably met their sisters.
g. 1. My father is probably at home.   2. Your uncle is probably at home.   3. The doctor is probably at home.   4. The professor is probably at home.   5. The teacher (*f.*) is probably at home. 6. The family is probably at home.
h. 1. The doctor likes to drink milk, he prefers to drink tea, but he likes best to drink coffee.   2. My friend likes to drink wine, he prefers to drink beer, but he likes best to drink water.   3. I like to eat vegetables, I prefer to eat meat, but I like best to eat cake.
i. 1. The girl is eating a piece of cake and drinking a cup of tea. 2. The woman is eating a piece of cake and drinking a cup of coffee. 3. The boy is eating a piece of cheese and drinking a glass of milk. 4. The man is eating a piece of cheese and drinking a bottle of beer.

C. GRAMMAR

1. Irregular verbs which change the **e** of the stem to **i** or **ie** in the second and third persons singular of the present indicative do the same in the familiar singular imperative. Such verbs omit the **-e** ending which regular verbs use.

geben to give   **du gibst** you give   **er, sie, es gibt** he, she, it gives
gib! give!

Verbs which have a similar change of stem vowel in the familiar singular imperative include the following.

essen	to eat	**iß!**	eat!
helfen	to help	**hilf!**	help!
lesen	to read	**lies!**	read!
nehmen	to take	**nimm!**	take!
sehen	to see	**sieh!**	see!
sprechen	to speak	**sprich!**	speak!

2. All other irregular verbs form the familiar singular imperative as regular verbs do.

gehen	to go	**gehe!**	go!
laufen	to run	**laufe!**	run!
schlafen	to sleep	**schlafe!**	sleep!

Note that these forms are to be used only for persons addressed as **du.**

a. **Gehe zu Bett und schlafe, mein Kind!**
   Go to bed and sleep, my child.

b. **Gib ihr das Geld und laufe nach Hause, Hans!**
   Give her the money and run home, Hans.

3. The familiar plural of the imperative of irregular verbs is identical with that of the present indicative, omitting the pronoun.
   Kommt ins Zimmer und lest euere Bücher, Richard und Klara!
   Come into the room and read your books, Richard and Klara.

4. The past perfect tense consists of the past tense of the auxiliary verb **haben** (or **sein**) and the past participle.

a. **Er hatte eine halbe Stunde auf mich gewartet.**
   He had waited half an hour for me.

b. **Ich war in der Stadt geblieben.**
   I had stayed in town.

5. The future perfect tense consists of the future tense of **haben** (or **sein**) and the past participle. The most frequent use of this tense is to indicate past probability, especially when used with **wohl** (probably).
   Sie werden (wohl) ihren Freund getroffen haben.
   They probably met their friend.

6. The future tense, with **wohl** (probably), frequently is used to express present probability.
   Mein Vater wird (wohl) zu Hause sein.
   My father is probably at home.

7. The comparative and superlative forms of **gerne** (gladly) are **lieber** (rather) and **am liebsten** (most gladly), respectively. **Lieber** plus a verb means "to prefer to," **am liebsten** plus a verb, "to like best to."
   Der Arzt trinkt gerne Milch, er trinkt lieber Tee, aber am liebsten trinkt er Kaffee.
   The doctor likes to drink milk, he prefers to drink tea, but he likes best to drink coffee.

8. When a noun of measure is followed by another noun, the second noun is not inflected.

Das Mädchen ißt ein Stück Kuchen und trinkt eine Tasse Tee.
The girl is eating a piece of cake and drinking a cup of tea.

D. EXERCISES

WRITE THE FOLLOWING SENTENCES IN GERMAN AND BE ABLE TO EXPRESS THEM ORALLY IN CLASS.

1. Speak more slowly, Hans.
2. They had gone home a week ago.
3. The children probably went to school at eight o'clock.
4. My sister likes to wear red hats best.
5. He had drunk two cups of tea.
6. We prefer to eat cake.
7. The boys are getting bigger and bigger.
8. Carry the chairs into the kitchen, Marie.
9. The girl had brought him a glass of cold water.
10. Does he prefer to drink beer or wine?
11. Give me two bottles of milk.
12. My uncle had become sixty years old in January.
13. His father probably believed it.
14. They had played a half hour.
15. Write your parents a letter, children.
16. My family had lived in that house half a year.
17. The man ate a piece of cheese.
18. I prefer to travel to Switzerland.
19. Bring me another cup of coffee, Mother.
20. They are probably sitting in the living room.
21. Read the lesson, Richard.
22. Eat a piece of meat, my son.
23. Do the students like to speak German best?
24. We are getting older and older.
25. Her mother is probably seventy years old.

E. READING AND SPEAKING

I. READ THE FOLLOWING ALOUD UNTIL YOU ARE THOROUGHLY FAMILIAR WITH IT.

Im Restaurant

Hans trifft seine Freundin Käthe in einem Restaurant in der Stadt.
„Hast du Walter gesehen?", fragt er sie.
„Nein. Ich habe ihn nicht gesehen."
5 „Ich sollte ihn um vier Uhr im Reisebüro (travel agency) treffen,
aber ich bin erst eine Stunde später gekommen. Er hatte eine halbe
Stunde auf mich gewartet, aber dann war es zu spät geworden. Er
wird wohl nach Hause gefahren sein. Was soll ich jetzt tun?"
„Rufe ihn doch an![1] Jetzt wird er wohl zu Hause sein."
10 „Du hast recht, aber erst (first) wollen wir essen. Was möchtest
du haben?"
„Ich glaube, ich werde Fleisch und Gemüse essen."
„Ich auch. Trinkst du gerne Milch?"
„Ja, aber ich trinke lieber Tee."
15 „Ich trinke am liebsten Kaffee. Gut. Eine Tasse Tee für dich und
eine Tasse Kaffee für mich. Und zum Nachtisch?"[2]
„Ein Stück Käse und einen Apfel."
„Nicht schlecht (bad), aber ich werde ein Eis essen."

II. ANSWER THE FOLLOWING QUESTIONS IN GERMAN.

1. Wo trifft Hans seine Freundin?
2. Wen soll sie gesehen haben?
3. Wie lange hatte Walter auf Hans gewartet?
4. Was will Käthe essen?
5. Was trinkt Hans am liebsten?
6. Was essen sie zum Nachtisch?

---

[1] **Rufe ihn doch an!** Why don't you call him up!   [2] **zum Nachtisch**   for dessert.

☛ UNIT 16

A. UNITS OF SPEECH AND VOCABULARY

I. STUDY AND READ ALOUD.

da kommt er	there he comes
ich würde singen	I would sing
sie würde gehen	she would go
würden Sie essen?	would you eat?
Bevor er singt, . . .	Before he sings, . . .
Weil sie lacht, . . .	Because she is laughing, . . .
Nachdem ich ging, . . .	After I went, . . .
Als sie arbeiteten, . . .	When they were working . . .
entweder blau oder gelb	either blue or yellow
sowohl der Vater als auch die Mutter	both the father and the mother
weder hell noch dunkel	neither light nor dark
nicht weiß, sondern schwarz	not white, but black

alles	everything	**schwarz**	black
nichts	nothing	**schwer**	heavy, difficult
blau	blue	**weiß**	white
dunkel	dark	**da** *adv.*	there
hell	light (*in color*), bright	**als**	when, as
		bevor *conj.*	before
leicht	light (*in weight*), easy	**bis**	until
		da *conj.*	because, since

117

daß *conj.*	that	sowohl . . . als	
ehe *conj.*	before	auch	both . . . and
entweder . . . oder	either . . . or	während	while
nachdem *conj.*	after	weder . . . noch	neither . . . nor
ob	whether	weil	because, since
obgleich	although	wenn	when, when-
sobald	as soon as		ever, if
sondern	but	arbeiten	to work
		lachen	to laugh

schwimmen	schwamm	ist geschwommen	to swim
singen	sang	gesungen	to sing

II. DRILL. EXPRESS ORALLY IN GERMAN. REPEAT UNTIL IT IS NO LONGER
NECESSARY TO REFER TO SECTION I.

a. 1. there he comes   2. there she comes   3. There comes the professor.
4. There come the students.   5. There come the children.   6. There
they come.

b. 1. I would sing   2. I would write   3. I would read   4. I would run

c. 1. she would go   2. she would swim   3. she would sing   4. he
would laugh   5. he would work   6. he would understand

d. 1. would you eat?   2. would you sing?   3. would you work?
4. would you laugh?   5. would you swim?

e. 1. Before he sings, . . .   2. Before he goes, . . .   3. Before he
swims, . . .   4. Whether he swims . . .   5. Whether she works . . .
6. Whether she comes . . .   7. Although she works, . . .   8. Although she laughs, . . .   9. Although she swims, . . .   10. Since
she swims, . . .   11. Since she laughs, . . .

f. 1. Because she is laughing, . . .   2. Because she is singing, . . .
3. Because she is working, . . .   4. Whenever she works, . . .
5. Whenever they work, . . .   6. If they swim, . . .   7. If they go, . . .
8. Until they work, . . .   9. Until they come, . . .   10. Until they
go, . . .

g. 1. After I went, . . .   2. After I swam, . . .   3. After I worked, . . .
4. As soon as I came, . . .   5. As soon as I saw, . . .   6. As soon as
I wrote, . . .   7. While I was writing, . . .   8. While I was swimming, . . .   9. While I was working, . . .

h. 1. When they were working, . . . 2. When they were swimming, . . .
3. When they were singing, . . . 4. As they traveled, . . . 5. As
they wrote, . . . 6. As they played, . . .

i. 1. . . . that they played. 2. . . . that they went. 3. . . . that
they came.

j. 1. either blue or yellow 2. either blue or black 3. either black or
white 4. either dark or light 5. either easy or difficult

k. 1. both the father and the mother 2. both the brother and the
sister 3. both white and black 4. both light and heavy 5. both
blue and white 6. both dark and light

l. 1. neither light nor dark 2. neither white nor black 3. neither
easy nor difficult 4. neither long nor short

m. 1. not white, but black 2. not light, but heavy 3. not here, but
there 4. not today, but tomorrow 5. not in summer, but in winter

n. 1. . . . everything. 2. They do everything. 3. They see everything. 4. They eat everything. 5. They drink everything.

o. 1. . . . nothing. 2. He wants nothing. 3. He eats nothing.
4. He drinks nothing. 5. He does nothing.

B. MODEL SENTENCES

I. STUDY UNTIL EACH SENTENCE CAN BE GIVEN CORRECTLY FROM THE
ENGLISH.

119. Er arbeitet nicht schnell, aber gut.
120. Das Haus ist nicht weiß, sondern schwarz.
121. Als ich nach Hause kam, war mein Vater nicht mehr da.
122. Wenn er in die Stadt ging, kaufte er viel.
123. Ich werde meinen Onkel sehen, wenn er uns besucht.
124. Da wir erst spät kommen können, werden wir ihn nicht sehen.
125. Da kommen sie.
126. Die Frau wußte, daß der Mann ihr einen Brief schreiben würde.
127. Ich glaube, er kommt morgen.

119. He does not work quickly, but well.
120. The house is not white, but black.
121. When I came home, my father was no longer there.
122. Whenever he went to town, he bought much (a lot).

123. I'll see my uncle when he visits us.
124. Since we cannot come until late, we will not see him.
125. There they come.
126. The woman knew that the man would write her a letter.
127. I believe he is coming tomorrow.

II. DRILL. EXPRESS ORALLY IN GERMAN.

a. 1. He does not work quickly, but well. 2. He does not work well, but quickly. 3. He does not learn well, but quickly. 4. He does not learn quickly, but well.

b. 1. The house is not white, but black. 2. The house is not new, but old. 3. The man is not old, but young. 4. The lesson is not easy, but hard. 5. The lesson is not long, but short.

c. 1. When I came home, my father was no longer there. 2. When I came to town, my brother was no longer there. 3. When I came to school, the teacher was no longer there. 4. When I came to church, my friend was no longer there.

d. 1. Whenever he went to town, he bought a lot. 2. Whenever he went to church, he sang a lot. 3. Whenever he went to the movies, he laughed a lot. 4. Whenever he went to the seashore, he swam a lot.

e. 1. I'll see my uncle when he visits us. 2. I'll see my aunt when she visits us. 3. We'll see our cousins when they visit us. 4. We'll see our parents when they visit us.

f. 1. Since we cannot come until late, we will not see him. 2. Since they cannot come until late, they will not see us. 3. Since she cannot come until late she will not see me. 4. Since he cannot come until late, he will not see her.

g. 1. There they come. 2. There come the neighbors. 3. There come the coeds. 4. There come the teachers (*f.*). 5. There comes the doctor. 6. There comes your girl friend. 7. There comes the girl.

h. 1. The woman knew that the man would write her a letter. 2. The man knew that his son would write him a letter. 3. The boy knew that his father would write him a letter. 4. The children knew that their parents would write them a letter. 5. The parents knew that their children would write them a letter.

i. 1. I believe he is coming tomorrow. 2. I believe she is singing tomorrow. 3. I believe they are working tomorrow. 4. I believe we are working tomorrow. 5. I believe we are meeting him tomorrow.

C. GRAMMAR

1. In main clauses, the finite (conjugated) verb is usually the second element. In normal word order, the first element is the subject; in inverted word order—with the subject after the verb—the first element may be an adverb, a prepositional phrase, an object, or any element used emphatically (see page 28, C6).

   Main clauses may be introduced by co-ordinating conjunctions, which usually do not affect word order, either normal or inverted. The principal co-ordinating conjunctions follow.

aber	but	**oder**	or
denn	for	**sondern**	but
entweder . . . oder		either . . . or	
sowohl . . . als auch		both . . . and	
weder . . . noch		neither . . . nor	

2. **Sondern** (but) is used only after a negative, such as **nicht** (not), when the elements preceding and following are mutually exclusive. Otherwise, **aber** (but) is used.

   a. **Das Haus ist nicht weiß, sondern schwarz.**
      The house is not white, but black.

   Note: **Sondern** suggests "but on the contrary."

   b. **Er arbeitet nicht schnell, aber gut.**
      He does not work quickly, but well.

   c. **Sein Onkel hat wenig Geld, aber viele Freunde.**
      His uncle has little money, but many friends.

3. Subordinating conjunctions introduce subordinate (dependent) clauses, in which the finite verb is usually last (transposed word order).

   a. **Ich werde meinen Onkel sehen, wenn er uns besucht.**
      I'll see my uncle when he visits us.

   When the subordinate clause precedes the main clause, the subject must follow the verb in the main clause (inverted word order).

b. **Als ich nach Hause kam, war mein Vater nicht mehr da.**

When I came home, my father was no longer there.

Note: Subordinate clauses are always set off by commas.

4. The principal subordinating conjunctions.

als	when, as	**daß**	that	**sobald**	as soon as
bevor, ehe	before	**nachdem**	after	**während**	while
bis	until	**ob**	whether	**wenn**	whenever
da, weil	because, since	**obgleich**	although		when, if

5. When a question is asked indirectly, the indirect question is a subordinate clause.

Ich weiß nicht, wann er kommt.

I don't know when he is coming.

Other interrogative words, in addition to **wann**, may introduce indirect questions.

warum?	why?	**wer?**	who?
was?	what?	**wo?**	where?
welcher? welche? welches?	which?	**wohin?**	where to?

6. **Als** (when, as) is generally used for a single past action.

a. **Als ich nach Hause kam, war mein Vater nicht mehr da.**

When I came home, my father was no longer there.

Wenn (whenever, when, if) is used for repeated action in any tense or for any future action.

b. **Wenn er in die Stadt ging, kaufte er viel.**

Whenever he went to town, he bought a lot.

c. **Ich werde meinen Onkel sehen, wenn er uns besucht.**

I'll see my uncle, when he visits us.

Note: The simple past tense is often preferred, even conversationally, in sentences of more than one clause, especially time clauses, such as *a* and *b*, above.

7. Distinguish between the adverb **da** (there) and the subordinating conjunction **da** (because, since).

a. **Da kommen sie.** (adverb)

There they come.

b. **Da wir erst spät kommen können, werden wir ihn nicht sehen.** (conjunction)

Since we cannot come until late, we will not see him.

Note that in *b* the subordinate clause has transposed word order: the subject (**wir**) immediately follows **da,** and the finite verb (**können**) is last.

8. The subordinating conjunction **daß** (that) may be omitted, in which case the word order is normal, rather than transposed.

    a. **Die Frau wußte, daß der Mann ihr einen Brief schreiben würde.** (transposed)

       The woman knew that the man would write her a letter.

    b. **Ich glaube, er kommt morgen.** (normal)

       I believe he is coming tomorrow.

Note: **Daß** represents "that" as a conjunction, whereas **das** represents "that" as an indefinite pronoun or "the" (*n.*) .

D. EXERCISES

WRITE THE FOLLOWING SENTENCES IN GERMAN AND BE ABLE TO EXPRESS THEM ORALLY IN CLASS.

1. After the neighbors had gone home, my cousins came.
2. When he eats supper, he always drinks tea.
3. Her brother always sings while he works.
4. I'll ask her whether her brother is at home.
5. Would you bring me a cup of coffee?
6. My mother knows that I am here.
7. There come the parents and the children.
8. He would not take the trip.
9. He is not a teacher, but a student.
10. I knew that they had to do their lessons.
11. Ask the boy what he has in his hand.
12. My brother usually eats a piece of cake before he goes to bed.
13. Her sister was reading a book while she was sitting at the table.
14. Both our uncle and our aunt know German.
15. Her hat is not white, but black.
16. If they see us, they will talk with us.
17. A year ago, they traveled to Germany because they wanted to see the Rhine.
18. His cousin knows when he is going to school again.
19. The children drink either milk or tea.
20. The girl ran until she fell.
21. Although he is old, the doctor works a lot.
22. The professor read the letter as soon as he saw it.
23. His girl friend is pretty, but she is very poor.

24. She knows neither my father nor my mother.
25. When the teacher came into the room, the students were writing the lesson.

E. READING AND SPEAKING

I. READ THE FOLLOWING ALOUD UNTIL YOU ARE THOROUGHLY FAMILIAR WITH IT.

Am Telefon[1]

Ehe er ins Reisebüro ging, war Hans in einen Laden gegangen, um etwas zu kaufen. Als er aus dem Laden kam, sah er, daß er eine Reifenpanne (flat tire) hatte. Weil er warten mußte, bis man den
5 Reifen repariert (repaired) hatte, konnte er erst um fünf Uhr ins Reisebüro gehen.

Da er Walter nicht im Reisebüro getroffen hatte, mußte Hans ihn anrufen (call up). „Walter", sagte er, „hier (this is) Hans. Es tut mir leid, daß ich zu spät ins Reisebüro gekommen bin. Ich habe eine
10 Reifenpanne gehabt."

„Das tut mir leid. Während ich im Büro gewartet habe, habe ich mit Herrn Schmidt gesprochen. Wenn er etwas von der Reederei erfährt,[2] wird er mich anrufen."

„Gut. Auf Wiederhören (good-by)."
15 „Auf Wiederhören."

Nachdem er telefoniert hatte, schrieb Hans einen Brief. Er hörte Radio, bis es spät wurde. Da er wieder Hunger hatte, ging er in die Küche und aß ein Stück Kuchen. Sobald er gegessen hatte, ging er auf sein Zimmer. Er wollte schlafen, aber er konnte es nicht. Er las ein
20 Buch und schlief dann ein.[3]

II. ANSWER THE FOLLOWING QUESTIONS IN GERMAN.

1. Wohin ging Hans, ehe er ins Reisebüro ging?
2. Warum ist er zu spät ins Reisebüro gekommen?

[1] **Am Telefon** On the Telephone.   [2] **Wenn er etwas von der Reederei erfährt** When he hears from the shipping company.   [3] **schlief dann ein** then fell asleep.

3. **Was tat Hans, nachdem er telefoniert hatte?**
4. **Was hat er gegessen?**
5. **Wann ist er auf sein Zimmer gegangen?**
6. **Was hat er dort getan?**

3. Was ist Hans, nachdem er Jahrzehnte hatte?
4. Was hat er gegessen?
5. Wenn ist er auf sein Zimmer gegangen?
6. Was hat er dort getan?

☞ UNIT 17

A. UNITS OF SPEECH AND VOCABULARY

I. STUDY AND READ ALOUD.

Er fährt heute ab.	He's leaving today.
Ich rufe ihn an.	I'm calling him up.
Wir machen die Fenster auf.	We're opening the windows.
Sie steht früh auf.	She's getting up early.
Er geht jetzt fort.	He's going away now.
Er kommt morgen zurück.	He's coming back tomorrow.
Die Frau kommt ins Gebäude herein.	The woman is coming into the building.
Mein Bruder geht aus dem Zimmer hinaus.	My brother is going out of the room.
Das Haus gefällt mir.	I like the house.
Der wievielte ist heute?	What day of the month is today?
Heute ist der erste Februar.	Today is the first of February.

der Bleistift, -s, -e	the pencil	der, die, das erste	the first
der Dampfer, -s, -	the steamer, ship	der, die, das zweite	the second
		der, die, das dritte	the third
die Geschichte, -, -n	the story	der, die, das vierte	the fourth
das Heft, -es, -e	the notebook	der, die, das siebte	the seventh
das Papier, -s, -e	the paper	der, die, das achte	the eighth
der Zug, -s, ⸚e	the train		

126

der, die, das	the	**der, die, das**	the
zwanzigste	twentieth	**einundzwanzigste**	twenty-first

ab-fahren[1]	**fuhr . . . ab**	**ist abgefahren**	**fährt . . . ab**
			to leave, depart
an-rufen	**rief . . . an**	**angerufen**	**ruft . . . an**
			to call up, telephone
auf-machen	**machte . . . auf**	**aufgemacht**	**macht . . . auf**
			to open
auf-stehen	**stand . . . auf**	**ist aufgestanden**	**steht . . . auf**
			to get up, stand up
empfehlen	**empfahl**	**empfohlen**	**empfiehlt**
			to recommend
erzählen	**erzählte**	**erzählt**	to tell, narrate
entscheiden	**entschied**	**entschieden**	to decide
fort-gehen	**ging . . . fort**	**ist fortgegangen**	**geht . . . fort**
			to go away
gefallen	**gefiel**	**gefallen**	**gefällt**
			to please
herein-kommen	**kam . . . herein**	**ist hereingekommen**	**kommt . . . herein**
			to come in
hinaus-gehen	**ging . . . hinaus**	**ist hinausgegangen**	**geht . . . hinaus**
			to go out
zerreißen	**zerriß**	**zerrissen**	to tear to pieces
zurück-kommen	**kam . . . zurück**	**ist zurückgekommen**	**kommt . . . zurück**
			to come back

II. DRILL. EXPRESS ORALLY IN GERMAN. REPEAT UNTIL IT IS NO LONGER
NECESSARY TO REFER TO SECTION I.

a. 1. He's leaving today.   2. She's leaving today.   3. I'm leaving today.
    4. The train is leaving today.   5. The steamer is leaving today.
b. 1. I'm calling him up.   2. I'm calling her up.   3. She's calling me up.
    4. She's calling us up.   5. He's calling us up.
c. 1. We're opening the windows.   2. You're opening the windows.
    3. I'm opening the windows.   4. She's opening the windows.
    5. He's opening the windows.
d. 1. She's getting up early.   2. I'm getting up early.   3. He's getting

---

[1] The hyphen indicates that the verb has a separable prefix. Normally the infinitive is spelled **abfahren** (see page 131, C3).

up early.   4. They're getting up early.   5. We're getting up early.

e.   1. He's going away now.   2. She's going away now.   3. The doctor is going away now.   4. The teacher (*f.*) is going away now.   5. The student (*f.*) is going away now.

f.   1. He's coming back tomorrow.   2. She's coming back tomorrow. 3. The neighbor is coming back tomorrow.   4. The professor is coming back next week.   5. The physician is coming back next month.

g.   1. The woman is coming into the building.   2. The girl is coming into the building.   3. The child is coming into the building.   4. The teachers are coming into the building.   5. The students are coming into the building.

h.   1. My brother is going out of the room.   2. My uncle is going out of the room.   3. My cousin is going out of the room.   4. My aunt is going out of the room.   5. My mother is going out of the room.

i.   1. I like the house.   2. She likes the house.   3. He likes the house. 4. We like the house.   5. They like the house.   6. Do you like the house?

j.   1. What day of the month is today?   2. Today is the first of February.   3. Today is the twenty-first of February.   4. Today is the twentieth of July.   5. Today is the eighth of June.   6. Today is the third of March.   7. Today is the seventh of March.   8. Today is the fourth of October.   9. Today is the second of October.

k.   1. The pencil . . .   2. The pencil is yellow.   3. The pencil is white. 4. The pencil is black.   5. The pencils are blue.   6. The pencils are green.   7. The pencils are red.

l.   1. . . . is telling.   2. He is telling a story.   3. He is telling me a story.   4. She is telling me a story.   5. They are telling stories. 6. We are telling stories.

m.   1. . . . recommends.   2. She recommends this steamer.   3. He recommends this steamer.   4. They recommend this steamer. 5. They recommend this train.   6. We recommend this train.

n.   1. . . . decides.   2. He decides everything.   3. She decides everything.   4. She decides nothing.   5. He decides nothing.

o.   1. . . . are tearing to pieces.   2. They are tearing the paper to pieces.   3. We are tearing the paper to pieces.   4. He is tearing the paper to pieces.   5. He is tearing the notebook to pieces. 6. She is tearing the notebook to pieces.

B. MODEL SENTENCES

I. STUDY UNTIL EACH SENTENCE CAN BE GIVEN CORRECTLY FROM THE ENGLISH.

128. **Schreibt er mit dem Bleistift?—Ja, er schreibt damit.**
129. **Was legt sie auf die Stühle?—Sie legt die Hefte darauf.**
130. **Heute ist der neunzehnte Februar und morgen ist der zwanzigste Februar.**
131. **Wir fahren nicht ab, ehe die Kinder zurückkommen.**
132. **Er kam ins Wohnzimmer herein, während sie hinausging.**
133. **Bitte machen Sie die Fenster auf!**
134. **Obgleich er früh aufgestanden war, ist er spät zurückgekommen.**
135. **Er ist früh fortgegangen, um vor zwei Uhr zurückzukommen.**
136. **Haben Sie alles verstanden?**

128. Is he writing with the pencil?—Yes, he is writing with it.
129. What is she putting on the chairs?—She is putting the notebooks on them.
130. Today is the nineteenth of February and tomorrow is the twentieth of February.
131. We are not leaving before the children come back.
132. He was coming into the living room while she was going out.
133. Please open the windows.
134. Although he had gotten up early, he came back late.
135. He went away early in order to come back before two o'clock.
136. Did you understand everything?

II. DRILL. EXPRESS ORALLY IN GERMAN.

a. 1. Is he writing with the pencil? Yes, he is writing with it. 2. Is she writing with the pencil? Yes, she is writing with it. 3. Is the student (*f.*) writing with the pencil? Yes, she is writing with it. 4. Is the student writing with the pencil? Yes, he is writing with it.
b. 1. What is she putting on the chairs? She is putting the notebooks on them. 2. What is she putting on the tables? She is putting the books on them. 3. What is she putting on the table and the chair? She is putting the pencils on them.

c. 1. Today is the nineteenth of February and tomorrow is the twentieth of February.   2. Today is the first of March and tomorrow is the second of March.   3. Today is the third of April and tomorrow is the fourth of April.   4. Today is the thirtieth of May and tomorrow is the thirty-first of May.

d. 1. We are not leaving before the children come back.   2. The children are not leaving before we come back.   3. The children are not leaving before their friends come back.   4. Our friends are not leaving before their parents come back.

e. 1. He was coming into the living room while she was going out. 2. She was coming into the living room while he was going out. 3. They were coming into the living room while we were going out. 4. We were coming into the living room while you were going out.

f. 1. Please open the windows.   2. Please open the door.   3. Please come in.   4. Please call me up.   5. Please get up.

g. 1. Although he had gotten up early, he came back late.   2. Although she had gotten up early, she came back late.   3. Although they had gotten up early, they came back late.   4. Although we had gotten up early, we came back late.

h. 1. He went away early in order to come back before two o'clock. 2. She went away early in order to come back before two o'clock. 3. I went away early in order to come back before two o'clock. 4. They went away early in order to come back before six o'clock. 5. We went away early in order to come back before six o'clock.

i. 1. Did you understand everything?   2. Did you understand nothing? 3. Did you understand something?   4. Did he understand it? 5. Did she understand that?

C. GRAMMAR

1. Personal pronouns referring to inanimate objects are not used as objects of prepositions that govern the dative or accusative case. Pronouns are usually replaced by **da-** (or **dar-**) plus the preposition. (If the preposition begins with a consonant, it is combined with **da-**; if it begins with a vowel, it is combined with **dar-**.)

    a. **Schreibt er mit dem Bleistift?—Ja, er schreibt damit.**
      Is he writing with the pencil?—Yes, he is writing with it.

b. **Was legt sie auf die Stühle?—Sie legt die Hefte darauf.**

What is she putting on the chairs?—She is putting the notebooks on them.

Note: The form of the compound is the same regardless of whether the noun it replaces is singular, as in *a,* or plural, as in *b.*

2. Ordinal numbers up to and including **neunzehnte** (nineteenth) are formed by adding **-t** to the cardinal number and the appropriate descriptive adjective endings. From **zwanzigste** on, **-st** is added.

> **Heute ist der neunzehnte Februar und morgen ist der zwanzigste Februar.**
>
> Today is the nineteenth of February and tomorrow is the twentieth of February.

The forms **erste** (first), **dritte** (third), **siebte** (seventh), **achte** (eighth) are irregular.

3. Verbs with separable prefixes consist usually of an adverb or a preposition and a simple verb. The prefix is placed at the end of a main clause when the verb is in the present or past tense. In subordinate clauses, however, the prefix precedes the verb and is attached to it.

a. **Wir fahren nicht ab, ehe die Kinder zurückkommen.**

We are not leaving before the children come back.

b. **Er kam ins Wohnzimmer herein, während sie hinausging.**

He was coming into the living room while she was going out.

Note 1: **Nicht** immediately precedes a separated prefix in a main clause.

Note 2: **Hin** (hence, from here) and **her** (hither, [to] here) are frequently prefixed to other adverbial elements to indicate direction with relation to the speaker.

4. The separable prefix stands at the end of an imperative clause.

> **Bitte machen Sie die Fenster auf!**
>
> Please open the windows.

5. The past participle of a verb with separable prefix is formed by attaching the prefix to the past participle of the root verb.

> **auf-stehen**   to get up   **ist aufgestanden**
> **auf-machen**   to open   **aufgemacht**

6. In compound tenses, both in main clauses and in subordinate clauses, the prefix precedes the infinitive or past participle and is attached to it.

a. **Obgleich er früh aufgestanden war, ist er spät zurückgekommen.**
   Although he had gotten up early, he came back late.
b. **Ich werde die Tür aufmachen.**
   I'll open the door.
7. When the infinitive of a verb with separable prefix is governed by
   zu (to), **zu** is inserted between the prefix and the infinitive, and all
   three parts are written as one word.
   Er ist früh fortgegangen, um vor zwei Uhr zurückzukommen.
   He went away early in order to come back before two o'clock.
8. Verbs with inseparable prefixes consist of a prefix which cannot
   stand alone and a verb. Verbs with inseparable prefixes are never
   divided. The principal inseparable prefixes are **be-, emp-, ent-, er-,
   ge-, ver-, zer-.** Note the following examples. **beginnen** (to begin),
   empfehlen (to recommend), **entscheiden** (to decide), **erzählen** (to tell),
   gefallen (to please), **verstehen** (to understand), **zerreißen** (to tear to
   pieces).
9. The past participles of verbs with inseparable prefixes never
   add **ge-.**
   Haben Sie alles verstanden?
   Did you understand everything?
10. The principal parts of the verbs with inseparable prefixes intro-
    duced before this lesson are as follows.

begegnen	to meet	**begegnete**	**ist begegnet**
begrüßen	to greet	**begrüßte**	**begrüßt**
beginnen	to begin	**begann**	**begonnen**
bekommen	to get, to receive	**bekam**	**bekommen**
beschreiben	to describe	**beschrieb**	**beschrieben**
besuchen	to visit	**besuchte**	**besucht**
verstehen	to understand	**verstand**	**verstanden**

D. EXERCISES

WRITE THE FOLLOWING SENTENCES IN GERMAN AND BE ABLE TO EXPRESS
THEM ORALLY IN CLASS.

1. What is lying on the table?—A pencil is lying on it.
2. We have called them up already.
3. My uncle goes to bed early in order to get up early.
4. Do you like my hat?

5. Yesterday was the sixth of July.
6. My aunt did not know whether she would come back again.
7. Please open the doors.
8. They are not going away until their parents call up.
9. Tell me something, Hans.
10. While she was opening the window, her son was going out of the room.
11. Please come in.
12. Her sister likes the white flowers.
13. The mother is coming back into the living room in order to tell the children stories.
14. The boy was standing in front of the table and the girl was sitting in front of it.
15. Please go out of the kitchen, children.
16. Did you meet your cousins in town?
17. The doctor has already gone away.
18. The day before yesterday was the eleventh of October.
19. After the train had left, my cousin (f.) came back home.
20. The child has torn the paper to pieces.
21. What is lying under the chairs?—The books are lying under them.
22. Get up now, Marie.
23. My friend had recommended a good book to me.
24. I did not like that car.
25. Tomorrow will be the fourteenth of June.
26. He waited for his neighbor in order to come in with him.
27. As soon as she had gone away, her brother received the letter.

E. READING AND SPEAKING

I. READ THE FOLLOWING ALOUD UNTIL YOU ARE THOROUGHLY FAMILIAR WITH IT.

Im Reisebüro

Am nächsten Freitag klingelte es¹ bei Hans. Er ging an die Tür und machte sie auf. „Guten Tag, Walter'', sagte er. „Bitte, komme herein.''

¹ **klingelte es**   the bell rang.

5 „Guten Tag, Hans. Ich habe keine Zeit hereinzukommen. Herr
Schmidt hat mich angerufen. Kannst du mit mir ins Büro gehen?”
„Ja, ich kann es. Sollen wir jetzt gehen?”
„Ja. Wir fahren mit meinem Auto. Um zwei Uhr sind wir da.”
Als Hans und Walter ins Büro eingetreten waren,[2] zeigte ihnen Herr
10 Schmidt den Brief von der Reederei. „Sie können am ersten Juni von
New York abfahren.”
„Das ist zu früh”, sagte Walter. „Die Schule ist erst am dritten
Juni aus (over). Fährt ein anderer Dampfer ein wenig später?”
„Ja. Am achten. Dann sind Sie am fünfzehnten in Hamburg.
15 D e n[3] (that) Dampfer kann ich empfehlen. Der (It) ist ausgezeichnet
(excellent).”
„Schön”, sagte Hans, „und wann können wir wieder zurückkommen?”
„Am sechzehnten September können Sie von Hamburg abfahren
20 und am dreiundzwanzigsten sind Sie wieder in New York.”
„Ausgezeichnet”, sagten Hans und Walter. „Das gefällt uns.”

II. ANSWER THE FOLLOWING QUESTIONS IN GERMAN.

1. **Wann hat es bei Hans geklingelt?**
2. **Warum konnte Walter nicht hereinkommen?**
3. **Was hat ihnen Herr Schmidt gezeigt?**
4. **Wollten sie am ersten Juni abfahren?**
5. **In welchem Monat wollten sie wieder zurückkommen?**
6. **Wann würden sie wieder in New York sein?**

---

[2] **ins Büro eingetreten waren** had entered the (travel) agency.   [3]Note that emphasis in German is indicated by spacing the type.

☞ UNIT **18**

A. UNITS OF SPEECH AND VOCABULARY

I. STUDY AND READ ALOUD.

wir folgen ihm	we are following him
sie ist ihr gefolgt	she followed her
Wieviel kostet es?	How much does it cost?
mit dem Zug	by train
mit der Straßenbahn	by streetcar
alles Fremde	everything strange, foreign
etwas Angenehmes	something pleasant
nichts Schlechtes	nothing bad
ein deutsches Flugzeug	a German airplane
ein englischer Autobus	an English bus
die meisten Leute	most people

der Amerikaner,		die Deutsche,	the German
-s, -	the American	-n, -n	girl, the
die Amerikanerin,	the American		German
-, -nen	girl, the		woman
	American	der Engländer,	the English-
	woman	-s, -	man
der Deutsche,		die Engländerin,	the English-
-n, -n	the German	-, -nen	woman
ein Deutscher	a German		

135

der Autobus,		**angenehm**	pleasant
-busses, -busse	the bus	**billig**	cheap, inex-
das Flugzeug, -s, -e	the airplane		pensive
der Reisende, -n, -n	the traveler	**teuer**	dear, expensive
ein Reisender	a traveler	**schlecht**	bad, evil
die Straßenbahn,		**braun**	brown
-, -en	the streetcar	**grau**	gray
amerikanisch	American	**heiß**	hot
deutsch	German	**wieviel?**	how much?
englisch	English	**folgen** + *dat.* **(ist)**	to follow
fremd	strange,	**kosten**	to cost
	foreign		

an-kommen	**kam . . . an**	**ist angekommen**	to arrive

II. DRILL. EXPRESS ORALLY IN GERMAN. REPEAT UNTIL IT IS NO LONGER
NECESSARY TO REFER TO SECTION I.

a. 1. we are following him   2. The people are following him.   3. The
travelers are following him.   4. The Americans are following him.
5. The Englishwoman is following her.   6. The German girl is
following her.   7. The American girl is following her.

b. 1. she followed her   2. Her daughter followed her.   3. Her sister
followed her.   4. Her mother followed her.

c. 1. How much does it cost?   2. How much does that cost?   3. How
much does this cost?

d. 1.   . . . by train.   2. They travel by train.   3. They travel by bus.
4. They travel by plane.   5. They travel by steamer.   6. They travel
by streetcar.

e. 1. everything strange   2. everything inexpensive   3. everything
expensive   4. everything hot   5. everything pleasant   6. everything
bad   7. everything gray   8. everything brown   9. everything
German   10. everything American   11. everything English

f. 1. something pleasant   2. something bad   3. something hot
4. something foreign   5. something cheap   6. something dear
7. something English   8. something German   9. something
American

g. 1. nothing bad   2. nothing pleasant   3. nothing expensive   4. nothing cheap   5. nothing hot   6. nothing strange   7. nothing brown   8. nothing gray

h. 1. a German airplane   2. an English airplane   3. an American airplane   4. a foreign airplane   5. a gray airplane   6. a brown airplane

i. 1. an English bus   2. an American bus   3. a German bus   4. a brown bus   5. a gray bus   6. an expensive bus   7. an inexpensive bus

j. 1. most people   2. most Americans   3. most Germans   4. most Englishmen   5. most Englishwomen   6. most American girls   7. most travelers   8. most streetcars

k. 1. they are arriving   2. A German and an American are arriving. 3. An American girl and an Englishwoman are arriving.   4. A German woman and an American woman are arriving.   5. A German and an Englishman are arriving.   6. The people are arriving.   7. The travelers are arriving.

B. MODEL SENTENCES

I. STUDY UNTIL EACH SENTENCE CAN BE GIVEN CORRECTLY FROM THE ENGLISH.

137. **Womit schreibt die Studentin?**
138. **Worüber sprechen die Mädchen?**
139. **Ich habe die folgenden Bücher gelesen.**
140. **Das ist ein viel getragener Hut.**
141. **Der Deutsche liest ein englisches Buch.**
142. **Die Kleine saß im Wohnzimmer und schrieb ihre Aufgabe.**
143. **E i n Reisender stand und die anderen Reisenden saßen.**
144. **Das Neue ist nicht immer besser als das Alte.**
145. **Die Tante hat dem Kind etwas Schönes gegeben.**

137. With what is the student (*f.*) writing?
138. What are the girls talking about?
139. I have read the following books.
140. That is a much-worn hat.
141. The German is reading an English book.

142. The little girl was sitting in the living room and writing her lesson.
143. One traveler was standing and the other travelers were sitting.
144. The new is not always better than the old.
145. The aunt gave the child something nice.

II. DRILL. EXPRESS ORALLY IN GERMAN.

a. 1. With what is the student (*f.*) writing?   2. With what is the Englishman writing?   3. With what is the American writing?   4. With what is the traveler writing?   5. With what are the people writing?   6. With what are the children writing?

b. 1. What are the girls talking about?   2. What are the boys talking about?   3. What are the men talking about?   4. What are the women talking about?

c. 1. I have read the following books.   2. They have read the following books.   3. The German read the following books.   4. My friend read the following books.   5. Her son read the following books.

d. 1. That is a much-worn hat.   2. This is a much-worn hat.   3. It is a much-worn hat.

e. 1. The German is reading an English book.   2. The German girl is reading an English book.   3. A German is reading an English book.   4. These Germans are reading an English book.

f. 1. The little girl was sitting in the living room and writing her lesson.   2. The little girl was sitting in the dining room and writing her lesson.   3. The little girl was sitting in the dining room and eating lunch.   4. The little girl was sitting in the kitchen and eating lunch.   5. The little girl was sitting in the bedroom and reading a book.

g. 1. One traveler was standing and the other travelers were sitting.   2. One traveler was sitting and the other travelers were standing.   3. One traveler was writing and the other travelers were reading.   4. One traveler was reading and the other travelers were writing.

h. 1. The new is not always better than the old.   2. The new is not always more pleasant than the old.   3. The new is not always more expensive than the old.   4. The old is not always cheaper than the new.   5. The old is often better than the new.

i. 1. The aunt gave the child something nice.   2. The mother gave the girl something nice.   3. The father gave his son something nice.

4. The doctor gave his brother something nice. 5. The child gave his mother something nice. 6. My sister gave her daughter something nice.

C. GRAMMAR

1. **Was?** (what?) is rarely used as the object of a preposition governing the dative or the accusative case. It is usually replaced by **wo-** plus the preposition, if the preposition begins with a consonant. If the preposition begins with a vowel, it is attached to **wor-**.
   a. **Womit schreibt die Studentin?**
   With what is the student (*f.*) writing?
   b. **Worüber sprechen die Mädchen?**
   What are the girls talking about?
2. The present participle of most verbs can be obtained by adding **-d** to the infinitive. The present participle is most often used as an adjective and is inflected with weak or strong endings like other descriptive adjectives. (See Units 7 and 8.)
   Ich habe die folgenden Bücher gelesen.
   I have read the following books.
3. Past participles are also used as descriptive adjectives, with weak or strong endings.
   Das ist ein viel getragener Hut.
   That is a much-worn hat.
4. A descriptive adjective may be used as a noun, and is then capitalized like a noun, but inflected with weak or strong endings like an adjective.
   a. **Der Deutsche liest ein englisches Buch.**
   The German is reading an English book.
   b. **Die Kleine saß im Wohnzimmer und schrieb ihre Aufgabe.**
   The little girl was sitting in the living room and writing her lesson.
   c. **E i n Reisender stand und die anderen Reisenden saßen.**
   One traveler was standing and the other travelers were sitting.
   Masculine forms are used for male beings and feminine forms for female beings. Frequently English requires an extra word, such as "one," "man," "boy," "woman," or "girl," to translate a German adjective-noun. (See sentence *b*, above.)

Note: Descriptive adjectives referring to nationality are written with a small initial.

ein englisches Buch   an English book

5. The neuter form of a descriptive adjective may be used as a noun (capitalized!) to denote an abstraction.

Das Neue ist nicht immer besser als das Alte.
The new is not always better than the old.

6. When **alles** (everything), **etwas** (something) or **nichts** (nothing) is used with a descriptive adjective, the adjective is considered a noun, with neuter singular ending.

Die Tante hat dem Kind etwas Schönes gegeben.
The aunt gave the child something nice.

When **etwas** or **nichts** precedes, the noun-adjective has strong endings; when **alles** precedes, the noun-adjective has weak endings.

alles Fremde   everything strange, foreign

D. EXERCISES

WRITE THE FOLLOWING SENTENCES IN GERMAN AND BE ABLE TO EXPRESS THEM ORALLY IN CLASS.

1. I had met my friend on the street.
2. This is an often-read book.
3. The old do not like to travel by airplane.
4. What are you talking about?
5. Their aunt is departing in the coming month.
6. She reads everything interesting.
7. Do the rich help the poor?
8. On what are the books lying?
9. The teacher (*f.*) read the written lessons.
10. The big one (*m.*) was younger than the small one (*m.*).
11. One traveler was going by plane and the other by steamer.
12. On the following evening we went to the movies.
13. His daughter buys nothing cheap.
14. The American is traveling by car.
15. They had arrived by streetcar.
16. Spoken German is easy.
17. We had followed the Englishmen.

18. I'll meet the stranger in town.
19. Most Germans travel by train.
20. She sees the sleeping children.
21. Did the girl follow her brother?
22. The good is often cheaper than the bad.
23. Please bring me something good.
24. For what are they waiting?

E. READING AND SPEAKING

I. READ THE FOLLOWING ALOUD UNTIL YOU ARE THOROUGHLY FAMILIAR WITH IT.

Die Reisenden

Am Abend rief Hans Käthe an. „Käthe, hier Hans. Heute bin ich im Reisebüro gewesen und habe meine Karten für die Reise bestellt (ordered)."

„Womit fährst du?" 5

„Ich fahre mit dem Dampfer. Es kostet weniger Geld."

„Fahren mehr Reisende mit dem Dampfer oder mit dem Flugzeug?"

„Herr Schmidt sagt, immer mehr Leute fahren mit dem Flugzeug, aber die meisten Reisenden fahren noch mit dem Dampfer."

„Ich würde gerne mit dem Dampfer fahren, denn ich liebe (like) 10 das Meer (sea)."

„Ich auch. Eine Woche auf hoher See[1] wird schön sein."

„Kaufst du ein Auto, wenn du in Europa ankommst?"

„Nein. Wir werden mit dem Zug oder mit dem Autobus fahren. Es kostet zuviel, mit einem Auto zu reisen." 15

„Ich glaube, ich würde ein Auto kaufen. Ich fahre nicht gerne mit dem Zug oder mit dem Autobus."

„Ich sehe, es ist schon spät und ich habe noch viel zu tun. Das ist also alles für heute. Ich rufe dich wieder an, wenn ich dir etwas Neues berichten (report) kann. Auf Wiederhören." 20

„Auf Wiederhören."

[1] auf hoher See   on the high seas.

II. ANSWER THE FOLLOWING QUESTIONS IN GERMAN.

1. Wen ruft Hans an?
2. Womit fährt er nach Europa?
3. Fahren die meisten Leute mit dem Flugzeug?
4. Wird Hans ein Auto kaufen?
5. Womit wird er in Europa fahren?
6. Wann wird er Käthe wieder anrufen?

☞ UNIT 19

A. UNITS OF SPEECH AND VOCABULARY

I. STUDY AND READ ALOUD.

Sie bittet um die Rechnung.	She is asking for the bill.
Er stellt mir eine Frage.	He is asking me a question.
Wir steigen in den Wagen ein.	We are getting in the car.
Es ist Viertel vor eins.	It is a quarter of one.
Es ist Viertel nach sechs.	It is a quarter after six.
Ich gehe auch dahin.	I am also going there.
eine Weile	a (little) while

Amerika, -s	America	ein Verwandter	a relative
der Enkel, -s, -	the grandson, grandchild	die Frage, -, -n	the question
		das Paket, -s, -e	the package
die Geschwister *pl.*	the brothers and sisters	die Rechnung, -, -en	the bill
die Großmutter, -, ⸚	the grandmother	das Schiff, -s, -e	the ship
		die Speisekarte, -, -n	the menu
der Großvater, -s, ⸚	the grandfather	das Viertel, -s, -	the quarter
der Neffe, -n, -n	the nephew	die Weile, -	the while
die Nichte, -, -n	the niece	die Zigarette, -, -n	the cigarette
der Verwandte, -n, -n	the relative		

143

dahin *adv.*	(to) there, thither	**betrachten**	to consider, to look at
hinten *adv.*	behind, in back	**lächeln**	to smile
		plaudern	to chat
vorne *Adv.*	forward, up front	**rauchen**	to smoke
		stellen	to put
alle *pl.*	all		

bitten (um + acc.)	bat	gebeten		to ask (for), request
ein-steigen (in + acc.)	stieg . . . ein	ist eingestiegen		to get in, on
verlassen	verließ	verlassen	verläßt	to leave (*behind*)

II. DRILL. EXPRESS ORALLY IN GERMAN. REPEAT UNTIL IT IS NO LONGER NECESSARY TO REFER TO SECTION I.

a. 1. She is asking for the bill. 2. She is asking for the package. 3. She asked for the package. 4. She asked for the menu. 5. She had asked for the menu. 6. She had asked for the bill.

b. 1. He is asking me a question. 2. My relative is asking me a question. 3. My relative is asking me questions. 5. My relatives are asking me questions. 4. All my relatives are asking me questions. 6. All our relatives are asking me questions.

c. 1. We are getting in the car. 2. We are getting on the train. 3. We got on the train. 4. They got on the streetcar. 5. Did you get on the streetcar? 6. Did you get on the bus?

d. 1. It is a quarter of one. 2. It is a quarter of five. 3. It is a quarter of eight. 4. It is a quarter of two. 5. It is a quarter of eleven. 6. It is a quarter of seven.

e. 1. It is a quarter after six. 2. It is a quarter after four. 3. It is a quarter after nine. 4. It is a quarter after twelve. 5. It is a quarter after ten. 6. It is a quarter after three.

f. 1. I am also going there. 2. His grandson is also going there. 3. His nephew is also going there. 4. His niece is also going there. 5. His grandmother is also going there.

g. 1. . . . in back. 2. My grandmother is sitting in back. 3. My niece is sitting in back. 4. My nephew is sitting in back. 5. My grandson is sitting in back.

h. 1. . . . up front. 2. Your grandson is standing up front. 3. Your

nephew is standing up front. 4. Your niece is standing up front.
5. Your grandmother is standing up front.

i. 1. They are looking at . . . 2. They are looking at the package.
3. They are looking at the bill. 4. They are looking at the ship.
5. All are looking at the menu.

j. 1. They are smiling. 2. All are smiling. 3. The relatives are smiling. 4. The grandchild is smiling. 5. The nephew is smiling.
6. The niece is smiling.

k. 1. You are chatting. 2. All are chatting. 3. Your brothers and sisters are chatting. 4. The brothers and sisters are chatting.

l. 1. He is smoking. 2. My grandfather is smoking. 3. My grandfather is smoking a cigarette. 4. My grandfather smokes cigarettes.
5. Her grandfather smokes cigarettes. 6. Our grandfathers smoked a little while. 7. Your grandfathers smoked a little while. 8. They smoked a little while.

m. 1. They are leaving America. 2. We are leaving America. 3. He is leaving America. 4. She is leaving the ship. 5. She left the ship.
6. He left the ship. 7. I have left the ship. 8. You have left the ship.

B. MODEL SENTENCES

I. STUDY UNTIL EACH SENTENCE CAN BE GIVEN CORRECTLY FROM THE
ENGLISH.

146. Kennen Sie den Mann, der im Wohnzimmer sitzt?
147. Hier ist das Buch, das Sie wollen.
148. Ich sehe das Kind, dem ich das Heft gegeben habe.
149. Die Frau, der er hilft, ist sehr alt.
150. Die Mädchen, die hier waren, sind jetzt fortgegangen.
151. Die Armen, denen sie das Geld gegeben hat, haben ihr gedankt.
152. Der Junge, dessen Schwester in meiner Klasse ist, heißt Richard.
153. Wir besuchten die Studentin, deren Vater wir kannten.
154. Viele Leute, deren Kinder in der Stadt wohnen, wohnen auf dem
Lande.
155. Der Bleistift, womit er schreibt, ist gelb.

146. Do you know the man who is sitting in the living room?

147. Here is the book which you want.
148. I see the child to whom I gave the notebook.
149. The woman that he is helping is very old.
150. The girls who were here have now gone away.
151. The poor people to whom she gave the money thanked her.
152. The boy whose sister is in my class is called Richard.
153. We visited the student (*f.*) whose father we knew.
154. Many people whose children live in town live in the country.
155. The pencil (which) he is writing with is yellow.

II. DRILL. EXPRESS ORALLY IN GERMAN.

a. 1. Do you know the man who is sitting in the living room?   2. Do you know the boy who is sitting in the living room?   3. Do you know the student who is sitting in the dining room?   4. Do you know the teacher who is sitting in the dining room?

b. 1. Here is the book which you want.   2. Here is the notebook which you want.   3. Here is the money which you want.   4. Here is the house which we want.

c. 1. I see the child to whom I gave the notebook.   2. I see the girl to whom I gave the notebook.   3. He sees the girl to whom he gave the notebook.   4. She sees the child to whom she gave the notebook.

d. 1. The woman that he is helping is very old.   2. The teacher (*f.*) that he is helping is very old.   3. The grandmother that he is helping is very old.   4. The aunt that he is helping is very old.

e. 1. The girls who were here have now gone away.   2. The boys who were here have now gone away.   3. The children who were here have now gone away.   4. The grandchildren who were here have now gone away.   5. The relatives who were here have now gone away.

f. 1. The poor people to whom she gave the money thanked her.   2. The relatives to whom she gave the money thanked her.   3. The relatives to whom he gave the money thanked him.   4. The poor people to whom he gave the money thanked him.

g. 1. The boy whose sister is in my class is called Richard.   2. The boy whose cousin (*f.*) is in my class is called Richard.   3. The student whose cousin (*f.*) is in my class is called Richard.   4. The man whose niece is in my class is called Richard.

h. 1. We visited the student (*f.*) whose father we knew.   2. We visited the student (*f.*) whose cousin (*f.*) we knew.   3. He visited the woman whose cousin (*f.*) he knew.   4. He visited the woman whose mother he knew.

i. 1. Many people whose children live in town live in the country.
2. Many people whose children live in the country live in town.
3. Many parents whose children live in the country live in town.
4. Many parents whose children live in town live in the country.

j. 1. The pencil (which) he is writing with is yellow.   2. The pencil (which) I am writing with is black.   3. The pencil (which) she is writing with is green.   4. The pencil (which) you are writing with is white.

C. GRAMMAR

1. The relative pronoun **der, die, das** (who, which, that) has the following forms.

	MASCULINE	NEUTER	FEMININE	PLURAL
NOM.	**der**	**das**	**die**	**die**
GEN.	**dessen**	**dessen**	**deren**	**deren**
DAT.	**dem**	**dem**	**der**	**denen**
ACC.	**den**	**das**	**die**	**die**

Note: The forms of the relative pronoun are identical with those of the definite article, except for the four genitive forms and the dative plural.

2. The relative pronoun has the same gender and number as the antecedent, the noun in the main clause for which it stands. The case of the relative pronoun, however, depends on its function in the relative clause (subject, object, possessive).

a. **Kennen Sie den Mann, der im Wohnzimmer sitzt?**
Do you know the man (who is) sitting in the living room?

b. **Hier ist das Buch, das Sie wollen.**
Here is the book (which) you want.

c. **Ich sehe das Kind, dem ich das Heft gegeben habe.**
   I see the child (to) whom I gave the notebook.
d. **Die Frau, der er hilft, ist sehr alt.**
   The woman (that) he is helping is very old.
e. **Die Mädchen, die hier waren, sind jetzt fortgegangen.**
   The girls who were here have now gone away.
f. **Die Armen, denen sie das Geld gegeben hat, haben ihr gedankt.**
   The poor people (whom) she gave the money to thanked her.

Note: The relative pronoun *cannot* be omitted in German. You will observe that in some of the English translations of the model sentences the relative pronoun may be used or omitted with no difference in meaning. In the German sentences, however, the relative pronoun *must* be expressed.

3. The relative pronoun **welcher, welche, welches** has the following forms.

	MASCULINE	NEUTER	FEMININE	PLURAL
NOM.	welcher	welches	welche	welche
DAT.	welchem	welchem	welcher	welchen
ACC.	welchen	welches	welche	welche

4. **Welcher, welche, welches** may be used instead of **der, die, das** in any case but the genitive. The sentences in paragraph 2 above may be rewritten as follows with no change in meaning.
   a. **Kennen Sie den Mann, welcher im Wohnzimmer sitzt?**
   b. **Hier ist das Buch, welches Sie wollen.**
   c. **Ich sehe das Kind, welchem ich das Heft gegeben habe.**
   d. **Die Frau, welcher er hilft, ist sehr alt.**
   e. **Die Mädchen, welche hier waren, sind fortgegangen.**
   f. **Die Armen, welchen sie das Geld gegeben hat, haben ihr gedankt.**

Note: There is no distinction in German corresponding to that between "who" and "which" in English. Both **der** and **welcher** may refer to either persons or things. However, **der** is preferred over **welcher,** especially in informal usage.

5. In the genitive, only **dessen** and **deren** (whose, of which) may be used.
   a. **Der Junge, dessen Schwester in meiner Klasse ist, heißt Richard.**
      The boy whose sister is in my class is called Richard.
   b. **Wir besuchten die Studentin, deren Vater wir kannten.**
      We visited the student (*f.*) whose father we knew.

    c. **Viele Leute, deren Kinder in der Stadt wohnen, wohnen auf dem Lande.**

    Many people whose children live in town live in the country.

6. A **wo-** (or **wor-**) compound *may* be used to replace a preposition and a relative pronoun in the dative or accusative case, when the pronoun represents an inanimate object.

    Der Bleistift, womit er schreibt, ist gelb.

    The pencil (which) he is writing with is yellow.

The use of **wo-** (or **wor-**) compounds in a relative clause is not compulsory. The above sentence may be written as follows.

    a. **Der Bleistift, mit dem er schreibt, ist gelb.**

    b. **Der Bleistift, mit welchem er schreibt, ist gelb.**

7. Relative clauses are subordinate clauses; therefore, the finite verb is last in the clause.

    Note: Relative clauses are *always* set off by commas.

D. EXERCISES

WRITE THE FOLLOWING SENTENCES IN GERMAN AND BE ABLE TO EXPRESS THEM ORALLY IN CLASS.

1. All the relatives that were there asked him questions.
2. I was looking at the package my grandfather had given me.
3. It was cold in the room in which her niece was sitting.
4. This morning I saw the woman whose daughter was here yesterday.
5. The man who is smoking a cigarette is his nephew.
6. He is getting into his car, which his uncle bought for him a week ago.
7. The girl friend to whom he wrote a letter called him up.
8. My sister is playing with the little girl whose father taught us English.
9. The lesson the student (*f.*) was learning was long.
10. They like best to go to the movies.
11. My cousin probably smoked all the cigarettes.
12. I'm taking the bottle of milk that is standing on the table.
13. He is giving her the books she asked for.
14. We like to eat in a restaurant which is not too expensive.
15. Her brothers and sisters were laughing while we were singing.

16. The table he had laid the notebook on was black.
17. The plane in which he is traveling will arrive this evening.
18. His grandmother, at whose house he lives, knows German.
19. The relatives for whom we were waiting had already gone.
20. Yesterday I chatted with the doctor whose wife you know.
21. Your mother is probably chatting with the grandchildren.
22. What is your girl friend doing with the flowers you sent her?
23. Do you see the students whom you helped yesterday?
24. The children whose parents were chatting in the dining room were playing in the living room.

E. READING AND SPEAKING

I. READ THE FOLLOWING ALOUD UNTIL YOU ARE THOROUGHLY FAMILIAR WITH IT.

In New York

Am siebten Juni fuhr Hans mit seinen Eltern und seinen Geschwistern nach New York. Das Schiff, womit er fahren sollte, fuhr erst am achten ab, aber sie wollten den Großvater und die Großmutter besuchen, die in New York wohnten. Da sie vor Mittag ankommen wollten, fuhren sie sehr früh fort. Hans saß vorne mit den Eltern, während die anderen Kinder hinten saßen. Käthe konnte nicht mitkommen, denn sie mußte bei ihrer Mutter bleiben, aber sie hatte vor (intended), am achten nach New York zu fahren, bevor Hans Amerika verließ.

Um Viertel vor zwölf Uhr kamen sie in New York an. Sie gingen in ein Restaurant, in welchem Herr und Frau Braun oft gegessen hatten. Nachdem er eine Weile die Speisekarte betrachtet hatte, bestellte (ordered) Herr Braun. Während sie Kaffee tranken, rauchte Herr Braun eine Zigarette. Sie saßen noch eine Weile und plauderten. Dann bat Herr Braun um die Rechnung.

Als die Brauns bei dem Großvater ankamen, fanden sie viele Verwandte da. Hans' Onkel und Tanten, seine Vettern und seine Kusinen stellten ihm viele Fragen. Es war sehr spät in der Nacht, als die Verwandten fortgingen. Erst Viertel nach zwei konnten die Brauns zu Bett gehen.

II. ANSWER THE FOLLOWING QUESTIONS IN GERMAN.

1. **Wen wollten die Brauns in New York besuchen?**
2. **Warum konnte Käthe nicht mitkommen?**
3. **Wo haben Hans' Geschwister gesessen?**
4. **Um wieviel Uhr sind sie in New York angekommen?**
5. **In welchem Restaurant haben sie zu Mittag gegessen?**
6. **Warum konnten sie erst um Viertel nach zwei zu Bett gehen?**

☛ UNIT 20

A. UNITS OF SPEECH AND VOCABULARY

I. STUDY AND READ ALOUD.

Es ist halb neun (Uhr).	It's half past eight (o'clock).
Es ist zehn (Minuten) vor eins.	It's ten minutes of one.
Es ist fünf (Minuten) nach acht.	It's five minutes after eight.
Sie kommen punkt zwölf (Uhr).	They are coming at twelve o'clock sharp.
Sie reicht ihm die Hand.	She is shaking hands with him.
Wir wünschen Ihnen glückliche Reise.	We wish you a pleasant trip.
Er nimmt von seinen Freunden Abschied.	He is taking leave of his friends.
beim Abschied	at parting, while taking leave
acht Uhr morgens	eight A.M., eight o'clock in the morning
morgens	in the morning(s), A.M.
nachmittags	in the afternoon(s), P.M.
abends	in the evening(s), P.M.
nachts	at night
montags	on Monday(s)

der Abschied, -s, -e	the farewell, departure	**ein Beamter**	an official
der Beamte, -n, -n	the official	**der Bekannte, -n, -n**	the acquaintance

152

ein Bekannter	an acquaint-	**einige**	some *pl.*
	ance	**mehrere**	several
das Beste	the best (thing)	**glücklich**	happy
das Gepäck, -s	the baggage	**schlimm**	bad
die Minute, -, -n	the minute	**von** + *dat.*	from, of
die Sache, -, -n	the thing	**küssen**	to kiss
das Schlimmste	the worst	**reichen**	to extend,
	(thing)		to hand
beide	both	**weinen**	to weep
einander	one another	**wünschen**	to wish

halten	**hielt**	**gehalten**	**hält**	to hold
verlieren	**verlor**	**verloren**		to lose

II. DRILL. EXPRESS ORALLY IN GERMAN. REPEAT UNTIL IT IS NO LONGER
NECESSARY TO REFER TO SECTION I.

a. 1. It's half past eight.   2. It's half past two.   3. It's half past six.
4. It's ten minutes of one.   5. It's eighteen minutes of four.
6. It's twenty minutes of eleven.   7. It's five minutes after eight.
8. It's twenty-two minutes after eight.   9. It's twenty-two minutes
after three.   10. It's thirteen minutes after seven.

b. 1. They are coming at twelve o'clock sharp.   2. The officials are
coming at twelve o'clock sharp.   3. The official is coming at twelve
o'clock sharp.   4. An official is coming at twelve o'clock sharp.
5. Several men are coming at twelve o'clock sharp.

c. 1. She is shaking hands with him.   2. He is shaking hands with her.
3. The official is shaking hands with her.   4. An official is shaking
hands with her.   5. They are shaking hands with one another.
6. We are shaking hands with one another.

d. 1. We wish you a pleasant trip.   2. We wish one another a pleasant
trip.   3. They are wishing one another a pleasant trip.   4. The
friends are wishing one another a pleasant trip.

e. 1. He is taking leave of his friends.   2. The official is taking leave
of his friends.   3. An acquaintance is taking leave of several friends.
4. He is taking leave of several acquaintances.   5. She is taking
leave of several acquaintances.   6. She is taking leave of some
acquaintances.

f. 1. . . . at parting. 2. Some women weep at parting. 3. Both women weep at parting. 4. Many women weep at parting. 5. Several women are kissing their friends (*f.*) while taking leave. 6. Both women are kissing their relatives while taking leave. 7. Some women kiss their relatives at parting.

g. 1. eight A.M. 2. ten A.M. 3. two P.M. 4. five P.M. 5. nine P.M. 6. eleven P.M.

h. 1. In the morning(s) . . . 2. In the morning(s) I work. 3. In the morning(s) he sleeps. 4. In the afternoon(s) he plays. 5. In the afternoon(s) she studies. 6. In the evening(s) we study. 7. In the evening(s) they work. 8. At night they sleep. 9. At night we sleep.

i. 1. On Monday(s) . . . 2. On Monday(s) he goes to the movies. 3. On Monday(s) we go downtown. 4. On Monday(s) she drives to school. 5. On Monday(s) we drive to the country.

j. 1. . . . the baggage. 2. He is holding the baggage. 3. The official is holding the baggage. 4. They are holding the baggage. 5. Whose baggage are you holding?

k. 1. . . . the best thing. 2. That is the best thing. 3. This is the best thing. 4. This is the worst thing. 5. It's the worst thing. 6. It's bad. 7. That is bad.

l. 1. He is losing . . . 2. He is losing his things. 3. She is losing her things. 4. They lost their things. 5. We lost our things.

B. MODEL SENTENCES

I. STUDY UNTIL EACH SENTENCE CAN BE GIVEN CORRECTLY FROM THE ENGLISH.

156. **Er kommt um halb sieben.**
157. **Die Schule beginnt punkt neun (Uhr).**
158. **Er wollte alles, was sie hatten.**
159. **Das ist das Schlimmste, was wir tun können.**
160. **Es ging ihr besser, was ihn sehr glücklich machte.**
161. **Wir haben viele gute Freunde.**
162. **Kennen Sie ihren Bruder? Der ist mein bester Freund.**
163. **Die Frau ist mit ihrer Schwester und deren Sohn gekommen.**
164. **Sie weiß, daß er nicht in die Stadt hat gehen können.**

156. He is coming at half past six.
157. School begins at nine o'clock sharp.
158. He wanted everything (that) they had.
159. That's the worst thing we can do.
160. She was feeling better, (a fact) which made him very happy.
161. We have many good friends.
162. Do you know her brother? *He* is my best friend.
163. The woman came with her sister and the latter's son.
164. She knows that he wasn't able to go to town.

II. DRILL. EXPRESS ORALLY IN GERMAN.

a. 1. He is coming at half past six.   2. He is going at half past six.
   3. She eats at half past six.   4. They eat at half past six.
b. 1. School begins at nine o'clock sharp.   2. School begins at eight
   o'clock sharp.   3. School begins at twelve o'clock sharp.   4. School
   begins at one o'clock sharp.
c. 1. He wanted everything (that) they had.   2. He had everything
   they wanted.   3. They bought everything they wanted.   4. We
   bought everything we saw.   5. He learned everything he read.
d. 1. That's the worst thing we can do.   2. It's the worst thing you
   can do.   3. It's the best thing I can do.   4. This is the best thing
   we can do.
e. 1. She was feeling better, which made him very happy.   2. She was
   feeling better, which made her very happy.   3. We were feeling
   better, which made us very happy.   4. They were feeling better,
   which made them very happy.   5. I was feeling better, which made
   me very happy.
f. 1. We have many good friends.   2. They have many good friends.
   3. She has many good friends.   4. He has many good friends.
g. 1. Do you know her brother? *He* is my best friend.   2. Do you
   know their cousin? *He* is my best friend.   3. Do you know his
   uncle? *He* is my best friend.   4. Do you know our physician? *He* is
   my best friend.
h. 1. The woman came with her sister and the latter's son.   2. The
   woman came with her niece and the latter's son.   3. The woman
   came with her daughter and the latter's son.   4. The woman came
   with her friend (*f.*) and the latter's brother.   5. The woman came
   with her cousin (*f.*) and the latter's friend.

i.   1. She knows that he wasn't able to go to town. 2. She knows
that he wasn't able to go to school. 3. He knows that she wasn't
able to go to church. 4. He knows that she wasn't able to go to
the movies. 5. I know that they weren't able to go to the restaurant. 6. I know that they weren't able to go into the building.

C. GRAMMAR

1. The genitive of nouns denoting parts of the day or days of the week
   indicates habitual or repeated occurrence. Such words are used
   adverbially and therefore are written with a small initial letter.

morgens	in the morning(s)
nachmittags	in the afternoon(s)
abends	in the evening(s)
nachts	at night
montags	on Monday(s)

   Morgens, nachmittags, and **abends** are frequently added to clock
   time for clarity.

   acht Uhr morgens   eight A.M., eight o'clock in the morning

2. In expressing the half hour, German looks forward to the next hour.
   "Half past six" is therefore expressed as **halb sieben.** Most time
   expressions are preceded by **um** (at).

um fünf Uhr	at five o'clock
um Viertel vor elf	at a quarter of eleven
um fünf Minuten nach acht	at five minutes after eight

   However, when **punkt** (exactly) is used, **um** is omitted.

   Die Schule beginnt punkt neun Uhr.
   School begins at nine o'clock sharp.

3. **Was** is used as the relative pronoun

   a. when the antecedent is a neuter pronoun such as **alles** (every-
      thing), **etwas** (something), **nichts** (nothing).

      Er wollte alles, was sie hatten.
      He wanted everything (that) they had.

   b. when the antecedent is a neuter superlative adjective used as
      a noun.

      Das ist das Schlimmste, was wir tun können.
      That's the worst thing we can do.

c. when the antecedent is a whole clause.

Es ging ihr besser, was ihn sehr glücklich machte.

She was feeling better, (a fact) which made him very happy.

4. Indefinite numerical adjectives, such as **einige** (some, a few), **manche** (some), **mehrere** (several), **viele** (many), **wenige** (few), take strong endings, as do descriptive adjectives following them.

  a. **Wir haben viele gute Freunde.**

  We have many good friends.

  Alle (all), **beide** (both), and **keine** (no), being definite numbers, are treated like **der**-words and are followed by descriptive adjectives with weak endings.

  b. **Wir haben keine guten Freunde.**

  We have no good friends.

5. The demonstrative pronoun **der, die, das** (that one, he, she, that) has the same inflection as the relative pronoun **der, die, das**. It is frequently used as an emphatic substitute for **er, sie, es** (he, she, it).

  a. **Kennen Sie ihren Bruder? Der ist mein bester Freund.**

  Do you know her brother? *He* is my best friend.

  The genitive demonstrative forms **dessen** and **deren** are used instead of the possessives **sein** (his) and **ihr** (her, their) to avoid ambiguity, often in the sense of "the latter's."

  b. **Die Frau ist mit ihrer Schwester und deren Sohn gekommen.**

  The woman came with her sister and the latter's son.

  The sentence

  Die Frau ist mit ihrer Schwester und ihrem Sohn gekommen.

  might mean

  The woman came with her sister and her (own) son.

6. A "double infinitive" stands last in any clause, main or subordinate. In subordinate clauses, the finite verb immediately precedes the double infinitive.

  Sie weiß, daß er nicht in die Stadt hat gehen können.

  She knows that he wasn't able to go to town.

D. EXERCISES

WRITE THE FOLLOWING SENTENCES IN GERMAN AND BE ABLE TO EXPRESS THEM ORALLY IN CLASS.

1. We eat at five P.M.

2. Several old men were sitting there.
3. This is the best thing I have done.
4. They stayed at home on Monday, because they had had to work on Sunday.
5. Mr. Braun met his friend and the latter's wife on the street.
6. The students went away at twenty minutes after four.
7. She found nothing that she liked.
8. Do you study your lessons in the evenings?
9. Both young women were waiting for their relatives.
10. He visited his parents every week, which pleased them very much.
11. It was five minutes of six when he got up.
12. The officials come into the building at 9 A.M.
13. Not all new houses are beautiful.
14. His sisters wept because the traveler had wanted to depart.
15. The parents were playing with their children and the latter's friends.
16. The official lost something he had in his pocket.
17. Would you bring me a cup of coffee at half past seven?
18. Some happy people were shaking hands with one another.
19. Everything we have is old.
20. Did you see his cousin? *She* is not very pretty.
21. Her friend (*f.*) has few good books.
22. It is one o'clock sharp.
23. Whom do you visit on Thursdays?
24. Do you know why the student (*f.*) has not wanted to go to school?

E. READING AND SPEAKING

I.   READ THE FOLLOWING ALOUD UNTIL YOU ARE THOROUGHLY FAMILIAR WITH IT.

Glückliche Reise

Am achten fuhren alle zum Schiff, wo sie um halb zehn ankamen. Hans gab einem Beamten sein Gepäck, und sie gingen an Bord. Da fanden sie viele Leute. Viele Verwandte kamen, um von den Reisenden
5 **Abschied zu nehmen. Sie sahen Freunde, die sie lange** (for a long time) **nicht gesehen hatten. Alle lachten und waren guter Laune** (in a good mood).

Frau Braun sagte: „Ich möchte deine Kabine sehen." Also gingen sie in die Kabine.

„Alles ist sehr schön", sagte Herr Braun. „Schläft Walter auch 10 hier?"

„Ja, wir haben dieselbe (the same) Kabine", antwortete der Sohn.

„Hier ist etwas für euch beide", sagte Frau Braun und gab ihrem Sohn ein Paket. „Da habt ihr etwas zu essen auf der Reise."

Um halb zwölf mußten alle Freunde und Verwandten das Schiff 15 verlassen. Mehrere weinten beim Abschied. Sie warteten bis zwölf Uhr. Dann fuhr der große Dampfer ab. Alle riefen „Glückliche Reise" und schwenkten die Taschentücher (waved their handkerchiefs).

II. ANSWER THE FOLLOWING QUESTIONS.

1. Wem hat Hans sein Gepäck gegeben?
2. Wer wollte die Kabine sehen?
3. Was hat Frau Braun ihrem Sohn gegeben?
4. Wann mußten die Freunde und die Verwandten das Schiff verlassen?
5. Was haben mehrere beim Abschied getan?
6. Wer hat „Glückliche Reise" gerufen?

☛ **UNIT 21**

A. UNITS OF SPEECH AND VOCABULARY

I. STUDY AND READ ALOUD.

Sie geht zur Mutter; sie geht zu ihr.	She's going to her mother('s house); she's going to her (house).
Er fährt zum Postamt.	He's driving to the post office.
Es ist ein Soldat im Zimmer.	There is a soldier in the room.
Es sind heute hundert Gäste im Hotel.	There are a hundred guests in the hotel today.
Es gibt jetzt viel Regen.	There is a lot of rain now.
Die Uhr hat eben eins geschlagen.	The clock just struck one.
Ich trete in das Hotel ein.	I am entering the hotel.
Erstens bin ich müde, . . .	In the first place I am tired, . . .
Gott sei Dank!	Thank God!
Man sagt . . .	One says, they say, people say . . .
Es ist . . .	There is . . .
Es sind . . .	There are . . .
Es gibt . . .	There is, there are . . .

der Dank, -s	the thanks	**das Hotel, -s, -s**	the hotel
der Gast, -es, ⸚e	the guest	**die Mannschaft,**	
der Gott, -es, ⸚er	the God	**-, -en**	the team
das Heer, -es, -e	the army	**der Offizier, -s, -e**	the officer

das Postamt,		**gesund**	healthy, in good
-s, ⸚er	the post office		health, well
der Preis, -es, -e	the prize	**krank**	sick
der Regen, -s	the rain	**müde**	tired
der Schnee, -s	the snow	**eben**	just
der Soldat,		**erstens**	in the first place
-en, -en	the soldier	**zweitens**	in the second
das Spiel, -s, -e	game		place
die Uhr, -, -en	the clock, watch	**drittens**	in the third
man	one, they,		place
	people	**zu** + *dat.*	to
hundert	a hundred, (one)	**leben**	to live, to be
	hundred		alive
		verkaufen	to sell

ein-treten	**trat . . . ein**	**ist eingetreten**	**tritt . . . ein**	to enter
gewinnen	**gewann**	**gewonnen**		to win
schlagen	**schlug**	**geschlagen**	**schlägt**	to strike, to beat

II. DRILL. EXPRESS ORALLY IN GERMAN. REPEAT UNTIL IT IS NO LONGER NECESSARY TO REFER TO SECTION I.

a. 1. She's going to her mother. 2. She's going to her. 3. The soldier is going to his mother. 4. He is going to her. 5. The officer is going to his mother's house. 6. He is going to her house. 7. Our guest is going to his mother's house. 8. Our guest is going to her house.

b. 1. He's driving to the post office. 2. The officer is driving to the post office. 3. The soldier is driving to the post office. 4. The guest is driving to the post office. 5. The guests are driving to the post office.

c. 1. There is a soldier in the room. 2. There is an officer in the room. 3. There is a guest in the room. 4. There is a boy in the room.

d. 1. There are a hundred guests in the hotel today. 2. There are a hundred travelers in the hotel today. 3. There are a hundred people in the hotel today. 4. There are one hundred people in the post office today. 5. There are one hundred people in the post office now.

e. 1. There is a lot of rain now. 2. There is a lot of rain today.

162   *Unit Twenty-One*

3. There is a lot of rain in April.   4. There is a lot of snow in January.   5. There is a lot of snow today.   6. There is a lot of snow now.

f.   1. The clock just struck one.   2. The clock just struck eleven. 3. The clock just struck four.   4. The clock just struck seven. 5. The clock is just striking six.   6. The clock is just striking nine.

g.   1. I am entering the hotel.   2. They are entering the hotel.   3. The soldiers are entering the house.   4. He is entering the house.   5. He is entering the building.   6. She is entering the building.   7. She is entering the store.

h.   1. In the first place I am tired . . .   2. In the first place I am tired, in the second place I am sick, and in the third place I have no money.   3. In the first place he is tired, in the second place he is sick, and in the third place he is poor.   4. In the first place she is tired, in the second place she is not healthy, and in the third place she is not here.   5. In the first place we are sick, in the second place our parents are not in good health, and in the third place we don't want to go.

i.   1. Thank God!   2. Thank God they're alive.   3. Thank God she's alive.   4. Thank God he's alive.

j.   1. They say . . .   2. They say that the team is winning the game. 3. They say that the team is winning the prize.   4. They say the team won the prize.   5. People say we have won the game.   6. People say he won the prize.   7. People say she has won the game.

k.   1. . . . are selling.   2. We are selling watches.   3. They are selling watches.   4. He is selling his watch.   5. She is selling her watch.

B. MODEL SENTENCES

I.   STUDY UNTIL EACH SENTENCE CAN BE GIVEN CORRECTLY FROM THE ENGLISH.

165.   **Gehen Sie zur Großmutter?—Ja, ich gehe zu ihr.**
166.   **Der Mann fährt zum Hotel.**
167.   **Es ist ein Offizier im Hause.**
168.   **Es sind viele Soldaten im Postamt.**
169.   **Es gibt einen Gott.**
170.   **Es gibt viele große Städte in Deutschland.**

171. Man sagt, sie lebt nicht mehr.
172. Man spricht Deutsch in Österreich.
173. Gott sei Dank, daß er wieder gesund wird.
174. Er lebe hoch!

165. Are you going to your grandmother?—Yes, I'm going to her.
166. The man is driving to the hotel.
167. There is an officer in the house.
168. There are many soldiers in the post office.
169. There is a God.
170. There are many large cities in Germany.
171. They say she is no longer alive.
172. They speak German in Austria.
173. Thank God that he is getting well again.
174. Long may he live!

II. DRILL. EXPRESS ORALLY IN GERMAN.

a. 1. Are you going to your grandmother?—Yes, I'm going to her.
2. Are you going to your aunt?—Yes, I'm going to her. 3. Are you going to your uncle?—Yes, I'm going to him. 4. Are you going to your grandfather?—Yes, I'm going to him.

b. 1. The man is driving to the hotel. 2. The officer is driving to the hotel. 3. The officer drove to the hotel. 4. The soldier drove to the hotel. 5. They drove to the hotel. 6. We drove to the hotel.

c. 1. There is an officer in the house. 2. There is a soldier in the house. 3. There is a boy in the room. 4. There is a student (*f.*) in the room. 5. There is a teacher (*f.*) in the room.

d. 1. There are many soldiers in the post office. 2. There are a hundred soldiers in the building. 3. There are a hundred children in school. 4. There are one hundred boys in school. 5. There are one hundred people in church.

e. 1. There is a God. 2. There is only one God. 3. There is no other God.

f. 1. There are many large cities in Germany. 2. There are many large cities in Europe. 3. There are many large cities in the United States. 4. There are some large cities in Switzerland.

g. 1. They say she is no longer alive. 2. They say the soldier is no longer alive. 3. They say the officer is no longer alive. 4. They say the teacher is no longer alive. 5. They say he is no longer alive.

h. 1. They speak German in Austria. 2. They speak German in Switzerland. 3. People speak German in Germany. 4. People speak English in the United States. 5. One speaks English in America.

i. 1. Thank God that he is getting well again. 2. Thank God that she is getting well again. 3. Thank God that they are getting well again. 4. Thank God that your parents are getting well again. 5. Thank God that your relatives are getting well again.

j. 1. Long may he live! 2. Long may she live! 3. Long may they live!

C. GRAMMAR

1. The ordinal adverbs **erstens** (in the first place), **zweitens** (in the second place), **drittens** (in the third place), and so on, are formed by adding **-ens** to the stem of the ordinal numbers **(der) erst e** (the first), **(der) zweit e** (the second), **(der) dritt e** (the third), and so on.

2. The preposition **zu** (to) is used after verbs of motion with nouns or pronouns referring to persons.

   Gehen Sie zur Großmutter?—Ja, ich gehe zu ihr.

   Are you going to your grandmother?—Yes, I'm going to her.

   This sentence may also mean

   Are you going to your grandmother's (house)?—Yes, I'm going to her house.

   Note that **zur** is the contraction for **zu + der.**

3. **Zu** may also be used after verbs of motion with other nouns.

   Der Mann fährt zum Hotel.

   The man is driving to the hotel.

   Note that **zum** is the abbreviation for **zu + dem.**

4. **Es ist** (there is) and **es sind** (there are) are used to indicate a temporary or a specific situation.

   a. **Es ist ein Offizier im Hause.**

      There is an officer in the house.

   b. **Es sind viele Soldaten im Postamt.**

      There are many soldiers in the post office.

Note that the noun following **es ist** or **es sind** is in the *nominative* case. **Es ist** is used before a singular noun, **es sind** before a plural noun.

5. **Es gibt** (there is, there are) is used for statements of a general or universal nature and for descriptions of weather conditions.
   a. **Es gibt einen Gott.**
      There is a God.
   b. **Es gibt viele große Städte in Deutschland.**
      There are many large cities in Germany.
   c. **Es gibt jetzt viel Regen.**
      There is a lot of rain now.

Note that the noun following **es gibt** is an *accusative direct object*; therefore, the verb (**gibt**) does not change, whether the following noun is singular or plural.

6. The pronoun **man** (one) is used as an indefinite subject referring to people in general. It is frequently translated by "they" or "people."
   a. **Man sagt, sie lebt nicht mehr.**
      They say she is no longer alive.
   b. **Man spricht Deutsch in Österreich.**
      They speak German in Austria.

The **man** construction is frequently equivalent to the passive construction in English. Sentence *b* may also mean "German is spoken in Austria."

7. The present subjunctive I of **sagen** (to say) follows.

ich sag e	wir sag en
[du sag est]	[ihr sag et]
er, sie, es sag e	sie sag en
	Sie sag en

The present subjunctive I of almost all other verbs is formed in the same way by adding the subjunctive endings to the *infinitive* stem. The present subjunctive I of **nehmen** (to take) is

ich nehm e	wir nehm en
[du nehm est]	[ihr nehm et]
er, sie, es nehm e	sie nehm en
	Sie nehm en

The infinitive, the third person singular present indicative, and the third person singular present subjunctive I of a few typical irregular verbs follow.

nehmen	to take	**er nimmt**	he takes	**er nehme**	(pres. subj. I)
lesen	to read	**er liest**	he reads	**er lese**	(pres. subj. I)
fallen	to fall	**er fällt**	he falls	**er falle**	(pres. subj. I)
laufen	to run	**er läuft**	he runs	**er laufe**	(pres. subj. I)
können	to be able	**er kann**	he can	**er könne**	(pres. subj. I)
müssen	to have to	**er muß**	he must	**er müsse**	(pres. subj. I)
wollen	to want	**er will**	he wants	**er wolle**	(pres. subj. I)

8. The only verb which is irregular in the present subjunctive I is **sein** (to be).

ich sei	**wir sei en**
[du sei st]	**[ihr sei et]**
er, sie, es sei	**sie sei en**
	Sie sei en

9. The present subjunctive I may be used for realizable wishes.
   a. **Gott sei Dank!**
      Thank God!
      Thanks be to God. (literally)
   b. **Er lebe hoch!**
      Long may he live!

Note that the present subjunctive I used in this way is frequently translated into English by means of "may" and "let."

D. EXERCISES

WRITE THE FOLLOWING SENTENCES IN GERMAN AND BE ABLE TO EXPRESS THEM ORALLY IN CLASS.

1. People say this hotel is very beautiful.
2. Was there much rain last summer?
3. Thank God that you are well again.
4. There are many people in town today.
5. Our friends have gone to their cousin's house.
6. In the first place the weather isn't nice, in the second place we are tired, and in the third place it isn't interesting.
7. His friends and relatives said: "Long may he live!"
8. There is only one chair in the living room.
9. Did you drive to church on Sunday?
10. There are three countries where German is spoken.

11. My parents came to our house three days ago.
12. Thank God that our friends are no longer sick.
13. They say the weather will be nice tomorrow.
14. Were there airplanes a hundred years ago?
15. There were many soldiers on the street.
16. German is spoken here.
17. Please bring this letter to the post office.
18. I rode to school by bus.
19. There was much snow last month.
20. Many books are sold in this store.
21. They'll come to my father's later.
22. People believe the soldiers will depart next week.
23. We must go to their house.

E. READING AND SPEAKING

I. READ THE FOLLOWING ALOUD UNTIL YOU ARE THOROUGHLY FAMILIAR WITH IT.

Ein Brief

den 13. Juni.

Liebe Mutter,

Seit sechs Tagen sind wir schon an Bord. Zuerst ist das Wetter sehr schön gewesen, und ich bin viel an Deck geblieben. Ich habe einen 5 großen Appetit gehabt und habe viel gegessen. Am dritten Tage aber ist der Wind sehr stark (strong) geworden. Dann hat es viel geregnet (rained). Der Sturm ist so schlimm gewesen, daß ich seekrank (seasick) geworden bin und habe zwei Tage im Bett liegen müssen. Ich habe nichts essen können und habe geglaubt, ich würde sterben (die), aber 10 dann ist es mir besser gegangen. Heute geht es mir sehr gut.

Jetzt ist das Wetter wieder schön und wir sitzen an Deck. Ich kann jetzt essen und habe wieder einen großen Appetit. Ich esse alles, was serviert wird.[1] Mache Dir keine Sorgen,[2] denn es geht mir jetzt gut.

Mit herzlichsten Grüßen an alle[3], 15
Dein Hans.

---

[1] alles, was serviert wird everything that is served. [2] Mache dir keine Sorgen Don't worry about me. [3] Mit herzlichsten Grüßen an alle Best wishes to everyone.

Hans gab Walter, der neben ihm saß, den Brief. Nachdem er ihn gelesen hatte, sagte Walter: „Auch ich werde einen Brief schreiben, denn ich habe noch nichts geschrieben. Kannst du mir einen Bleistift
20 und ein Stück Papier geben?"

Hans gab ihm, was er verlangte (asked for) **und nun** (now) **begann** Walter zu schreiben. Aber er gab es bald auf (up), denn er schrieb nicht gern Briefe.

II. ANSWER THE FOLLOWING QUESTIONS IN GERMAN.

1. **Wann hat Hans der Mutter geschrieben?**
2. **Wie war das Wetter am dritten Tage gewesen?**
3. **Warum war Hans seekrank geworden?**
4. **Hatte es viel geregnet?**
5. **Wann hat er seinen Appetit wieder zurückbekommen?**
6. **Wem hat er den Brief gegeben?**

☞ UNIT 22

A. UNITS OF SPEECH AND VOCABULARY

I. STUDY AND READ ALOUD.

Mir tut der Arm weh.	My arm hurts.
Ihm tun die Augen weh.	His eyes hurt.
Es regnet.	It's raining.
Die Sonne scheint.	The sun is shining.
Es scheint richtig zu sein.	It seems to be right.
Ich denke an ihn.	I'm thinking of him.
Er hat aufgehört zu lesen.	He has stopped reading.
acht Tage	a week
am Himmel	in the sky

der Arm, -s, -e	the arm	**die Antwort,**	
das Auge, -s, -n	the eye	**-, -en**	the answer
der Fuß, -es, ⸚e	the foot	**die Füllfeder,**	
der Kopf, -es, ⸚e	the head	**-, -n**	the fountain pen
das Ohr, -s, -en	the ear	**der Rat, -s**	the advice,
der Himmel, -s, -	the sky		counsel
der Mond, -es, -e	the moon	**der Teil, -s, -e**	the part
die Sonne, -, -n	the sun	**möglich**	possible
der Stern, -s, -e	the star	**richtig**	right, correct
der Sturm, -s, ⸚e	the storm	**stark**	strong
der Wind, -es, -e	the wind	**wichtig**	important

| brauchen | to need | suchen | to look for, to |
| regnen | to rain | | seek |

auf-hören	hörte ... auf	aufgehört	to stop, to cease
denken	dachte	gedacht	to think
genießen	genoß	genossen	to enjoy
scheinen	schien	geschienen	to shine; to seem
verbringen	verbrachte	verbracht	to spend (*time*)

II. DRILL. EXPRESS ORALLY IN GERMAN. REPEAT UNTIL IT IS NO LONGER NECESSARY TO REFER TO SECTION I.

a. 1. My arm hurts. 2. My eye hurts. 3. My foot hurts. 4. My head hurts. 5. My ear hurts. 6. Her ear hurts. 7. Her head hurts. 8. Her foot hurts. 9. Her eye hurts. 10. His arm hurts. 11. His head hurts. 12. Your head hurts.

b. 1. His eyes hurt. 2. His ears hurt. 3. His arms hurt. 4. His feet hurt. 5. Her feet hurt. 6. Her arms hurt. 7. Her ears hurt. 8. Her eyes hurt.

c. 1. It's raining. 2. It's raining now. 3. It's raining today. 4. It's raining this afternoon. 5. It's raining already.

d. 1. The sun is shining. 2. The sun is shining in the sky. 3. The moon is shining. 4. The moon is shining in the sky. 5. The stars are shining in the sky. 6. The moon and the stars are shining in the sky. 7. Is the moon shining in the sky? 8. Is the sun shining in the sky?

e. 1. It seems to be right. 2. It seems to be possible. 3. This seems to be important. 4. This seems to be right. 5. That doesn't seem to be right. 6. That doesn't seem to be possible. 7. The answer doesn't seem to be important. 8. The answer doesn't seem to be possible. 9. The answer seems to be important.

f. 1. I am thinking of him. 2. I am thinking of you. 3. He thought of you. 4. She thought of him. 5. We have thought of him. 6. We have thought of you.

g. 1. He has stopped reading. 2. He has stopped working. 3. They have stopped working. 4. They have stopped smoking. 5. It has stopped raining.

h. 1. ... a week. 2. He is spending a week in Cologne. 3. I am spending a week in Cologne. 4. She is spending a week in Berlin.

5. She spent a week in Hamburg.   6. They spent a week in Heidelberg.

i.   1. He needs . . .   2. He needs advice.   3. He needs the pen.   4. I need the pen.   5. I need advice.

j.   1. They are seeking . . .   2. They are seeking advice.   3. We are looking for advice.   4. He is looking for advice.   5. I am looking for advice.   6. I am looking for the pens.   7. They are looking for the pens.

k.   1. We are enjoying . . .   2. We are enjoying this part of the book. 3. They are enjoying this part of the story.   4. He is enjoying this part of the story.   5. She enjoyed this part of the book.   6. We enjoyed this part of the book.

B. MODEL SENTENCES

I.   STUDY UNTIL EACH SENTENCE CAN BE GIVEN CORRECTLY FROM THE ENGLISH.

175.   **Er sagte, er besuche seinen Freund.**
       Er sagte, er besuchte seinen Freund.

176.   **Sie sagten, er gehe nach Hause.**
       Sie sagten, er ginge nach Hause.

177.   **Er glaubte, sie seien reich.**
       Er glaubte, sie wären reich.

178.   **Sie schrieb, sie habe ihre Kusine gesehen.**
       Sie schrieb, sie hätte ihre Kusine gesehen.

179.   **Sie glaubten, daß ihr Vater nach Hause gegangen sei.**
       Sie glaubten, daß ihr Vater nach Hause gegangen wäre.

180.   **Ich sagte, daß meine Verwandten fortgegangen waren.**

181.   **Er wußte, daß sein Vetter in der Stadt war.**

182.   **Er sagt, es hat geregnet.**

183.   **Sie fragten, ob mein Bruder das Buch habe.**
       Sie fragten, ob mein Bruder das Buch hätte.

184.   **Der Lehrer sagte, daß der Student die Aufgabe lernen solle.**
       Der Lehrer sagte, daß der Student die Aufgabe lernen sollte.

175.   He said he was visiting his friend.

176. They said he was going home.
177. He believed they were rich.
178. She wrote she had seen her cousin (*f.*).
179. They believed that their father had gone home.
180. I said that my relatives had gone away.
181. He knew that his cousin was in town.
182. He says it rained.
183. They asked whether my brother had the book.
184. The teacher said that the student should study the lesson.

II. DRILL. EXPRESS ORALLY IN GERMAN.

a. 1. He said he was visiting his friend.   2. She said he was visiting his friend.   3. She said she was visiting her friend (*f.*).   4. He said she was visiting her friend (*f.*).

b. 1. They said he was going home.   2. They said the boy was going home.   3. They said the woman was going home.   4. They said she was going home.

c. 1. He believed they were rich.   2. He believed his friends were rich. 3. He believed his friends were poor.   4. He believed they were poor.

d. 1. She wrote she had seen her cousin (*f.*).   2. She wrote she had seen her aunt.   3. He wrote he had seen her aunt.   4. He wrote he had seen his aunt.   5. He wrote he had seen his mother.

e. 1. They believed that their father had gone home.   2. They believed that their uncle had gone home.   3. They believed that the doctor had gone home.   4. They believed that the teacher had gone home. 5. They believed that the student had gone home.

f. 1. I said that my relatives had gone away.   2. I said that my parents had gone away.   3. I said that my friends had gone away.   4. I said that my aunt and my uncle had gone away.

g. 1. He knew that his cousin was in town.   2. She knew that her niece was in town.   3. She knew that her niece was at church. 4. She knew that her cousin (*f.*) was at school.   5. He knew that his grandfather was at home.

h. 1. He says it rained.   2. My brother says it rained.   3. My sister says it rained.   4. She says it rained.

i. 1. They asked whether my brother had the book.   2. They asked whether my father had the book.   3. They asked whether my mother had the book. 4. They asked whether my sister had the book.

j. 1. The teacher said that the student should study the lesson. 2. The teacher said that the student (*f.*) should study the lesson. 3. The teacher (*f.*) said that the student (*f.*) should study the lesson. 4. The teacher (*f.*) said that the student should study the lesson.

C. GRAMMAR

1. The present subjunctive II forms of most weak verbs are identical with those of the past indicative. The present subjunctive II of **sagen** (to say) follows.

ich sagte	wir sagten
[du sagtest]	[ihr sagtet]
er, sie, es sagte	sie sagten
	Sie sagten

2. The present subjunctive II of strong verbs is formed by adding the subjunctive endings to the stem of the *past indicative*, plus umlaut if the vowel can be umlauted.

INFINITIVE	PAST INDICATIVE	PRESENT SUBJUNCTIVE II
bleiben to stay	**ich blieb**	**ich bliebe**
sehen to see	**ich sah**	**ich sähe**
ziehen to pull	**ich zog**	**ich zöge**
werden to become	**ich wurde**	**ich würde**

The present subjunctive II of **sein** (to be) and **werden** (to become) follows.

ich wär e	wir wär en
[du wär est]	[ihr wär et]
er, sie, es wär e	sie wär en
	Sie wär en

ich würd e	wir würd en
[du würd est]	[ihr würd et]
er, sie, es würd e	sie würd en
	Sie würd en

3. Indirect discourse is the reporting or paraphrasing of someone's statement without quoting his exact words. When the statement is

introduced by a verb of saying, thinking, believing, or communicating in a past tense (simple past, present perfect, or past perfect), the following verb is usually in the subjunctive, unless it is an obvious fact (see paragraph 6, below). The present subjunctive I or II is used when the original statement was in the present tense.

Direct discourse or statement.
a. **Er sagte: „Ich besuche meinen Freund."**
He said: "I'm visiting my friend."
b. **Sie sagten: „Er geht nach Hause."**
They said: "He's going home."
c. **Sie sind reich.**
They are rich.
Indirect Discourse.
a. **Er sagte, er besuche seinen Freund.**
Er sagte, er besuchte seinen Freund.
He said he was visiting his friend.
b. **Sie sagten, er gehe nach Hause.**
Sie sagten, er ginge nach Hause.
They said he was going home.
c. **Er glaubte, sie seien reich.**
Er glaubte, sie wären reich.
He believed they were rich.
Note 1: Both subjunctive I and II forms are used in indirect discourse. Subjunctive I is preferred in formal and literary usage; subjunctive II in informal writing and in conversation.
Note 2: In informal usage, the distinction between subjunctive and indicative in indirect discourse is no longer always carefully observed.
4. The past subjunctive I consists of the present subjunctive I of the auxiliary verb **haben** or **sein** plus the past participle. The past subjunctive I of **sehen** (to see) and **kommen** (to come) follows.

ich hab e   gesehen
[du hab est gesehen]
er, sie, es hab e   gesehen
wir hab en   gesehen
[ihr hab et   gesehen]
sie hab en   gesehen
Sie hab en   gesehen

ich sei	gekommen
[du sei st	gekommen]
er, sie, es sei	gekommen
wir sei en	gekommen
[ihr sei et	gekommen]
sie sei en	gekommen
Sie sei en	gekommen

The past subjunctive II consists of the present subjunctive II of **haben** or **sein** plus the past participle. The past subjunctive II of **sehen** (to see) and **kommen** (to come) follows.

ich hätte	gesehen
[du hättest	gesehen]
er, sie, es hätte	gesehen
wir hätten	gesehen
[ihr hättet	gesehen]
sie hätten	gesehen
Sie hätten	gesehen

ich wäre	gekommen
[du wärest	gekommen
er, sie, es wäre	gekommen
wir wären	gekommen
[ihr wäret	gekommen]
sie wären	gekommen
Sie wären	gekommen

5. The past subjunctive I or II is used when the direct statement was in the past, present perfect, or past perfect indicative.

   a. **Sie schrieb, sie habe ihre Kusine gesehen.**
      Sie schrieb, sie hätte ihre Kusine gesehen.
      She wrote she had seen her cousin (*f.*).

   The above is an indirect statement of one of the following.

      Sie schrieb: ,,Ich sah meine Kusine.''
      Sie schrieb: ,,Ich habe meine Kusine gesehen.''
      Sie schrieb: ,,Ich hatte meine Kusine gesehen.''

   b. **Sie glaubten, daß ihr Vater nach Hause gegangen sei.**
      Sie glaubten, daß ihr Vater nach Hause gegangen wäre.
      They believed that their father had gone home.

The above is an indirect statement of the thought contained in the following.

> **Unser Vater ging nach Hause.**
> **Unser Vater ist nach Hause gegangen.**
> **Unser Vater war nach Hause gegangen.**

6. In indirect discourse, the verb is usually in the indicative (a) if the introductory verb is in the first person, in any tense; (b) if the introductory verb indicates knowledge of a fact; (c) if the introductory verb is in the present tense and reports an obvious fact.

   a. **Ich sagte, daß meine Verwandten fortgegangen waren.**
      I said that my relatives had gone away.
   b. **Er wußte, daß sein Vetter in der Stadt war.**
      He knew that his cousin was in town.
   c. **Er sagt, es hat geregnet.**
      He says it rained.

7. The subjunctive is usually used in indirect questions introduced by **ob** (whether, if), after a past introductory verb.

   > **Sie fragten, ob mein Bruder das Buch habe.**
   > **Sie fragten, ob mein Bruder das Buch hätte.**
   > They asked whether my brother had the book.

8. The subjunctive of **sollen** (to be supposed to) is used in indirect statements of command.

   > **Der Lehrer sagte, daß der Student die Aufgabe lernen solle.**
   > **Der Lehrer sagte, daß der Student die Aufgabe lernen sollte.**
   > The teacher said that the student should study the lesson.

   Note that the subjunctive of **sollen** means "should."

D. EXERCISES

WRITE THE FOLLOWING SENTENCES IN GERMAN AND BE ABLE TO EXPRESS THEM ORALLY IN CLASS.

1. His parents knew that he hadn't gone to school.
2. She said her head hurt.
3. My uncle thought that he had to go home.
4. Your mother writes that she is spending a week at the seashore.
5. The doctor asked where she had seen his cousin.
6. We believe that you are right.

7. Do you know why the children are not here?
8. Her grandfather believed that she should take a trip to Austria.
9. The little boy thought that he could stay home all day.
10. They know that their friends have been living here for a week.
11. His brother wrote that it had rained all summer in Germany.
12. The girls believed that their teacher (*f.*) had gone away a week ago.
13. My sister asked my father whether I might go to the movies.
14. These people said that our aunt was looking for us.
15. Your teacher believes that you haven't studied much.
16. They said that it was still raining.
17. My relatives wrote that I should visit them next month.
18. The little children say that their feet hurt.
19. She asked when it had begun to rain.
20. I believe that they are very strong.
21. All his friends said that he had departed the day before yesterday.
22. I don't know where he lives now.
23. My friend said that he had seen my brother in town.

E. READING AND SPEAKING

I. READ THE FOLLOWING ALOUD UNTIL YOU ARE THOROUGHLY FAMILIAR WITH IT.

In Hamburg

An einem Montag kamen Hans und Walter in Hamburg an. Sie gingen zu ihrem Hotel und packten ihre Koffer aus[1]. Es waren keine anderen Amerikaner im Hotel, und man sprach nur Deutsch. Die zwei Freunde sprachen auch Deutsch und fanden, daß man sie leicht 5 verstand. Sie gingen zum Postamt und fragten, ob man etwas für sie habe. Der Beamte gab Hans zwei Briefe und sagte, es tue ihm leid, aber er habe nichts für Walter.

Der eine Brief war von der Mutter und der andere von Käthe. Da sie noch keinen Brief von ihm bekommen hatten, hatten sie viele 10 Fragen. Am Ende ihres Briefes schrieb die Mutter: „Ich hoffe, daß ihr eine gute Reise habt und gesund wieder nach Hause kommt."

Vom Postamt gingen sie zur Alster, einem großen See mitten in

---

[1] packten ihre Koffer aus   unpacked their bags.

(in the middle of) **der Stadt. Es waren viele Segelboote** (sailboats)
15 **auf der Alster und sie waren sehr schön anzusehen** (to look at). **Hans**
wollte rudern (to row), **aber Walter wollte es nicht. Es hatte eben**
eins geschlagen und er sagte, er habe jetzt Hunger und möchte lieber
essen. Hans meinte (said), **sie könnten** (could) **nach dem Essen rudern.**
Walter war damit einverstanden² und sie gingen in ein Restaurant.
20   **Der Kellner** (waiter) **fragte, ob sie Amerikaner seien und sagte,**
er sei vor einigen Jahren in den Vereinigten Staaten gewesen. Er
wollte Englisch mit ihnen reden, aber sie sagten, sie würden in
Deutschland nur Deutsch sprechen. Er meinte (thought), **ihre Aus-**
sprache (pronunciation) **sei sehr gut. Nach dem Mittagessen gingen**
25 **sie wieder zur Alster und mieteten** (hired) **ein kleines Boot.**

II. ANSWER THE FOLLOWING QUESTIONS IN GERMAN.

1. **Wann sind die Freunde in Hamburg angekommen?**
2. **Was hat man im Hotel gesprochen?**
3. **Wohin sind sie vom Hotel gegangen?**
4. **Wer hat keine Briefe bekommen?**
5. **Was ist die Alster?**
6. **Warum wollte Walter nicht rudern?**
7. **Wieviel Uhr hatte es eben geschlagen?**
8. **Was haben die jungen Herren gemietet?**

²**war damit einverstanden**   agreed to that.

☛ UNIT 23

A. UNITS OF SPEECH AND VOCABULARY

I. STUDY AND READ ALOUD.

Sie biegen um die Ecke.	They are turning around the corner.
Dieser Weg führt zum Bahnhof.	This is the way to the railroad station.
Sie lernt ihre Nachbarin kennen.	She becomes acquainted with (meets) her neighbor (*f.*).
Er bleibt auf dieser Seite stehen.	He is stopping on this side.
Der Rhein fließt von Süden nach Norden.	The Rhine flows from south to north.
Der Hafen liegt in dieser Richtung.	The harbor is in this direction.
an der Ecke	on the corner, at the corner
um die Ecke	around the corner
nach rechts	to the right
nach links	to the left
von Osten	from (the) east
nach Westen	to (the) west
auf dieser Seite	on this side
auf der anderen Seite	on the other side
weit von hier	far from here

der Bahnhof, -s, ⸗e	the railroad station	**die Ecke, -, -n**	the corner
		der Hafen, -s, ⸗	the harbor

179

der Platz, -es, ⸚e	the square, place	die Schuld, -, -en	the debt
das Rathaus, -es, ⸚er	the city hall	die Seite, -, -n	the side, page
		der Zahn, -es, ⸚e	the tooth
die Richtung, -, -en	the direction	der Zahnarzt, -es, ⸚e	the dentist
der Weg, -s, -e	the way, road	tausend	a thousand, one thousand
der Norden, -s	the north		
der Osten, -s	the east	links	(on the) left
der Süden, -s	the south	rechts	(on the) right
der Westen, -s	the west	weit	far
der Kellner, -s, -	the waiter	um + acc.	around
die Nachbarin, -, -nen	the neighbor (f.)	bezahlen	to pay
		führen	to lead

biegen	bog	ist gebogen		to turn
fließen	floß	ist geflossen		to flow
kennen-lernen	lernte . . . kennen	kennengelernt		to become acquainted with, to meet (*for the first time*)
stehen-bleiben	blieb . . . stehen	ist stehengeblieben		to stop
sterben	starb	ist gestorben	stirbt	to die
ziehen	zog		gezogen	to pull

II. DRILL. EXPRESS ORALLY IN GERMAN. REPEAT UNTIL IT IS NO LONGER NECESSARY TO REFER TO SECTION I.

a. 1. They are turning around the corner. 2. We are turning around the corner. 3. You are turning around the corner. 4. He is turning around the corner. 5. He is turning to the right. 6. She is turning to the right. 7. She has turned to the right. 8. She has turned to the left. 9. We have turned to the left. 10. They have turned to the left.

b. 1. This is the way to the railroad station. 2. This is the way to the square. 3. This is the way to the city hall. 4. This is the way to the harbor.

c. 1. She becomes acquainted with her neighbor (f.). 2. She is becoming acquainted with my neighbor (f.). 3. She has met my neighbor (f.). 4. I have become acquainted with my neighbor (f.). 5. We have met our neighbor (f.).

d. 1. He is stopping on this side. 2. She is stopping on this side. 3. She stopped on this side. 4. We stopped on the other side. 5. We stopped on the other side of the street. 6. They stopped on the other side of the street. 7. They have stopped at the corner. 8. I am stopping at the corner. 9. Are you stopping at the corner?

e. 1. The Rhine flows from south to north. 2. The river flows from south to north. 3. These rivers flow from south to north. 4. The rivers flow from east to west. 5. This river flows from east to west. 6. Which river flows from west to east?

f. 1. The harbor is in this direction. 2. The city hall is in this direction. 3. The station is in this direction. 4. The square is in this direction.

g. 1. ... far from here. 2. Is the harbor far from here? 3. Is the city hall far from here? 4. Is the station far from here? 5. Is the square far from here?

h. 1. They are paying ... 2. They are paying the debts. 3. They are paying their debts. 4. He paid his debts. 5. She paid the waiter. 6. We have paid the waiter. 7. I have paid the waiter.

i. 1. They are dying. 2. A thousand people are dying. 3. A thousand soldiers died. 4. A thousand officers died. 5. The dentist has died. 6. The waiter has died. 7. He is dying. 8. She is dying.

j. 1. The dentist is pulling the tooth. 2. The dentist is pulling her tooth. 3. The dentist has pulled her tooth. 4. The dentist has pulled her teeth. 5. The dentist pulled my teeth.

B. MODEL SENTENCES

I. STUDY UNTIL EACH SENTENCE CAN BE GIVEN CORRECTLY FROM THE ENGLISH.

185. **Er sagte, daß er in die Schule gehen werde (würde).**
186. **Wenn er jetzt käme, würde ich mit ihm reden.**
187. **Wenn wir in die Stadt führen, könnten wir einige Sachen kaufen.**
188. **Wenn er sie nicht gesehen hätte, wäre er fortgegangen.**
189. **Sie sagte, er werde schon nach dem Frühstück abgefahren sein.**
190. **Wenn sie in die Kirche gekommen wären, würden sie ihre Freunde getroffen haben.**
191. **Dächte er öfter an seine Mutter, (so) würde er ihr schreiben.**
192. **Wenn er nur reich wäre!**

193. Wenn sie das gewußt hätten!
194. Ich möchte eine Tasse Kaffee haben.
195. Dürfte ich um ein Stück Kuchen bitten?
196. Könnten Sie mir einen neuen Hut zeigen?
197. Würden Sie heute nachmittag ins Kino gehen?

185. He said that he would go to school.
186. If he came now, I'd talk with him.
187. If we drove to town, we could buy some things.
188. If he hadn't seen her, he would have gone away.
189. She said he probably left already after breakfast.
190. If they had come to church, they would have met their friends.
191. If he thought of his mother more often, he would write her.
192. If he were only rich!
193. If they had known that!
194. I'd like to have a cup of coffee.
195. Might I ask for a piece of cake?
196. Could you show me a new hat?
197. Would you go to the movies this afternoon?

II. DRILL. EXPRESS ORALLY IN GERMAN.

a. 1. He said that he would go to school. 2. The boy said that he would go to school. 3. The student (*f.*) said that she would go to school. 4. She said that she would go to school.

b. 1. If he came now, I'd talk with him. 2. If my friend came now, I'd talk with him. 3. If my acquaintance came now, I'd talk with him. 4. If my relative came now, I'd talk with him.

c. 1. If we drove to town, we could buy some things. 2. If they drove to town, they could buy some things. 3. If the girls drove to town, they could buy some things. 4. If the women drove to town, they could buy some things. 5. If our parents drove to town, they could buy some things.

d. 1. If he hadn't seen her, he would have gone away. 2. If her cousin hadn't seen her, he would have gone away. 3. If her brother hadn't seen her, he would have gone away. 4. If his sister hadn't seen him, she would have gone away. 5. If his niece hadn't seen him, she would have gone away.

e. 1. She said he probably left already after breakfast. 2. She said her father probably left already after breakfast. 3. She said her brother probably left already after breakfast. 4. She said her uncle probably left already after breakfast.

f. If they had come to church, they would have met their friends. 2. If the students had come to church, they would have met their friends. 3. If the boys had come to church, they would have met their friends. 4. If the men had come to church, they would have met their friends.

g. 1. If he thought about his mother more often, he would write her. 2. If your friend thought about his mother more often, he would write her. 3. If your cousin (*f.*) thought about her mother more often, she would write her. 4. If your niece thought about her mother more often, she would write her.

h. 1. If he were only rich! 2. If my father were only rich! 3. If my grandfather were only rich! 4. If my grandmother were only well!

i. 1. If they had known that! 2. If your neighbors had known that! 3. If your parents had known that! 4. If we had known that!

j. 1. I'd like to have a cup of coffee. 2. I'd like to have a cup of tea. 3. I'd like to have a glass of water. 4. I'd like to have a glass of milk. 5. I'd like to have a bottle of milk.

k. 1. Might I ask for a piece of cake? 2. Might I ask for a piece of cheese? 3. Might I ask for a cup of tea? 4. Might I ask for a glass of milk?

l. 1. Could you show me a new hat? 2. Could you show me a brown hat? 3. Could you show me a green hat? 4. Could you show me a black hat?

m. 1. Would you go to the movies this afternoon? 2. Would you go to the movies this evening? 3. Would you go to the restaurant this evening? 4. Would you go to the restaurant tomorrow afternoon?

C. GRAMMAR

1. The future subjunctive consists of the present subjunctive I of **werden** and the infinitive of the main verb. The future subjunctive of **gehen** (to go) follows.

ich werde gehen
[du werdest gehen]
er, sie, es werde gehen
wir werden gehen
[ihr werdet gehen]
sie werden gehen
Sie werden gehen

The conditional consists of the present subjunctive II of **werden** and the infinitive of the main verb. The conditional of **gehen** (to go) follows.

ich würde gehen
[du würdest gehen]
er, sie, es würde gehen
wir würden gehen
[ihr würdet gehen]
sie würden gehen
Sie würden gehen

2. The future subjunctive and the conditional are used in indirect discourse to report a direct statement in future time.

   Er sagte, daß er in die Schule gehen werde (würde).

   He said that he would go to school.

   The future subjunctive is preferred in formal literary style, the conditional in conversation and informal writing.

3. Some irregular weak verbs umlaut the past-stem vowel in the present subjunctive II.

INFINITIVE		PAST INDICATIVE	PRESENT SUBJUNCTIVE II
bringen	to bring	brachte	brächte
denken	to think	dachte	dächte
dürfen	may, to be permitted to	durfte	dürfte
haben	to have	hatte	hätte
können	can, to be able to	konnte	könnte
mögen	to like, care to	mochte	möchte
müssen	must, to have to	mußte	müßte
wissen	to know	wußte	wüßte

Irregular weak verbs which have **a** as the stem vowel in the past indicative, have **e** in the present subjunctive II.

kennen	to know		kannte	kennte

4. There are two types of conditional sentences: real and unreal. Real conditions are expressed in the indicative.

   a. **Ich werde meinen Onkel sehen, wenn er uns besucht.**

      I'll see my uncle if he visits us.

   Unreal conditions are expressed in the subjunctive. If the condition refers to the present or the future, the present subjunctive II is used in the **wenn** clause, and the conditional in the main clause.

   b. **Wenn er jetzt käme, würde ich mit ihm reden.**

      If he came now, I'd talk with him.

5. For modal auxiliaries, the present subjunctive II is preferred to the conditional in the *conclusion* of present unreal conditions.

   Wenn wir in die Stadt führen, könnten wir einige Sachen kaufen.

   If we drove to town, we could buy some things.

6. The past subjunctive II is usually used in both clauses in unreal conditions referring to the past.

   Wenn er sie nicht gesehen hätte, wäre er fortgegangen.

   If he hadn't seen her, he would have gone away.

7. The future perfect subjunctive, which is rare in German, consists of the present subjunctive I of **werden** plus the past participle of the main verb and the infinitive of **haben** or **sein.**

   er werde gesehen haben

   er werde gegangen sein

8. The conditional perfect, which is also rare in German, consists of the present subjunctive II of **werden** plus the past participle of the main verb and the infinitive of **haben** or **sein.**

   er würde gesehen haben

   er würde gegangen sein

9. The future perfect subjunctive is used in indirect discourse to report a direct statement that was expressed in future perfect.

   Sie sagte, er werde schon nach dem Frühstück abgefahren sein.

   She said he probably left already after breakfast.

   The conditional perfect may be used in the main clause of a past unreal condition (see paragraph 6, above).

   Wenn sie in die Kirche gekommen wären, würden sie ihre Freunde getroffen haben.

   If they had come to church, they would have met their friends.

10. The conjunction **wenn** (if) may be omitted; the finite verb then stands before the subject.

Dächte er öfter an seine Mutter, (so) würde er ihr schreiben.
If he thought of his mother more often, he would write her.

Note: The main clause following an unreal condition may be introduced by **so** or **dann**, particularly if **wenn** is omitted. **So** is preferred for logical, **dann** for temporal conclusions. Their meaning, "then," is usually omitted in English.

The model sentences cited in the above paragraphs may be re-written as follows with no change in meaning.

    a. **Käme er jetzt, (dann) würde ich mit ihm reden.**
    b. **Führen wir in die Stadt, (so) könnten wir einige Sachen kaufen.**
    c. **Hätte er sie nicht gesehen, (so) wäre er fortgegangen.**
    d. **Wären sie in die Kirche gekommen, (so) würden sie ihre Freunde getroffen haben.**

11. The **wenn**-clause of an unreal condition may be used alone to express an unrealizable wish.

    a. **Wenn er nur reich wäre!**
        If he were only rich!
    b. **Wenn sie das gewußt hätten!**
        If they had known that!

Note that in these expressions, too, the conjunction **wenn** may be omitted; the finite verb is then placed before the subject.

    c. **Wäre er nur reich!**
        Were he only rich!
    d. **Hätten sie das gewußt!**
        Had they known that!

12. The present subjunctive II or the conditional is used in expressions of polite request.

    a. **Ich möchte eine Tasse Kaffee haben.**
        I'd like to have a cup of coffee.
    b. **Dürfte ich um ein Stück Kuchen bitten?**
        Might I ask for a piece of cake?
    c. **Könnten Sie mir einen neuen Hut zeigen?**
        Could you show me a new hat?
    d. **Würden Sie heute nachmittag ins Kino gehen?**
        Would you go to the movies this afternoon?

D. EXERCISES

WRITE THE FOLLOWING SENTENCES IN GERMAN AND BE ABLE TO EXPRESS THEM ORALLY IN CLASS.

1. If the doctor had not come, my friend would have died.
2. Would she go to the seashore next summer?
3. If I only had a new hat!
4. If the bus stops at the corner, we'll get on.
5. Might I have the menu?
6. If you paid the waiter, we could go.
7. Would your friend like to have a cup of tea?
8. If they knew my uncle, they would help him.
9. Were it only warmer!
10. I would read the book, if he brought it to me.
11. Had the train only left later!
12. I'll see you in church tomorrow, if you are there.
13. He would not get up now.
14. They would be tired, if they worked longer.
15. Could you do something for me?
16. If the boy ran faster, he'd be home at one.
17. My sister would like to buy a new house.
18. I'd have gone to the movies, if it hadn't rained.
19. Had we only lived one hundred years ago!
20. If the children don't go to school, they will not learn much.
21. We'd like to take a trip to Europe.
22. If our relatives had come to the station, we'd have seen them there.
23. The weather would be nice, if the sun were shining.
24. I am thirsty and could drink a glass of beer.

E. READING AND SPEAKING

I. READ THE FOLLOWING ALOUD UNTIL YOU ARE THOROUGHLY FAMILIAR
WITH IT.

Die Stadtrundfahrt[1]

**Am nächsten Morgen standen Hans und Walter sehr früh auf, um
eine Stadtrundfahrt zu machen. Sie frühstückten im Hotel und gingen
dann zum Platz vor dem Bahnhof. Dort kauften sie zwei Fahrscheine
(tickets) und stiegen in den Autobus ein. Vor ihnen saß ein junges** 5
**deutsches Ehepaar (couple), das auf Urlaub (vacation) war. Sie
begannen, miteinander zu reden, und es gab vieles (many things) zu
fragen.**

[1] **Die Stadtrundfahrt**   The Sightseeing Tour of the City.

„Wohin fahren Sie von Hamburg?" fragte der junge Mann, der
10 Herr Müller hieß.

„Von Hamburg fahren wir nach Köln", sagte Hans.

„Wir sind aus Berlin und fahren jetzt nach Berlin zurück. Wenn
Sie nach Berlin kämen, würden wir Ihnen die Sehenswürdigkeiten
(points of interest) der Stadt gern zeigen."

15 „Das wäre schön", sagte Walter, „aber in acht Tagen sollen wir
einige Freunde, die wir auf dem Schiff kennengelernt haben, in Köln
treffen."

„Wenn Sie später nach Berlin kommen, können Sie uns dann
besuchen. Wenn Sie wünschen, können wir Ihnen unsere Berliner
20 Adresse geben."

„Vielen Dank, das ist sehr nett (nice) von Ihnen", sagte Hans.

„Wir wollen in einigen Wochen nach Berlin fahren", sagte Walter,
„und dann werden wir Sie besuchen."

Der Autobus fuhr durch die ganze Stadt. Sie g ngen in das Rathaus
25 und in einige Museen (museums) der Stadt. Der Hafen interessierte
(interested) die Reisenden sehr und sie blieben dort eine Weile. Nach
der Rundfahrt nahmen die zwei Amerikaner Abschied von dem jungen
Ehepaar und gingen ins Hotel zurück.

II. ANSWER THE FOLLOWING QUESTIONS IN GERMAN.

1. Was wollten Hans und Walter am nächsten Morgen machen?
2. Wo haben Sie gefrühstückt?
3. Was haben sie gekauft?
4. Wen haben sie im Autobus kennengelernt?
5. Wann sollten sie Freunde in Köln treffen?
6. Wo wohnt das junge Ehepaar?
7. Wo sind die Reisenden eine Weile geblieben?
8. Wohin sind die beiden Freunde nach der Rundfahrt gegangen?

☞ UNIT **24**

A. UNITS OF SPEECH AND VOCABULARY

I. STUDY AND READ ALOUD.

er wäscht sich	he's washing himself
ich ziehe mich an	I'm dressing (myself)
Sie setzt sich an den Tisch.	She's sitting down at the table.
Sie sieht sich den Kölner Dom an.	She's looking at the Cathedral of Cologne.
Der Zug nähert sich dem Dorf.	The train is approaching the village.
Ich hole eine Medizin von der Apotheke.	I'm getting medicine from the drugstore.

der Anzug, -s, ⸗e	the suit	der Geschäfts-	
die Apotheke,	the pharmacy,	mann, -s,	
-, -n	drugstore	Geschäftsleute	the businessman
der Berg, -es, -e	the mountain	das Gesicht,	
die Dame, -, -n	the lady	-s, -er	the face
der Dom, -s, -e	the cathedral	das Kaufhaus,	the department
das Dorf, -es, ⸗er	the village	-es, ⸗er	store
das Feld, -es, -er	the field	die Medizin, -	the medicine
das Geschäft,	the shop,	der Schaffner,	
-s, -e	business	-s, -	the conductor

189

der Schuh, -s, -e	the shoe	uns	ourselves
der Speisewagen,		[euch	yourselves]
-s, -	the dining car	sauber	clean
mich	myself	Kölner	(of) Cologne
[dich	yourself]	bestellen	to order
sich	himself, herself,	bürsten	to brush
	itself, your-	holen	to fetch, to get
	self, your-	sich nähern	
	selves, them-	+ *dat*.	to approach
	selves	sich setzen	to sit down

sich an-sehen	sah sich . . . an	angesehen	sieht sich . . . an	to look at
an-ziehen	zog . . . an	angezogen		to dress, to put on
schließen	schloß	geschlossen		to close
waschen	wusch	gewaschen	wäscht	to wash

II. DRILL. EXPRESS ORALLY IN GERMAN. REPEAT UNTIL IT IS NO LONGER NECESSARY TO REFER TO SECTION I.

a. 1. he's washing himself 2. she's washing herself 3. they are washing themselves 4. we washed ourselves 5. I washed myself 6. he washed himself 7. The child washed himself. 8. Did you wash yourself?

b. 1. I'm dressing (myself) 2. we are dressing (ourselves) 3. they are dressing (themselves) 4. he has dressed (himself) 5. she has dressed (herself) 6. you have dressed (yourselves) 7. we have dressed (ourselves)

c. 1. She's sitting down at the table. 2. The lady is sitting down at the table. 3. The ladies sat down at the table. 4. They sat down at the table. 5. She sat down at the table. 6. The conductor sat down at the table.

d. 1. She's looking at the Cathedral of Cologne. 2. The lady is looking at the Cathedral of Cologne. 3. The lady looked at the Cathedral of Cologne. 4. The lady looked at the village. 5. She looked at the village. 6. The ladies looked at the field. 7. They looked at the field.

e. 1. The train is approaching the village. 2. The train is approaching the field. 3. The train is approaching the mountain. 4. The train approached the mountain.   5. Did the train approach the mountain?

f.   1. I'm getting medicine from the drugstore.   2. We are getting medicine from the drugstore.   3. They are getting medicine from the drugstore.   4. She's getting medicine from the drugstore.   5. He's getting medicine from the drugstore.   6. The lady is getting medicine from the drugstore.

g.   1. His face ...   2. His face is clean.   3. Her face is clean.   4. The child's face is clean.   5. The children's faces are clean.

h.   1. We are ordering ...   2. We are ordering coffee.   3. We are ordering coffee in the dining car.   4. They are ordering tea in the dining car.   5. The travelers are ordering tea in the dining car.

i.   1. He's brushing ...   2. He's brushing the suit.   3. Are you brushing the suit?   4. Are you brushing the shoe?   5. I'm brushing the shoe.   6. I'm brushing the shoes.   7. He's brushing the shoes.   8. He's brushing the suits.

j.   1. She's closing ...   2. She's closing the shop.   3. The businessman is closing the shop.   4. The businessman closed the shop.   5. He closed the shop.   6. He closed the department store.   7. The businessman closed the department store.   8. They closed the department store.

B. MODEL SENTENCES

I. STUDY UNTIL EACH SENTENCE CAN BE GIVEN CORRECTLY FROM THE ENGLISH.

198. Ich wasche mir das Gesicht.
199. Die Reisenden haben sich den Kölner Dom angesehen.
200. Der Junge zieht sich die Schuhe an.
201. Der Zug hat sich dem Dorf genähert.
202. Die Freunde begrüßen sich.
203. Mein Onkel sagte, daß seine Söhne nach Hause kämen.
204. Der Kellner fragte, ob ich eine Tasse Kaffee bestellt hätte.
205. Das Kind tat, als ob es krank wäre.
206. Es schien ihnen, als ob der Frühling schon gekommen wäre.
207. Sollte Ihr Bruder morgen kommen, (so) bringen Sie ihn zu mir.

198. I'm washing my face.

199. The travelers looked at the Cologne Cathedral.
200. The boy is putting on his shoes.
201. The train approached the village.
202. The friends are greeting one another.
203. My uncle said that his sons were coming home.
204. The waiter asked whether I had ordered a cup of coffee.
205. The child acted as if he were sick.
206. It seemed to them as if spring had already come.
207. Should your brother come tomorrow, bring him to my house.

II. DRILL. EXPRESS ORALLY IN GERMAN.

a. 1. I'm washing my face.   2. I'm washing my hands.   3. I'm washing my feet.   4. I'm washing my ears.

b. 1. The travelers looked at the Cologne Cathedral.   2. The brothers and sisters looked at the Cologne Cathedral.   3. The ladies looked at the Cologne Cathedral.   4. The gentlemen looked at the Cologne Cathedral.   5. The students looked at the Cologne Cathedral.

c. 1. The boy s putting on his shoes.   2. The conductor is putting on his shoes.   3. The man is putting on his shoes.   4. The student is putting on his shoes.   5. The girl is putting on her shoes.

d. 1. The train approached the village.   2. The car approached the village.   3. The bus approached the village.   4. The plane approached the village.

e. 1. The friends are greeting one another.   2. The relatives are greeting one another.   3. The acquaintances are greeting one another.   4. The businessmen are greeting one another.   5. The ladies are greeting one another.

f. 1. My uncle said that his sons were coming home.   2. My cousin said that his sons were coming home.   3. My cousin said that his brothers were coming home.   4. My aunt said that her children were coming home.   5. My niece said that her parents were coming home.

g. 1. The waiter asked whether I had ordered a cup of coffee.   2. The waiter asked whether I had ordered a cup of tea.   3. He asked whether I had ordered a piece of cake.   4. She asked whether I had ordered a piece of cheese.   5. They asked whether I had ordered a glass of milk.

h. 1. The child acted as if he were sick. 2. The girl acted as if she were sick. 3. The salesman acted as if he were sick. 4. The woman acted as if she were sick. 5. The student (*f.*) acted as if she were sick.

i. 1. It seemed to them as if spring had already come. 2. It seemed to us as if summer had already come. 3. It seemed to me as if fall had already come. 4. It seemed to her as if winter had already come.

j. 1. Should your brother come tomorrow, bring him to my house. 2. Should your grandson come tomorrow, bring him to my house. 3. Should your nephew come tomorrow, bring him to our house. 4. Should your cousin come tomorrow, bring him to our house. 5. Should your friend come tomorrow, bring him to our house.

C. GRAMMAR

1. If the subject of a verb is in the first person: **ich** (I), **wir** (we), or in the familiar second person: **du** (you), **ihr** (you), and the object is in the same person, then the appropriate direct-object pronoun is used with reflexive meaning.

> **Ich wasche mich.**
> I'm washing myself.
> **Wir ziehen uns an.**
> We are dressing ourselves.

2. If both the subject and the object of a verb are in the third person, or in the polite **Sie** (you) form, the reflexive pronoun **sich** (himself, herself, itself, themselves, yourself, yourselves) is used as the direct-object pronoun.

> **Er wäscht sich.**
> He is washing himself.

3. The complete present tense of **waschen,** used reflexively, follows.

ich wasche mich	I am washing myself, I am getting washed
[du wäscht dich	you are washing yourself, are getting washed]
er, sie, es wäscht sich	he, she, it is washing himself, herself, itself, is getting washed
wir waschen uns	we are washing ourselves, are getting washed

> **[ihr wascht euch**   you are washing yourselves, are getting
>   washed]
>
> **sie waschen sich**   they are washing themselves, are getting
>   washed
>
> **Sie waschen sich**   you are washing yourself (yourselves), are
>   getting washed

4. If a reflexive verb has a direct noun object, the reflexive pronoun is
   in the dative case.

   a. **Ich wasche <u>mir</u> das Gesicht.**
      I am washing my face.

   b. **Die Reisenden haben <u>sich</u> den Kölner Dom angesehen.**
      The travelers looked at the Cologne Cathedral.

   c. **Der Junge zieht <u>sich</u> die Schuhe an.**
      The boy is putting on his shoes.

   Note that the reflexive pronoun **sich** has the same form for both
   the dative and the accusative cases.

5. In contrast to verbs like **waschen** (to wash) and **anziehen** (to dress),
   which can be used both as simple verbs and as reflexive verbs, there
   are some verbs which are never used without the reflexive pronoun;
   for example, **sich nähern** (to approach).

   > **Der Zug hat sich dem Dorf genähert.**
   > The train approached the village.

6. The reflexive pronoun may be used in a reciprocal sense.

   > **Die Freunde begrüßen sich.**
   > The friends are greeting one another.

   Note: **Einander** (one another) may replace **sich** in a reciprocal
   sense (a) and must replace it in order to avoid ambiguity (b).

   a. **Die Freunde begrüßen einander.**
      The friends are greeting one another.

   b. **Die Kinder waschen einander.**
      The children are washing one another.

   Compare with the following.

   > **Die Kinder waschen sich.**
   > The children are washing themselves.

7. Adjectives formed from names of cities end in **-er** and are not
   inflected. They are always capitalized.

   > **Die Reisenden haben sich den Kölner Dom angesehen.**
   > The travelers looked at the Cologne Cathedral.

8. In indirect discourse or in indirect questions, the present subjunctive I is avoided if the form is identical with the present indicative. It is replaced by the corresponding form of the present subjunctive II.
   a. **Mein Onkel sagte, daß seine Söhne nach Hause kämen.**
   My uncle said that his sons were coming home.
   If the past subjunctive I form is identical with the present perfect indicative, it is replaced by the past subjunctive II.
   b. **Der Kellner fragte, ob ich eine Tasse Kaffee bestellt hätte.**
   The waiter asked whether I had ordered a cup of coffee.
9. Clauses introduced by **als ob** (as if) use the subjunctive forms as they are used in the **wenn**-clause of unreal conditions.
   a. **Das Kind tat, als ob es krank wäre.**
   The child acted as if he were sick.
   b. **Es schien ihnen, als ob der Frühling schon gekommen wäre.**
   It seemed to them as if spring had already come.
10. The present subjunctive II of **sollen** (to be supposed to) is frequently used with a dependent infinitive in the **wenn**-clause of a condition and is translated by "should." Note that **wenn** may be omitted and the finite verb stands first.
   Sollte Ihr Bruder morgen kommen, so bringen Sie ihn zu mir.
   Should your brother come tomorrow, bring him to my house.

D. EXERCISES

WRITE THE FOLLOWING SENTENCES IN GERMAN AND BE ABLE TO EXPRESS THEM ORALLY IN CLASS.

1. The teachers and the students greeted one another.
2. Please sit down.
3. We want to look at the Hamburg City Hall.
4. The conductor thought that I had lost my baggage.
5. As we were approaching the school, the students were going home.
6. The traveler said that the trains were leaving soon.
7. After he had washed his face, the boy went to bed.
8. The girls are telling each other stories.
9. Should it rain this afternoon, then I'll stay in town.
10. My sisters wrote that their girl friends had taken a long trip.
11. Children, wash your hands.

12. Did you see the Heidelberg railroad station?
13. Their grandmother believed that they were going to the movies.
14. The boys ate the cake as if they had eaten nothing the whole day.
15. I have already dressed.
16. It seemed to the neighbors as if he were very rich.
17. Should you come to town at twelve o'clock, we could eat with you.
18. We visited the Cologne Cathedral.
19. The man asked whether we wanted to buy something.
20. They acted as if they didn't know their friends.
21. The guest had sat down on a chair in the living room.
22. We will see one another tomorrow.
23. The lady said that I had gotten medicine in the drugstore.
24. Marie, put on your shoes.

E. READING AND SPEAKING

I. READ THE FOLLOWING ALOUD UNTIL YOU ARE THOROUGHLY FAMILIAR
    WITH IT.

In Köln

Als die beiden Freunde Hamburg verließen, fuhren sie nach Bremen,
wo sie einige Tage verbrachten, und fuhren dann nach Köln weiter.
Als sie aus dem Kölner Bahnhof auf die Straße herauskamen, sahen
5 sie den Dom vor sich. „Der Dom ist sehr, sehr schön", sagte Walter.
„Ja", sagte Hans, „aber jetzt kann ich mir nichts ansehen. Mir
tut der Kopf weh. Ich glaube, ich erkälte mich."[1]
„Gehen wir zum Hotel. Dann werde ich dir eine Medizin von der
Apotheke holen."
10 Nachdem Hans die Medizin eingenommen (taken) hatte, fühlte er
sich (he felt) besser. Dann wollte er sich den Dom ansehen. Man
führte sie durch den alten Dom und zeigte ihnen viel Interessantes.
„Ich habe nicht gewußt, daß der Dom so alt ist", sagte Hans.
„Ich auch nicht. Man sagt, man hat sechshundert Jahre lang daran
15 gebaut."[2]
„Es ist gut, daß er nicht während des Krieges zerstört worden ist
(was destroyed)."

---

[1] erkälte mich   am catching cold.   [2] man hat ... daran gebaut   they worked
on it.

„Ja. Man hat den Bahnhof auf der anderen Seite des Platzes schwer getroffen,[3] aber man wollte den Dom schonen (to spare)."

Später fuhren Hans und Walter durch die Stadt und über den Rhein. 20 Von der anderen Seite des Flusses konnten sie den Dom photographieren.

Als sie müde wurden, gingen sie wieder zum Hotel zurück (back) und schliefen ein wenig, denn sie waren sehr früh aufgestanden und hatten den ganzen Tag sehr viel getan. 25

II. ANSWER THE FOLLOWING QUESTIONS IN GERMAN.

1. Wohin sind die beiden Freunde von Hamburg gefahren?
2. Wem hat der Kopf weh getan?
3. Was hat Walter von der Apotheke geholt?
4. Welches interessante Gebäude haben sie sich in Köln angesehen?
5. Wie viele Jahre hat man daran gebaut?
6. Welches Gebäude hat man während des Krieges schwer getroffen?
7. Wie heißt der Fluß, an dem Köln liegt?
8. Was haben sie von der anderen Seite des Flusses photographiert?

[3] **man hat den Bahnhof schwer getroffen** the railroad station was hard hit.

☞ UNIT 25

A. UNITS OF SPEECH AND VOCABULARY

I. STUDY AND READ ALOUD.

Es macht mir Freude.	It gives me pleasure.
Die Schüler nennen ihre Namen.	The pupils give their names.
Hat sie ein Paar Handschuhe?	Does she have a pair of gloves?
Er spricht ein paar Worte.	He is speaking a few words.
Diese Wörter haben dieselbe Bedeutung.	These words have the same meaning.
Ich sende es mit der Post.	I am sending it by mail.
Was bedeutet der Satz?	What does the sentence mean?
Er beeilt sich nie.	He never hurries.
Selbst sein Feind glaubt ihm.	Even his enemy believes him.
Haben Sie es je versucht?	Have you ever tried it?

die Bedeutung, -, -en	the meaning	die Post, -	the mail, post office
die Fahrt, -, -en	the ride	der Satz, -es, =e	the sentence
der Feind, -es, -e	the enemy	der Schüler, -s, -	the pupil
die Freude, -, -n	the joy, pleasure	die Schülerin, -, -nen	the pupil f.
der Glaube, -ns	the faith		
der Handschuh, -s, -e	the glove	der Wald, -es, =er	the forest, woods
der Name, -ns, -n	the name	das Wort, -es	the word
das Paar, -s, -e	the pair, couple		

die Worte	the words (*in a phrase*)	**schwach**	weak
die Wörter	the words (*individually*)	**je**	ever
		nie	never
selbst	even, self	**bedeuten**	to mean, to signify
ein paar	a few	**sich beeilen**	to hurry
derselbe, dieselbe, dasselbe	the same	**versuchen**	to try

brennen	brannte	gebrannt	to burn
nennen	nannte	genannt	to name
rennen	rannte	ist gerannt	to run
senden	sandte	gesandt	to send

II. DRILL. EXPRESS ORALLY IN GERMAN. REPEAT UNTIL IT IS NO LONGER NECESSARY TO REFER TO SECTION I.

a. 1. It gives me pleasure. 2. The ride gives me pleasure. 3. The ride gives us pleasure. 4. The ride gives them pleasure. 5. The ride gives him pleasure. 6. The ride gives her pleasure.

b. 1. The pupils give their names. 2. The pupils (*f.*) give their names. 3. The pupil (*f.*) gives her name. 4. The pupil gives his name. 5. The pupil gave his name. 6. The pupil (*f.*) gave her name. 7. The pupils (*f.*) gave their names. 8. The pupils gave their names.

c. 1. Does she have a pair of gloves? 2. Does he have a pair of gloves? 3. Does the boy have a pair of gloves? 4. Does the child have a pair of gloves? 5. Is the child wearing a pair of shoes? 6. Are you wearing a pair of shoes?

d. 1. He is speaking a few words. 2. She is speaking a few words. 3. The teacher (*f.*) is speaking a few words. 4. The teacher is speaking a few words.

e. 1. These words have the same meaning. 2. Some words have the same meaning. 3. Several words have the same meaning. 4. The two words have the same meaning.

f. 1. I am sending it by mail. 2. He is sending it by mail. 3. He was sending it by mail. 4. She was sending it by mail. 5. She has sent it by mail. 6. They have sent it by mail.

g. 1. What does the sentence mean? 2. What does this sentence mean?

3. What do these sentences mean?   4. What does the word mean?
5. What does this word mean?   6. What does the other word mean?

h. 1. He never hurries.   2. She never hurries.   3. She has never
hurried.   4. We have never hurried.   5. I have never hurried.

i. Even his enemy believes him.   2. Even his enemy believed him.
3. Even their enemies believed them.   4. Even their enemies believe
them.

j. 1. Have you ever tried it?   2. Has he ever tried it?   3. Has she
ever tried that?   4. Have they ever tried that?

k. 1. the same glove   2. the same sentence   3. the same forest   4. the
same post office   5. the same school   6. the same book   7. the
same couple   8. the same word

l. 1. . . . weak.   2. Her faith is weak.   3. His faith is weak.
4. Their faith is weak.

m. 1. It is burning.   2. The forest is burning.   3. The forest was
burning.   4. The post office was burning.   5. It has burned.
6. The forest has burned.   7. The forests have burned.

n. 1. He's running.   2. He's running into the forest.   3. She's running
into the forest.   4. She has run into the woods.   5. They have run
into the woods.

B. MODEL SENTENCES

I.   STUDY UNTIL EACH SENTENCE CAN BE GIVEN CORRECTLY FROM THE
ENGLISH.

208. **Die Wörter „Samstag" und „Sonnabend" haben dieselbe Bedeutung.**

209. **Das Buch hat mit diesen Worten geendet.**

210. **Wir sind mit einem jungen Paar gereist.**

211. **Er ist mit ein paar Freunden angekommen.**

212. **Mein Großvater hat es selbst getan.**

213. **Ich selbst habe sie gesehen.**

214. **Selbst ein Kind könnte das tun.**

215. **Seine Geschichten waren nie kurz.**

216. **Er war nie mein Feind.**

217. **Ihr Kind ist nie gerne in die Schule gegangen.**

218. **Er ruft mich nie an.**

208. The words "Samstag" and "Sonnabend" have the same meaning.
209. The book ended with these words.
210. We traveled with a young couple.
211. He arrived with a few friends.
212. My grandfather did it himself.
213. I myself saw them.
214. Even a child could do that.
215. His stories were never short.
216. He was never my enemy.
217. Her child never liked to go to school.
218. He never calls me up.

II. DRILL. EXPRESS ORALLY IN GERMAN.

a. 1. The words "Samstag" and "Sonnabend" have the same meaning.
2. The words "bevor" and "ehe" have the same meaning. 3. The words "schicken" and "senden" have the same meaning. 4. The words "rennen" and "laufen" have often the same meaning.

b. 1. The book ended with these words. 2. The story ended with these words. 3. The sentence ended with these words. 4. The lesson ended with these words.

c. 1. We traveled with a young couple. 2. My friends traveled with a young couple. 3. Her friends traveled with an elderly couple. 4. His parents traveled with an elderly couple.

d. 1. He arrived with a few friends. 2. My uncle arrived with a few friends. 3. Your cousin left with a few friends. 4. The teacher left with a few students.

e. 1. My grandfather did it himself. 2. My nephew did it himself. 3. The boy did it himself. 4. The student did it himself. 5. The man did it himself.

f. 1. I myself saw them. 2. I myself visited them. 3. I myself sent them. 4. I myself tried them. 5. I myself paid them.

g. 1. Even a child could do that. 2. Even a child could say that. 3. Even a child could find that. 4. Even a child could learn that. 5. Even a child could try that.

h. 1. His stories were never short. 2. Her stories were never long. 3. Their stories were never interesting. 4. Their books were never interesting.

i. 1. He was never my enemy. 2. I was never his enemy. 3. You were never his enemy. 4. You were never his friend. 5. He was never your friend.

j. 1. Her child never liked to go to school. 2. Our son never liked to go to school. 3. Our grandmother never liked to go to town. 4. My mother never liked to go to town.

k. 1. He never calls me up. 2. My brother never calls me up. 3. My cousin never calls me up. 4. My friend never calls me up. 5. They never call me up.

C. GRAMMAR

1. Some nouns, such as **der Glaube** (the faith) and **der Name** (the name), add **-ns** for the genitive singular, **-n** for all other forms.

	SINGULAR	PLURAL
NOMINATIVE	der Name	die Namen
GENITIVE	des Namens	der Namen
DATIVE	dem Namen	den Namen
ACCUSATIVE	den Namen	die Namen

2. The verbs **brennen** (to burn), **nennen** (to name), **rennen** (to run), and **senden** (to send) form their various tenses like **kennen** (to know). The principal parts, plus the present subjunctive II, follow.

INFINITIVE	PAST INDICATIVE	PAST PARTICIPLE	PRESENT SUBJUNCTIVE II
brennen	brannte	gebrannt	brennte
nennen	nannte	genannt	nennte
rennen	rannte	ist gerannt	rennte
senden	sandte	gesandt	sendete

3. The adjective **derselbe, dieselbe, dasselbe** (the same) consists of the definite article plus **selb-** with weak adjective endings; the combination is always written as one word.

	MASCULINE	FEMININE	NEUTER	PLURAL
NOMINATIVE	derselbe	dieselbe	dasselbe	dieselben
GENITIVE	desselben	derselben	desselben	derselben
DATIVE	demselben	derselben	demselben	denselben
ACCUSATIVE	denselben	dieselbe	dasselbe	dieselben

4. **Das Wort** (the word) has two plural forms: **die Wörter** is used for isolated words (a); **die Worte,** for words in a phrase, clause, or longer statement (b).

   a. **Die Wörter „Samstag" und „Sonnabend" haben dieselbe Bedeutung.**

     The words "Samstag" and "Sonnabend" have the same meaning.

   b. **Das Buch hat mit diesen Worten geendet.**

     The book ended with these words.

5. When **ein Paar** is used as a noun, meaning "a pair, a couple," **ein** is inflected and **Paar** is capitalized.

   a. **Wir sind mit einem jungen Paar gereist.**

     We traveled with a young couple.

   b. **Hat sie ein Paar Handschuhe?**

     Does she have a pair of gloves?

When **ein paar** is used as an adjective, meaning "a few," **ein** is not inflected and **paar** is written with a small initial letter.

   c. **Er ist mit ein paar Freunden angekommen.**

     He arrived with a few friends.

6. The pronoun **selbst** (self) is used after the verb and its objects (a) or immediately after the noun or pronoun it emphasizes (b).

   a. **Mein Großvater hat es selbst getan.**

     My grandfather did it himself.

   b. **Ich selbst habe sie gesehen.**

     I myself saw them.

These two sentences may also be expressed as follows.

   c. **Der Großvater selbst hat es getan.**

   d. **Ich habe sie selbst gesehen.**

Note that **selbst** may be translated "myself," "himself," "herself," "itself," "themselves," "yourself," "yourselves," "ourselves," depending on the subject.

7. As an adverb, **selbst** precedes the element it emphasizes and means "even."

            Selbst ein Kind könnte das tun.

            Even a child could do that.

8. **Nie** (never), like **nicht** (not), usually *follows* the conjugated form of the verb and its objects in main clauses.

   a. **Er beeilt sich nie.**

     He never hurries.

Nie, like **nicht,** usually *precedes* predicate adjectives (b) or nouns (c), adverbs or prepositional phrases of manner or place (d), past participles (d), infinitives (e), and separable prefixes (f).

b. **Seine Geschichten waren nie kurz.**
His stories were never short.

c. **Er war nie mein Feind.**
He was never my enemy.

d. **Ihr Kind ist nie gerne in die Schule gegangen.**
Her child never liked to go to school.

e. **Ihr Kind wird nie gerne in die Schule gehen.**
Her child will never like to go to school.

f. **Er ruft mich nie an.**
He never calls me up.

D. EXERCISES

WRITE THE FOLLOWING SENTENCES IN GERMAN AND BE ABLE TO EXPRESS THEM ORALLY IN CLASS.

1. My sister never wears gloves.
2. You can try it yourself.
3. The children believed that the buildings were burning.
4. They never come into this room.
5. My uncle has always lived in the same house.
6. Your cousin (*f.*) is buying a pair of shoes.
7. Her niece never became a teacher.
8. The last words in your letter are very interesting.
9. The boy had run into the house.
10. Can we find his name in the book?
11. His son has never eaten in a restaurant.
12. We are learning a few new words today.
13. The parents had called the child Karl.
14. Our relatives were never here.
15. Did he give his name?
16. A few books are lying on the table.
17. Do you know what these two words mean?
18. Their enemies will never find them.
19. Her brother sent the package by mail.

20. He did it in good faith.
21. Her aunt was never poor.
22. The girl and her cousin have the same teacher.
23. His words gave me pleasure.
24. The woman could not write her name.

E. READING AND SPEAKING

I. READ THE FOLLOWING ALOUD UNTIL YOU ARE THOROUGHLY FAMILIAR WITH IT.

Die Rheinreise

Hans und Walter besuchten ihre Kölner Freunde, die sie auf dem Schiff kennengelernt hatten. Als sie am Tisch saßen und plauderten, sagten die Amerikaner, sie möchten das ganze Rheinland sehen. Die deutschen Freunde meinten, man könnte den Rhein am besten auf einer Fahrt mit dem Rheindampfer sehen. Also kauften Hans und Walter Fahrkarten und stiegen früh am nächsten Morgen in das weiße Schiff ein.

Es war ein schöner Sommertag. Als der Dampfer von Köln abfuhr, sahen sich die Reisenden den großen Dom noch einmal an, aber bald (soon) konnte man ihn nicht mehr sehen. Es waren über hundert Menschen an Bord und sie sprachen nicht nur Deutsch, sondern auch Englisch und noch andere Sprachen. Die zwei Amerikaner lernten ein paar andere Reisende kennen und unterhielten sich (conversed) mit ihnen.

Nach einer Weile sahen sie Bonn, die Hauptstadt der Bundesrepublik.[1] Vom Schiffe konnten sie die Regierungsgebäude (government buildings) sehen. Hinter Koblenz waren viele Hügel (hills) und Weinberge (vineyards) zu sehen (to be seen). Alles war grün und schön. Dann kamen die vielen alten Burgruinen (castle ruins). Ein paar deutsche Reisende nannten die Namen der Ruinen und erzählten den Amerikanern viele Geschichten über die alten Zeiten.

„Das Rheintal (Rhine Valley) ist sehr schön", sagte Hans. „Ich verstehe jetzt, warum man so viel vom Rheinland spricht."

„Ja", sagte Walter. „Diese Fahrt macht mir Freude. Es ist gut, daß wir mit dem Rheindampfer gefahren sind."

---

[1] die Hauptstadt der Bundesrepublik   the capital of the Federal Republic.

Die beiden Freunde aßen im Schiffsrestaurant zu Mittag. Als sie wieder an Deck gingen, war es sehr warm geworden. Also zogen sie sich die Jacken aus.[2] Hier und da sah man Leute, die im Rhein
30 schwammen. Einige Kinder lachten und spielten. Die Kinder amüsierten sich glänzend.[3] Am späten Nachmittag war es nicht mehr so warm, und es wurde immer dunkler. Hans und Walter mußten sich die Jacken wieder anziehen. Um neun Uhr stiegen sie in Wiesbaden aus.

II. ANSWER THE FOLLOWING QUESTIONS IN GERMAN.

1. Wohin sind Hans und Walter früh am Morgen gegangen?
2. Was haben sie sich noch einmal angesehen?
3. Wie heißt die Hauptstadt der Bundesrepublik?
4. Was war hinter Koblenz zu sehen?
5. Wo haben Hans und Walter zu Mittag gegessen?
6. Was haben sie nach dem Mittagessen (lunch) getan?
7. Wann und wo sind sie ausgestiegen?

[2] **zogen sie sich die Jacken aus** they took off their jackets.   [3] **amüsierten sich glänzend** had a splendid time.

☞ UNIT 26

A. UNITS OF SPEECH AND VOCABULARY

I. STUDY AND READ ALOUD.

Man ändert das Gesetz.	The law is being changed.
Dieses Land besteht aus vielen Staaten.	This country consists of many states.
Er hat viel in seinem Leben erfahren.	He has experienced a lot in his life.
Jeder Mensch liebt die Freiheit und den Frieden.	Every human being loves freedom and peace.
Sie liebt die Natur.	She loves nature.
Ich besitze mein eigenes Haus.	I own my own house.
Er hat ein schwaches Herz.	He has a weak heart.
Sie war ein einziges Mal bei uns.	She was at our house only once.
Sie hat das Kleid einmal getragen.	She wore the dress one time.
Jedesmal geht der Junge zu spät fort.	The boy leaves too late every time.
Manchmal kommt er zu früh an.	Sometimes he arrives too early.
Solche Menschen wird man selten finden.	You will seldom find such people.
auf dem Bild	in the picture

das Bild, -es, -er	the picture	**das Gesetz, -es, -e**	the law
die Freiheit, -	(the) freedom	**das Herz,**	
der Friede, -ns	(the) peace	**-ens, -en**	the heart

das Kleid, -es	the dress	solcher, solche,	
die Kleider *pl.*	the clothes	solches	such
das Mal, -s, -e	the time, occa-	bald	soon
	sion	selten	seldom
der Mensch	the human	einmal	once, one time
-en, -en	being	zweimal	twice, two times
die Natur, -	(the) nature	dreimal	three times
der Ring, -s, -e	the ring	jedesmal	every time
der Staat, -es, -en	the state	manchmal	sometimes
das Tier, -s, -e	the animal	ändern	to change
eigen	own	lieben	to love, to like
einzig	only, single	töten	to kill

besitzen	besaß	besessen		to own, to possess
bestehen (+ aus + *dat.*)	bestand	bestanden		to consist (of)
erfahren	erfuhr	erfahren	erfährt	to experience, to find out
erkennen	erkannte	erkannt		to recognize

II. DRILL. EXPRESS ORALLY IN GERMAN. REPEAT UNTIL IT IS NO LONGER NECESSARY TO REFER TO SECTION I.

a. 1. The law is being changed. 2. The law is being changed soon. 3. The law was soon changed. 4. The laws were soon changed.

b. 1. This country consists of many states. 2. This country consists of several states. 3. This country consists of forty-nine states. 4. Europe consists of many states.

c. 1. He has experienced a lot in his life. 2. The traveler has experienced a lot in his life. 3. My grandmother has experienced a lot in her life. 4. My aunt has experienced a lot in her life.

d. 1. Every human being loves freedom and peace. 2. Every American loves freedom and peace. 3. Every German loves freedom and peace. 4. Every Englishman loves freedom and peace.

e. 1. She loves nature. 2. He loves nature. 3. They love nature. 4. We love nature. 5. Do you love nature? 6. Does every human being love nature?

f. 1. I own my own house. 2. We own our own house. 3. They owned their own house. 4. She owned her own house. 5. He had owned his own house. 6. They had owned their own house.

g. 1. He has a weak heart.   2. She has a weak heart.   3. The teacher (*f.*) has a weak heart.   4. The teacher has a weak heart.   5. The salesman has a weak heart.

h. 1. She was at our house only once.   2. His girl friend was at our house only once.   3. Our cousin (*f.*) was at our house only once. 4. Her cousin was at our house only once.   5. My acquaintance was at our house only once.

i. 1. She wore the dress one time.   2. My sister wore this dress one time.   3. My mother wore this dress one time.   4. My mother wore these clothes one time.   5. My aunt wore these clothes one time. 6. She wore these clothes one time.

j. 1. The boy leaves too late every time.   2. My brother leaves too late every time.   3. His son leaves too late every time.   4. The children leave too late every time.

k. 1. Sometimes he arrives too early.   2. Sometimes the boy arrives too early.   3. Sometimes the man arrives too early.   4. Sometimes we arrive too early.

l. 1. You will seldom find such people.   2. You will seldom find such children.   3. You will seldom find such pupils.   4. You will seldom find such teachers.   5. You will seldom find such businessmen.

m. 1. . . . in the picture.   2. They recognize him in the picture. 3. She recognized me in the picture.   4. They recognized her in the picture.   5. He recognized the ring in the picture.   6. She had recognized the ring in the picture.   7. I had recognized the ring in the picture.

B. MODEL SENTENCES

I. STUDY UNTIL EACH SENTENCE CAN BE GIVEN CORRECTLY FROM THE ENGLISH.

219. **Das Leben ist kurz.**
220. **Solch eine Stadt haben wir nie gesehen.**
221. **Er lehrt die Schüler die Aufgabe.**
222. **Der Mann tat, als erkennte er den Ring.**
223. **Gestern hätten wir unsere Tante besuchen können.**
224. **Er hätte das arme Tier nicht töten sollen.**

219. Life is short.
220. We've never seen such a city.
221. He is teaching the pupils the lesson.
222. The man acted as if he recognized the ring.
223. We could have visited our aunt yesterday.
224. He should not have killed the poor animal.

II. DRILL. EXPRESS ORALLY IN GERMAN.

a. 1. Life is short. 2. Life is interesting. 3. Life is hard. 4. Life is dear.

b. 1. We've never seen such a city. 2. We've never seen such a woman. 3. You've never seen such a house. 4. I've never had such a car.

c. 1. He is teaching the pupils the lesson. 2. He is teaching the pupils (*f.*) the lesson. 3. She is teaching the pupils (*f.*) the lesson. 4. She is teaching the pupils the lesson. 5. She is teaching us the lesson. 6. He is teaching me the lesson.

d. 1. The man acted as if he recognized the ring. 2. The boy acted as if he recognized the ring. 3. The pupil acted as if he recognized the ring. 4. The woman acted as if she recognized the ring. 5. The woman acted as if she recognized the man. 6. The girl acted as if she recognized the woman. 7. The child acted as if he recognized the boy.

e. 1. We could have visited our aunt yesterday. 2. You could have visited your grandmother yesterday. 3. He could have visited his uncle yesterday. 4. He could have seen his cousin this morning. 5. She could have seen her brother this afternoon. 6. You could have seen their parents this evening.

f. 1. He should not have killed the poor animal. 2. You should not have killed the poor animal. 3. You should not have killed the poor animals. 4. We should not have killed the old animals. 5. They should not have killed the old animals.

C. GRAMMAR

1. The neuter noun **das Herz** (the heart) has the following inflection.

	SINGULAR	PLURAL
NOMINATIVE	das Herz	die Herzen
GENITIVE	des Herzens	der Herzen
DATIVE	dem Herzen	den Herzen
ACCUSATIVE	das Herz	die Herzen

2. **Das Mal** may be used as a noun or combined with cardinal numbers or certain **der**-words to form adverbs.

        ein einziges Mal   only once, one single time

einmal	once, one time	**jedesmal**	every time
zweimal	twice, two times	**manchmal**	sometimes
dreimal	three times		

3. Abstract nouns are used *with* the definite article.
   a. **Sie liebt die Natur.**
      She loves nature.
   b. **Jeder Mensch liebt die Freiheit und den Frieden.**
      Every human being loves freedom and peace.
   c. **Das Leben ist kurz.**
      Life is short.
4. Inflected singular forms of **solcher, solche, solches** (such) are *preceded* by the indefinite article.
       Ein solcher Mensch liebt die Natur.
       Such a man loves nature.
       Solche Menschen lieben die Natur.
       Such people love nature.
   The uninflected form **solch** is *followed* by the indefinite article.
       Solch eine Stadt haben wir nie gesehen.
       We have never seen such a city.
5. Some verbs, such as **lehren** (to teach), are used with two accusative objects.
       Er lehrt die Schüler die Aufgabe.
       He is teaching the pupils the lesson.
6. **Als** may be used alone in place of **als ob** (as if), with the finite verb immediately following the conjunction.
       Der Mann tat, als erkennte er den Ring.
       The man acted as if he recognized the ring.
7. The past subjunctive II of the modal auxiliary **können** (can, to be able to) plus dependent infinitive is equivalent to English "could have" plus past participle.

>   **Gestern hätten wir unsere Tante besuchen können.**
>   We could have visited our aunt yesterday.

8. The past subjunctive II of the modal auxiliary **sollen** (to be supposed to) plus dependent infinitive is equivalent to English "should have" plus past participle.

>   **Er hätte das arme Tier nicht töten sollen.**
>   He should not have killed the poor animal.

D. EXERCISES

WRITE THE FOLLOWING SENTENCES IN GERMAN AND BE ABLE TO EXPRESS THEM ORALLY IN CLASS.

1. Does your girl friend wear such big hats?
2. My grandfather has taught me German.
3. It seemed to me as if they had gone home.
4. Your acquaintance visited us twice.
5. All human beings should love peace.
6. Could you have come yesterday evening?
7. Germany lies in the heart of Europe.
8. I should have written my mother a letter yesterday.
9. Is nature always beautiful?
10. You should have stayed home.
11. Will you teach him English?
12. Next time we'll go to your house.
13. My brother could have traveled to Austria last summer.
14. I never was in such a house.
15. Did our new teacher (*f.*) teach you the lesson?
16. He should have told the children a story.
17. My parents have seen you only once.
18. The boys acted as if they were no longer tired.
19. Does she like to wear such dresses?
20. Life in Germany is very interesting.
21. She called him up four times while he was sick.
22. My heart hurts when I see that.
23. We should have known that.
24. This is the last time.

E. READING AND SPEAKING

I. READ THE FOLLOWING ALOUD UNTIL YOU ARE THOROUGHLY FAMILIAR WITH IT.

Wiesbaden, Mainz und Frankfurt

Als Hans und Walter am nächsten Morgen aufstanden, führte sie ein Angestellter des Hotels nach unten in die Bäder[1] und sagte ihnen, die Stadt habe ihren Namen von solchen Bädern bekommen. Die Bäder gefielen ihnen sehr, und sie blieben eine Weile dort. Später zogen sie 5 sich an und gingen durch das Herz der Stadt. Einige Deutsche sagten ihnen, daß Wiesbaden die Hauptstadt des Staates Hessen sei, aber sie sagten nicht „Staat", sondern „Land", da die Deutschen ihre Staaten „Länder" nennen. Die Amerikaner sahen, daß die Stadt während des Krieges schwer getroffen worden war.[2] Man sagte ihnen, 10 sie sollten auch Mainz und Frankfurt besuchen, da diese beiden Städte nicht weit von Wiesbaden sind.

Am Nachmittag fuhren sie nach Mainz, der Hauptstadt des Landes Rheinland-Pfalz.

„Weißt du, daß Gutenberg hier die Buchdruckerkunst (art of print- 15 ing) erfunden (invented) hat?" fragte Hans.

„Ja", sagte Walter. „Wir werden uns sein Denkmal (monument) ansehen können. Was liest du im Reiseführer (guide book)?"

„Mainz ist eine der ältesten deutschen Städte und war der erste Bischofssitz Deutschlands."[3] 20

„Ich habe einmal gelesen, daß die Erzbischöfe (archbishops) von Mainz die deutschen Kaiser (emperors) gekrönt (crowned) hätten."

„Ich glaube, du hast recht, aber hat man die Kaiser hier gekrönt?"

„Nein, in Frankfurt. Wir wollen morgen dahinfahren."

„Gut." 25

Am nächsten Tage fuhren die beiden Freunde mit dem Autobus nach Frankfurt. Sie besuchten das Haus, wo Goethe, Deutschlands größter Dichter, geboren wurde.[4]

---

[1] **führte sie ein Angestellter des Hotels nach unten in die Bäder** an employee of the hotel took them downstairs to the (mineral) baths.   [2] **schwer getroffen worden war** had been hard hit.   [3] **der erste Bischofssitz** the residence of the first German bishop.   [4] **Deutschlands größter Dichter geboren wurde** Germany's greatest poet was born.

„Jetzt wollen wir den Dom sehen, wo man die deutschen Kaiser
30 gekrönt hat", sagte Hans.

Nachdem sie sich den Dom angesehen hatten, gingen sie zur Paulskirche (St. Paul's Church), wo 1848 das erste deutsche Parlament
zusammenkam (came together). Später besuchten sie das Messegelände
(fair grounds), wo die berühmte (famous) Frankfurter Messe abge-
35 halten wird (is held). Dann fuhren sie wieder nach Wiesbaden zu ihrem
Hotel.

II. ANSWER THE FOLLOWING QUESTIONS IN GERMAN.

1. **Wovon hat Wiesbaden seinen Namen bekommen?**
2. **In welchem Land liegt diese Stadt?**
3. **Wie heißt die Hauptstadt des Landes Rheinland-Pfalz?**
4. **Wer hat die Buchdruckerkunst erfunden?**
5. **Wer hat die deutschen Kaiser gekrönt?**
6. **In welcher Stadt hat man sie gekrönt?**
7. **Womit sind die beiden Freunde nach Frankfurt gefahren?**
8. **Welcher große Dichter wurde in dieser Stadt geboren?**

☞ UNIT 27

A. UNITS OF SPEECH AND VOCABULARY

I. STUDY AND READ ALOUD.

Wie ist die Aussicht von der Brücke?	How is the view from the bridge?
Er hat Glück.	He is lucky.
Sie wohnt in der Nähe des Turms.	She lives near the tower.
Sie blicken auf das Schloß.	They glance at the castle.
Der Präsident dient dem Volk.	The President serves the people.
Er erinnert sich an die Stadt.	He remembers the city.
Sie erklärt alles auf französisch.	She explains everything in French.
Die Kunst interessiert mich.	Art interests me.
Mein Freund sammelt Gemälde.	My friend collects paintings.
Die Schweiz ist wegen ihrer Berge berühmt.	Switzerland is famous for its mountains.
Das Volk wählt den Präsidenten.	The people elect the President.

die Aussicht, -, -en	the view	**das Glück, -s**	the (good) luck
Bayern, -s	Bavaria	**der König, -s, -e**	the king
der Berg, -es, -e	mountain	**die Kunst, -, -̈e**	(the) art
die Brücke, -, -n	the bridge	**der Maler, -s, -**	the painter
der Franzose, -n, -n	the Frenchman	**die Nähe, -**	the vicinity
der Italiener, -s, -	the Italian	**der Präsident,**	
der Spanier, -s, -	the Spaniard	**-en, -en**	the president
das Gemälde, -s, -	the painting		

215

das Schloß		**wie?**	how?
des Schlosses,		**blicken + auf**	
die Schlösser	the castle	**+ *acc.***	to glance (at)
der Turm, -s, ⸗e	the tower	**dienen + *dat.***	to serve
das Volk, -es, ⸗er	the people,	**sich erinnern + an**	
	nation	**+ *acc.***	to remember
berühmt	famous	**erklären**	to explain
französisch	French	**interessieren**	to interest
italienisch	Italian	**sammeln**	to collect
spanisch	Spanish	**wählen**	to elect

II. DRILL. EXPRESS ORALLY IN GERMAN. REPEAT UNTIL IT IS NO LONGER
NECESSARY TO REFER TO SECTION I.

a. 1. How is the view from the bridge? 2. How is the view from the
tower? 3. How is the view from the castle? 4. How is the view
from the castles? 5. How is the view from the towers? 6. How
is the view from the bridges?

b. 1. He is lucky. 2. The Frenchman is lucky. 3. The Italian is lucky.
4. The Spaniard is lucky. 5. The painter is lucky.

c. 1. She lives near the tower. 2. The painter lives near the tower.
3. The Frenchman lives near the castle. 4. The Italian lives near
the mountains. 5. The Spaniard lives near the bridge.

d. 1. They glance at the castle. 2. He glanced at the painting. 3. She
glanced at the bridge. 4. We glanced at the tower.

e. 1. The President serves the people. 2. The President served the
people. 3. The King served the nation. 4. The King had served
the nation.

f. 1. He remembers the city. 2. She remembers the country. 3. We
remember the village. 4. They remember Munich. 5. I remember
Bavaria.

g. 1. She explains everything in French. 2. The painter explains
everything in French. 3. The Frenchman explains everything in
French. 4. The Italian explains everything in Italian. 5. The
painter is explaining something in Italian. 6. He is explaining
something in Italian. 7. They are explaining something in Spanish.
8. The painter is explaining something in Spanish. 9. The Spaniard
is explaining something in Spanish.

h. 1. Art interests me. 2. Art interested him. 3. Art interested her. 4. Bavaria does not interest them. 5. Munich did not interest us.
i. 1. My friend collects paintings. 2. The King collects paintings. 3. The President collects paintings. 4. The President collected paintings.
j. 1. Switzerland is famous for its mountains. 2. Germany is famous for its castles. 3. Bavaria is famous for its castles. 4. Munich is famous for its art. 5. Munich is famous for its beer. 6. Is Germany famous for its mountains? 7. Is Austria famous for its mountains?
k. 1. The people elect the President. 2. We elect him. 3. We elected them. 4. They elected her.

B. MODEL SENTENCES

I. STUDY UNTIL EACH SENTENCE CAN BE GIVEN CORRECTLY FROM THE ENGLISH.

225. Die Geschichte wird von dem Jungen gelesen.
226. Die Tür wurde von der Frau geschlossen.
227. Die Aufgaben werden von den Schülern geschrieben werden.
228. Der Brief ist gestern geschrieben worden.
229. Sein Leben war durch den Krieg geändert worden.
230. Dem Mann wird von seinen Kindern geholfen.
231. Es wurde gestern abend viel gesungen.
232. Die Tür war geschlossen.

225. The story is being read by the boy.
226. The door was (being) closed by the woman.
227. The lessons will be written by the pupils.
228. The letter was written yesterday.
229. His life had been changed by the war.
230. The man is being helped by his children.
231. There was a lot of singing yesterday evening.
232. The door was closed.

II. DRILL. EXPRESS ORALLY IN GERMAN.

a. 1. The story is being read by the boy. 2. The story is being read by the student.   3. The book is being read by the student.   4. The book is being read by the teacher.   5. The book is being read by the dentist.

b.   1. The door was (being) closed by the woman.   2. The door was (being) closed by the teacher (*f.*).   3. The window was (being) closed by the teacher (*f.*).   4. The window was (being) closed by the student (*f.*).

c.   1. The lessons will be written by the pupils.   2. The lessons will be written by the pupils (*f.*).   3. The letters will be written by the children.   4. The letters will be written by the parents.   5. The letters will be written by the friends.

d.   1. The letter was written yesterday.   2. The lesson was written yesterday.   3. The sentence was written yesterday.   4. The story was written yesterday.

e.   1. His life had been changed by the war.   2. Her life had been changed by the war.   3. Life in Europe had been changed by the war.   4. Life in Germany had been changed by the war.   5. Life in the United States had been changed by the war.

f.   1. The man is being helped by his children.   2. The man is being helped by his friends.   3. The boy is being helped by his brothers.   4. The boy is being helped by his sisters.   5. The boy is being helped by his relatives.

g.   1. There was a lot of singing yesterday evening.   2. There was a lot of singing yesterday afternoon.   3. There was little singing this morning.   4. There was little singing last week.

h.   1. The door was closed.   2. The window was closed.   3. The house was closed.   4. The building was closed.   5. The store was closed.

C. GRAMMAR

1.   The passive voice consists of a conjugated form of **werden** as the auxiliary verb and the past participle of the main verb.

   Die Geschichte wird gelesen.
   The story is being read.

2.   The different tense forms are obtained by changing the tense of **werden.**

   a.   **Die Tür wurde geschlossen.**
   The door was (being) closed.

b. **Die Aufgaben werden geschrieben werden.**

The lessons will be written.

Note the word order of a passive infinitive: **geschrieben werden.**

3. When the past participle of **werden** is used in a compound tense in the passive voice, its form is shortened to **worden** (in place of **geworden**).

a. **Der Brief ist gestern geschrieben worden.** (Note word order.)

The letter was written yesterday.

b. **Sein Leben war geändert worden.** (Note word order.)

His life had been changed.

Note that the sentence **Der Brief ist geschrieben worden** may be equivalent to both of the following.

The letter was written.

The letter has been written.

4. The agent (*by whom* something is done) is expressed as the dative object of the preposition **von** (by).

a. **Die Geschichte wird von dem Jungen gelesen.**

The story is being read by the boy.

b. **Die Tür wurde von der Frau geschlossen.**

The door was (being) closed by the woman.

c. **Die Aufgaben werden von den Schülern geschrieben werden.**

The lessons will be written by the pupils.

5. The instrument (*by means of which* something is done) is expressed as the accusative object of **durch** (through, by).

Sein Leben war durch den Krieg geändert worden.

His life had been changed by the war.

6. A verb which requires its object to be in the dative case in the active voice also requires the dative case in the passive voice.

Dem Mann wird von seinen Kindern geholfen.

The man is being helped by his children.

7. **Es** is frequently used as the impersonal subject of verbs in the passive voice. English uses an equivalent *active* construction.

Es wurde gestern abend viel gesungen.

There was a lot of singing yesterday evening.

8. The verb **sein** (to be) is used with a past participle to express a state or a condition, rather than an action.

    a. **Die Tür war geschlossen.**

       The door was closed.

Compare this sentence with

    b. **Die Tür wurde geschlossen.**

       The door was (being) closed.

D. EXERCISES

WRITE THE FOLLOWING SENTENCES IN GERMAN AND BE ABLE TO EXPRESS
THEM ORALLY IN CLASS.

1. These paintings have been collected by my uncle.
2. Is the door closed?
3. When was the president elected?
4. Everything was explained to us in German.
5. The package was sent last month.
6. The letter had been written a week ago.
7. I was helped by my friends.
8. There is a lot of talking in school today.
9. The laws were changed last year.
10. The bill will be paid by my father.
11. The story was being explained by the pupils when we came into
     the room.
12. Are the windows closed?
13. The little child will be dressed by his sister.
14. Our car was already sold.
15. The paintings were bought by my cousin.
16. He was helped by the medicine.
17. This bill must be paid today.
18. The meal will be ordered by my mother.
19. There was laughing and weeping when the ship left.
20. The new house has already been sold.
21. My lessons are written.
22. Many pictures have been collected by my grandfather.

E. READING AND SPEAKING

I. READ THE FOLLOWING ALOUD UNTIL YOU ARE THOROUGHLY FAMILIAR
   WITH IT.

Nach München

Von Wiesbaden fuhren Hans und Walter mit dem Zug nach Heidelberg am Neckar.[1] Sie besuchten die alte Universität, die auch in Amerika sehr berühmt ist, und dann gingen sie zum Schloß. Die alten Gebäude interessierten alle Touristen sehr, aber die meisten Leute 5 sah man in der Nähe des Großen Fasses (near the Big Cask), das mehr als zweihunderttausend Flaschen Wein halten kann. Da sie vom Schloß eine gute Aussicht hatten, photographierten sie den Fluß, die Brücke und die Stadt.

Als sie später durch die Stadt gingen, sagte Walter: „Ich habe nicht 10 gewußt, daß Heidelberg so groß ist. Ich hatte geglaubt, es wäre eine kleine Universitätsstadt."

Von Heidelberg fuhren sie den Neckar entlang (along the Neckar) über (via) Stuttgart und Tübingen in den Schwarzwald. Sie verbrachten ein paar Tage am Titisee, wo sie schwammen und sich amüsierten.[2] 15 Dann fuhren sie nach München, der Hauptstadt von Bayern.

„München wird die Stadt der Kunst genannt", sagte Hans. „Ich möchte die alten Gemäldesammlungen (collections of paintings) sehen."

„Du hast recht", sagte Walter, während er durch den Reiseführer 20 blätterte (leafed).

Sie gingen zum Haus der Kunst, und beide machten große Augen, als sie die berühmten Gemälde von deutschen und vielen anderen Malern sahen.

„Ich glaube, Dürers Werke (works) gefallen mir am besten", sagte 25 Hans.

„Sie sind sehr schön", sagte Walter, „aber ich sehe mir lieber die Werke von Rubens an. Ich möchte eine ganze Woche hierbleiben."

„Weißt du, daß Leute aus allen Ländern zum Haus der Kunst kommen? Siehst du die Frau dort, die den Mädchen alles auf fran- 30 zösisch erklärt?"

„Ja", antwortete Walter, „und vor einer Weile habe ich auch Spanisch und Italienisch gehört."

Am nächsten Morgen standen sie schon um elf Uhr vor dem Rathaus und hörten das Glockenspiel (chimes), während sie die Turnierszene 35

---

[1] am Neckar   on the Neckar river.   [2] sich amüsierten   had a good time.

mit den historisch gekleideten Figuren beobachteten.[3] Dann stiegen sie auf[4] den Turm des Rathauses, um sich die Stadt anzusehen.

II. ANSWER THE FOLLOWING QUESTIONS IN GERMAN.

1. **Welche berühmte Universität haben Hans und Walter besucht?**
2. **Wieviel Wein kann das Große Faß halten?**
3. **Was haben die beiden Freunde photographiert?**
4. **Welchen Fluß entlang sind sie gefahren?**
5. **Welche Stadt ist wegen ihrer Kunst berühmt?**
6. **Welcher Maler hat Hans am besten gefallen?**
7. **Um wieviel Uhr haben sie das Glockenspiel gehört?**
8. **Warum sind sie auf den Turm gestiegen?**

[3] während sie die Turnierszene mit den historisch gekleideten Figuren beobachteten
while they observed the tournament scene with the figures in historical costume.
[4] stiegen sie auf   they went up to.

☞ UNIT 28

A. UNITS OF SPEECH AND VOCABULARY

I. STUDY AND READ ALOUD.

es freut mich	I'm glad
es gelingt mir	I succeed
es ist schade	it's a shame
Es klopft.	Someone is knocking (at the door).
Ich amüsiere mich glänzend.	I'm having a splendid time.
Sie sehen gut aus.	You look good.
Er bindet die Krawatte.	He's tying his tie.
Wo sind Sie geboren?	Where were you born?
Was für einen Grund hat er?	What kind of reason does he have?
Was für Gründe hat sie?	What kind of reasons does she have?
Sie lassen ein Haus bauen.	They are having a house built.
Er wohnt mitten in der Stadt.	He lives in the middle of town.
was für (ein)?	what kind of?

der Grund, -es, ⸚e	the reason	geboren	born
die Krawatte, -, -n	the necktie	glänzend	splendid
das Museum, -s, Museen	the museum	mitten + in + *dat.*	in the middle of
das Werk, -es, -e	the work (of art)	überall	everywhere

223

doch	nevertheless, after all, yet	**bauen**	to build
sich amüsieren	to have a good time	**freuen**	to give pleasure to
		klopfen	to knock

aus-sehen	sah . . . aus	ausgesehen	sieht . . . aus	to look, to appear
binden	band	gebunden		to tie
gelingen	gelang	ist gelungen		to succeed
lassen	ließ	gelassen	läßt	to let

II. DRILL. EXPRESS ORALLY IN GERMAN. REPEAT UNTIL IT IS NO LONGER NECESSARY TO REFER TO SECTION I.

a. 1. I'm glad 2. he's glad 3. She's glad nevertheless. 4. They are glad nevertheless. 5. We are glad after all. 6. You are glad after all.

b. 1. I succeed 2. she succeeds 3. he succeeded 4. you succeeded 5. we have succeeded 6. they have succeeded

c. 1. it's a shame 2. It's a shame that you didn't see his works. 3. It's a shame that we didn't see their works. 4. It's a shame that we didn't see Dürer's works.

d. 1. Someone is knocking (at the door). 2. Someone knocked at the door. 3. Someone had knocked at the door.

e. 1. I'm having a splendid time. 2. He's having a splendid time. 3. They are having a splendid time. 4. They are having a good time everywhere. 5. She's having a good time everywhere. 6. We are having a good time everywhere.

f. 1. You look good. 2. She looked good. 3. He had looked bad. 4. They had looked bad.

g. 1. He's tying his tie. 2. I'm tying my tie. 3. I tied my tie. 4. He tied his tie. 5. Did you tie your tie?

h. 1. Where were you born? 2. Where was he born? 3. Where was the child born? 4. When was the child born? 5. When were the children born?

i. 1. What kind of reason has he? 2. What kind of reason has she? 3. What kind of reasons has she? 4. What kind of reasons have they?

j. 1. They are having a house built. 2. We are having a house built.

3. He's having a house built.   4. The President is having a museum built.

k. 1. He lives in the middle of town.   2. He works in the middle of town.   3. She is standing in the middle of the room.   4. The child is sitting in the middle of the room.

B. MODEL SENTENCES

I. STUDY UNTIL EACH SENTENCE CAN BE GIVEN CORRECTLY FROM THE ENGLISH.

233. Es freut mich, daß Sie hier sind.
234. Es ist ihm gelungen, die Aufgabe zu lernen.
235. Ich bin in den Vereinigten Staaten geboren.
236. Goethe wurde in Frankfurt geboren.
237. Mein Onkel hat ein neues Haus bauen lassen.
238. Sie hatte ihn singen hören.
239. Die Mädchen haben ihre Freundinnen kommen sehen.
240. Mit was für einem Bleistift schreiben Sie?
241. Im Jahre 1955 (neunzehnhundertfünfundfünfzig) haben unsere Verwandten uns besucht.
242. 1949 (Neunzehnhundertneunundvierzig) sind wir nach Deutschland gefahren.

233. I am glad (that) you are here.
234. He succeeded in learning the lesson.
235. I was born in the United States.
236. Goethe was born in Frankfurt.
237. My uncle had a new house built.
238. She had heard him sing.
239. The girls saw their girl friends coming.
240. What kind of pencil are you writing with?
241. Our relatives visited us in (the year) 1955.
242. We went to Germany in 1949.

II. DRILL. EXPRESS ORALLY IN GERMAN.

a. 1. I am glad (that) you are here.   2. I am glad (that) my relatives are here.   3. He is glad (that) his friends are here.   4. We are glad (that) our acquaintances are here.   5. They are glad (that) their parents are here.

b. 1. He succeeded in learning the lesson.   2. She succeeded in writing the lesson.   3. She succeeded in writing the letter.   4. I succeeded in reading the letter.   5. Did you succeed in reading the book?

c. 1. I was born in the United States.   2. He was born in the United States.   3. He was born in Switzerland.   4. She was born in Germany.   5. They were born in Austria.

d. 1. Goethe was born in Frankfurt.   2. Goethe was born in Germany. 3. Schiller was born in Germany.   4. Brahms was born in Hamburg. 5. Beethoven was born in Bonn.

e. 1. My uncle had a new house built.   2. Her father had a new house built.   3. His brother had a new house built.   5. Our acquaintance had a small house built.

f. 1. She had heard him sing.   2. The teacher (*f.*) had heard the pupil sing.   3. The teacher had heard the pupils (*f.*) sing.   4. The children had heard the teacher sing.   5. The parents had heard the children sing.

g. 1. The girls saw their girl friends coming.   2. My cousins (*f.*) saw their girl friends coming.   3. Our cousins saw their friends coming. 4. Her grandfather saw his grandchildren coming.   5. The man saw the president coming.

h. 1. What kind of pencil are you writing with?   2. What kind of pencil is he writing with?   3. What kind of fountain pen is he writing with?   4. What kind of fountain pen is she writing with?

i. 1. Our relatives visited us in (the year) 1955.   2. Their relatives visited them in (the year) 1955.   3. His friends visited him in (the year) 1955.   4. My cousins visited me in (the year) 1955.   5. Her children visited her in (the year) 1955.

j. 1. We went to Germany in 1949.   2. They went to Austria in 1949. 3. The doctor went to Europe in 1949.   4. The businessman went to Munich in 1949.   5. The dentist went to Vienna in 1949.

C. GRAMMAR

1. Some verbs are used with the neuter pronoun **es** (it) as subject and are called impersonal verbs. To this group belong the following expressions.

es freut mich	I am glad
es klopft	someone is knocking (at the door)
es gelingt mir	I succeed
es regnet	it is raining
es schneit	it is snowing
es ist schade	it's a shame
es tut mir leid	I'm sorry

2. Some of these expressions may be followed by **zu** + an infinitive or by a clause introduced by **daß** (that).

   a. **Es ist ihm gelungen, die Aufgabe zu lernen.**
   He has succeeded in learning the lesson.

   b. **Es freut mich, daß Sie hier sind.**
   I'm glad (that) you are here.

3. The present tense of the auxiliary verb **sein** is used with the past participle **geboren** (born) when referring to living persons.

   Ich bin in den Vereinigten Staaten geboren.
   I was born in the United States.

4. The past tense of **werden** is used with **geboren** when referring to persons who are no longer alive.

   Goethe wurde in Frankfurt geboren.
   Goethe was born in Frankfurt.

5. The verb **lassen** (to let) is used with a dependent infinitive to express causative action, that is, having or letting someone perform something.

   Sie lassen ein Haus bauen.
   They are having a house built.

6. When **lassen** is used in a compound tense with a dependent infinitive, the past participle is replaced by a form identical with the infinitive, thus forming a "double infinitive."

   Mein Onkel hat ein neues Haus bauen lassen (in place of **gelassen**).
   My uncle had a new house built.

   Note that this "double infinitive" is similar to that involving modal auxiliary verbs (page 106, C5).

7. The verbs **hören** (to hear) and **sehen** (to see), when used in compound tenses, also form a "double infinitive" if an infinitive depends upon them. Note that English uses either the infinitive or the present participle.

   a. **Sie hatte ihn singen hören** (in place of **gehört**).

      She had heard him sing.

   b. **Die Mädchen haben ihre Freundinnen kommen sehen** (in place of **gesehen**).

      The girls saw their girl friends coming.

8. In the interrogative expression **was für ein?** (what kind of?), the indefinite article **ein** is inflected and agrees with the noun it modifies, but **was** and **für** remain unchanged.

   a. **Was für einen Grund hat er?**

      What kind of reason does he have?

   b. **Mit was für einem Bleistift schreiben Sie?**

      What kind of pencil are you writing with?

   In the plural the form is **was für?**

   c. **Was für Gründe hat sie?**

      What kind of reasons does she have?

9. Dates may be expressed by the phrase **im Jahre** (in the year) plus the number of the year (a), or by the number of the year alone (b).

   a. **Im Jahre 1955 (neunzehnhundertfünfundfünfzig) haben unsere Verwandten uns besucht.**

      Our relatives visited us in (the year) 1955.

   b. **1949 (Neunzehnhundertneunundvierzig) sind wir nach Deutschland gefahren.**

      We went to Germany in 1949.

D. EXERCISES

WRITE THE FOLLOWING SENTENCES IN GERMAN AND BE ABLE TO EXPRESS THEM ORALLY IN CLASS.

1. We are glad to see you.
2. Washington was born in 1732.
3. She is having another table made.
4. In what kind of town do they live?
5. My aunt succeeded in selling her house.
6. Have you seen the children eating?
7. The king had had a castle built in 1600.
8. It looked as if it had rained.

9. When was your brother born?
10. The teacher was having the lesson written.
11. We had never seen him work.
12. Where was Bismarck born?
13. My brother is having a brown suit made.
14. It was a shame that we had to go away.
15. We'll have the door closed.
16. We had seen them play last summer.
17. My cousins were born in 1950.
18. He was sorry that you did not go in his store.
19. My grandfather had the window opened.
20. What kind of shoes does he like to wear?
21. When was Napoleon born?
22. Has your friend succeeded in finding a dentist?
23. Did you hear the students talking?
24. The war began in the year 1939.

E. READING AND SPEAKING

I. READ THE FOLLOWING ALOUD UNTIL YOU ARE THOROUGHLY FAMILIAR WITH IT.

Wien

Von München fuhren Hans und Walter in die Alpen, wo ihnen die hohen, schneebedeckten (snow-covered) Berge sehr gefielen und zu manchen schönen Ausflügen (excursions) verlockten (attracted). Dann fuhren sie nach Wien, der Hauptstadt von Österreich. Als sie 5 ankamen, war es sehr warm in der Stadt. Hans wollte sich die Stadt ansehen, aber Walter wollte lieber schwimmen gehen. Also fragten sie die Leute im Hotel, wo sie ein gutes Freiluftbad (outdoor swimming pool) finden könnten. Man riet ihnen, mit der Straßenbahn nach Grinzing zu fahren und dann mit dem Autobus zum Krapfenwaldl. 10 Als sie ankamen, fanden sie ein schönes Freiluftbad mitten im Wald, wo sie den ganzen Tag schwimmen konnten. Von dort konnten sie auch die ganze Stadt und die Donau (Danube) sehen.

Am nächsten Morgen gingen sie durch die Stadt und besuchten die Hofburg, die Winterresidenz der Kaiser des Heiligen Römischen 15

Reiches[1]. In der Nähe sahen sie Standbilder (statues) von Mozart,
Goethe, Schiller und Grillparzer, dem größten Dramatiker (dramatist)
Österreichs. Natürlich gingen sie auch in die alten Kirchen. Im
Stephansdom[2] sahen sie die Grabstätten (tombs) der Kardinäle und
20 der alten Habsburger Herzöge (dukes).

Was sie am meisten interessierte war das Schloß Schönbrunn, wo
die Habsburger während der Sommermonate wohnten. Maria Theresia
ließ es im Jahre 1794 bauen. Es waren viele Zimmer im Schloß, und
sie waren alle sehr schön eingerichtet (furnished).

25 Überall sahen sie Erinnerungen (mementos) an die zweitausend-
jährige Geschichte (history) Wiens und Österreichs. Sie sahen die
Reste (remains) eines alten römischen Lagers (camp) und viele
Denkmäler (monuments) für die Feldherren (generals) in den Kriegen
(wars) gegen (against) Österreichs Feinde (enemies), von den Kriegen
30 gegen die Türken bis zum ersten Weltkrieg (World War).

II. ANSWER THE FOLLOWING QUESTIONS IN GERMAN.

1. Was gefiel Hans und Walter in den Alpen?
2. Wer wollte schwimmen gehen?
3. Womit sind sie nach Grinzing gefahren?
4. Wo liegt das Freiluftbad?
5. Was konnten sie vom Freiluftbad sehen?
6. Wo hatten die alten Kaiser des Heiligen Römischen Reiches im
     Winter gewohnt?
7. Wessen Grabstätten haben sie im Stephansdom gesehen?
8. Wer hat das Schloß Schönbrunn bauen lassen?
9. In welcher Jahreszeit hatten die Habsburger in Schönbrunn gewohnt?
10. Was haben Hans und Walter überall gesehen?

[1] das Heilige Römische Reich   the Holy Roman Empire.   [2] Stephansdom   St.
Stephen's Cathedral.

☛ UNIT 29

A. UNITS OF SPEECH AND VOCABULARY
I. STUDY AND READ ALOUD.

Er macht das Licht an.	He's putting on the light.
Sie ärgert sich über das Kind.	She's annoyed at the child.
Man errichtet ihm ein Denkmal.	They are erecting a monument to him.
Sie kämmt sich die Haare.	She's combing her hair.
Das Konzert findet morgen statt.	The concert is taking place tomorrow.
Je mehr er sieht, desto mehr will er.	The more he sees, the more he wants.
Ich packe die Hosen in den Koffer.	I'm packing my trousers in the bag.
Die Stadt hat eine Million Einwohner.	The city has a million inhabitants.
Der Dichter hat im vorigen Jahrhundert gelebt.	The poet lived in the last century.

das Denkmal, -s, -er	the monument	**das Haar, -s, -e**	the hair
der Dichter, -s, -	the poet	**die Hose, -, -n**	the (pair of) trousers
der Einwohner, -s, -	the inhabitant	**die Jacke, -, -n**	the jacket

231

das Jahrhundert,		**niemand**	no one, nobody
-s, -e	the century	**voriger, vorige,**	
die Katze, -, -n	the cat	**voriges**	previous, last
der Koffer, -s, -	the bag, trunk	**je** (+ *comp.*)	the (+ *comp.*)
das Konzert, -s, -e	the concert	**. . . desto** (+	. . . the (+
das Licht, -es, -er	the light	*comp.*)	*comp.*)
die Maus, -, ⸗e	the mouse	**sich ärgern**	to be annoyed
die Million, -, -en	the million	**+ über + acc.**	at
laut	loud	**errichten**	to erect
jeder	everyone,	**kämmen**	to comb
	everybody	**packen**	to pack
jemand	someone,		
	somebody		

an-machen	machte . . . an	angemacht		to put on (a light)
fangen	fing	gefangen	**fängt**	to catch
statt-finden	fand . . . statt	stattgefunden		to take place

II. DRILL. EXPRESS ORALLY IN GERMAN. REPEAT UNTIL IT IS NO LONGER
NECESSARY TO REFER TO SECTION I.

a. 1. He's putting on the light. 2. Someone is putting on the light.
3. Someone put on the light. 4. No one put on the light. 5. No
one is putting on the light.

b. 1. She's annoyed at the child. 2. Everyone is annoyed at my friend.
3. Everyone was annoyed at my friend. 4. We were annoyed at
the boy. 5. They were annoyed at the boy. 6. I was annoyed at
his son and his daughter. 7. No one was annoyed at them.

c. 1. They are erecting a monument to him. 2. They are erecting a
monument to the poet. 3. They erected a monument to the poet.
4. We erected a monument to the poet. 5. We erected a monument
to the poets.

d. 1. She's combing her hair. 2. He's combing his hair. 3. Everybody
is combing his hair. 4. The child is combing his hair. 5. The
man is combing his hair.

e. 1. The concert is taking place tomorrow. 2. The concert is taking
place next week. 3. The concert took place yesterday. 4. The
concert has just taken place.

f. 1. The more he sees, the more he wants. 2. The more she sees, the more she wants. 3. The more the girl sees, the more she wants. 4. The more the child sees, the more he wants. 5. The more the children see, the more they want.

g. 1. I'm packing my trousers in the bag. 2. He's packing his trousers in the bag. 3. He packed his trousers in the bag. 4. He packed his jacket in the trunk. 5. I've packed my jacket in the bag. 6. I had packed my jacket and my trousers in the trunk.

h. 1. The city has a million inhabitants. 2. This city has a million inhabitants. 3. This state has a million inhabitants. 4. That village has a thousand inhabitants. 5. My village has a thousand inhabitants.

i. 1. The poet lived in the last century. 2. The poet died in the last century. 3. The king died in the last century. 4. The king lived in the last century.

j. 1. The cat... 2. The cat is catching the mouse. 3. The cat caught the mouse. 4. These cats had caught many mice.

k. 1. ...loud 2. The children are very loud. 3. They sing too loud. 4. Speak louder, please.

B. MODEL SENTENCES

I. STUDY UNTIL EACH SENTENCE CAN BE GIVEN CORRECTLY FROM THE ENGLISH.

243. Hunderte von Kindern gehen in die Schule.
244. Tausende von Menschen waren auf der Straße.
245. Berlin hat drei Millionen Einwohner.
246. Je langsamer das Kind spricht, desto besser verstehe ich es.
247. Es versteht sich.
248. Kein Wasser war zu haben.
249. Das Lernen ist schwer.
250. Beim Lesen spricht er nie.
251. Sie denkt daran, nach Hause zu gehen.
252. Er wartet darauf, daß seine Freunde kommen.
253. Bitte seien Sie nicht so laut!

243. Hundreds of children go to school.

244. Thousands of people were on the street.
245. Berlin has three million inhabitants.
246. The slower the child speaks, the better I understand him.
247. It's understood.
248. No water was to be had.
249. Learning is difficult.
250. He never speaks while reading.
251. She's thinking of going home.
252. He's waiting for his friends to come.
253. Please don't be so loud.

II. **EXPRESS ORALLY IN GERMAN.**

a. 1. Hundreds of children go to school.   2. Hundreds of children go to the movies.   3. Hundreds of persons go to this restaurant. 4. Hundreds of people go into that building.

b. 1. Thousands of people were on the street.   2. Thousands of people were in town.   3. Thousands of travelers were in town.   4. Thousands of travelers were visiting the cities.

c. 1. Berlin has three million inhabitants.   2. Hamburg has almost two million inhabitants.   3. Vienna has almost two million inhabitants.   4. Switzerland has almost five million inhabitants.

d. 1. The slower the child speaks, the better I understand him.   2. The slower the girl speaks, the better I understand her.   3. The slower the boy speaks, the better I understand him.   4. The slower the children speak, the better I understand them.

e. 1. It's understood.   2. That's understood.   3. This is understood.

f. 1. No water was to be had.   2. No coffee was to be had.   3. No tea was to be had.   4. No bread was to be had.   5. No cheese was to be had.

g. 1. Learning is difficult.   2. Learning is important.   3. Learning is not easy.

h. 1. He never speaks while reading.   2. He never smiles while reading. 3. He never smokes while reading.   4. He never eats while reading. 5. He never drinks while reading.

i. 1. She's thinking of going home.   2. He's thinking of going home. 3. He's thinking of going to town.   4. We are thinking of going to town.   5. They are thinking of going to the restaurant.   6. They are thinking of going to the store.

j. 1. He's waiting for his friends to come. 2. He's waiting for his relatives to come. 3. She's waiting for her parents to come. 4. She's waiting for her girl friends to come. 5. We are waiting for our cousins to come. 6. We are waiting for our acquaintances to come.

k. 1. Please don't be so loud. 2. Please don't be so loud, Mr. Schmidt. 3. Please don't be so loud, Miss Meyer.

C. GRAMMAR

1. **Hundert** (hundred) and **Tausend** (thousand), when used as nouns, are capitalized, form their plural by adding **-e,** and are followed by **von** (of) with the dative case.
   a. **Hunderte von Kindern gehen in die Schule.**
      Hundreds of children go to school.
   b. **Tausende von Menschen waren auf der Straße.**
      Thousands of people were on the street.

2. **Million** (million) is always a noun and therefore always capitalized. It is followed directly by a noun.
   a. **Die Stadt hat eine Million Einwohner.**
      The city has a million inhabitants.
   b. **Berlin hat drei Millionen Einwohner.**
      Berlin has three million inhabitants.

3. **Je . . . desto** (the . . . the) is used as follows: **je** plus the comparative form of an adjective or adverb in the subordinate clause, **desto** plus the comparative form in the main clause, to indicate a proportional relationship.
   a. **Je mehr er sieht, desto mehr will er.**
      The more he sees, the more he wants.
   b. **Je langsamer das Kind spricht, desto besser verstehe ich es.**
      The slower the child speaks, the better I understand him.

4. Reflexive constructions are sometimes substituted for passive forms. Note that their English equivalents are expressed in the passive voice.
   a. **Es versteht sich.**
      It's understood.
   b. **Das lernt sich leicht.**
      That is easily learned.

5. The verb **sein** (to be) plus **zu** and an infinitive can also be substituted for the passive.

Kein Wasser war zu haben.

No water was to be had.

Note: For a substitute construction with **man,** see page 165, C6.

6. An infinitive may be used as a neuter noun.

a. **Das Lernen ist schwer.**

Learning is difficult.

b. **Beim Lesen spricht er nie.**

He never speaks while reading.

Note that such verbal nouns are usually equivalent to English verbal nouns ending in -ing.

7. A **da(r)**-compound (see page 130, C1) is used to anticipate an infinitive clause that is dependent upon a verb followed by a preposition, such as **denken an** (to think of), **warten auf** (to wait for).

a. **Sie denkt daran, nach Hause zu gehen.**

She is thinking of going home.

A **daß**-clause is used when two different subjects are employed.

b. **Er wartet darauf, daß seine Freunde kommen.**

He is waiting for his friends to come.

8. The command forms of **sein** (to be) are

sei be (for persons addressed as **du**)

seid be (for persons addressed as **ihr**)

seien Sie be (for persons addressed as **Sie**)

D. EXERCISES

WRITE THE FOLLOWING SENTENCES IN GERMAN AND BE ABLE TO EXPRESS THEM ORALLY IN CLASS.

1. We saw hundreds of cars in town.
2. No one was to be seen on the street.
3. The longer he works, the more money he gets.
4. My parents are thinking of taking a trip to Europe.
5. Four million Americans have read this book.
6. The little boy was talking while eating.
7. Hans, be here at six o'clock.
8. These lessons are easily done.

9. Thousands of children have visited this museum.
10. I remembered that your cousin took a trip to Switzerland.
11. This painting is not to be sold.
12. Don't wait for me to put the light on.
13. Munich now has a million inhabitants.
14. Such shoes are not to be bought any more.
15. The man was smoking a cigarette while eating.
16. The professor has hundreds of books.
17. The less he sleeps, the more tired he looks.
18. These sentences are to be written in German.
19. Do you listen to the radio while dressing?
20. How many million inhabitants does this state have?
21. The more the pupils read, the more they learn.
22. Your book will soon be found.
23. They have built thousands of houses since the war.
24. Children, be at home when your friends come.

E. READING AND SPEAKING

I. READ THE FOLLOWING ALOUD UNTIL YOU ARE THOROUGHLY FAMILIAR
WITH IT.

In Nürnberg

Als sie im Zug von Wien nach Nürnberg fuhren, las Walter wieder
im Reiseführer.

„Was liest du jetzt?" fragte Hans.

„Ich lese das Kapitel (chapter) über Nürnberg und seine Geschichte. 5
Weißt du, daß Nürnberg die Stadt der Spielzeuge (toys) genannt
wird?"

„Das habe ich nicht gewußt. Kannst du mir noch mehr erzählen?"

„In Nürnberg macht man auch Fahrräder (bicycles) und Motor-
räder, aber die Stadt ist nicht nur wegen ihrer Industrie berühmt. Im 10
Jahre 1835 wurde hier die erste deutsche Eisenbahnstrecke (railroad),
Nürnberg-Fürth, eröffnet (opened). Jetzt werde ich nicht mehr lesen,
denn der Zug hält (is stopping). Wir können alles mit eigenen Augen
sehen."

Vom Bahnhof gingen sie über die Straße und sahen sich das Frauentor 15
an, das ein Teil der alten Stadtmauern (city walls) ist. Die Mauern und

Türme aus dem 14.¹ und 15. Jahrhundert sind sehr gut erhalten
(preserved). Die beiden Freunde besuchten das Haus, wo Albrecht
Dürer, der berühmte Nürnberger Maler des 16. Jahrhunderts, gewohnt
20 hatte. Sie sahen sich die alte Burg aus dem 12. Jahrhundert an, aber
was sie am meisten interessierte, war die neue Jugendherberge (youth
hostel), wo die jungen Leute für sehr wenig Geld übernachten² können.

Nachdem sie sich die Sehenswürdigkeiten der Stadt angesehen
hatten, aßen sie zu Mittag. Dann gingen sie die Königstraße entlang
25 und besuchten einige Kaufhäuser, wo sie Geschenke (gifts) für ihre
Verwandten kauften. Am Abend gingen sie ins Kino.

II. ANSWER THE FOLLOWING QUESTIONS IN GERMAN.

1. Welche Stadt wird die Stadt der Spielzeuge genannt?
2. Wann ist die erste deutsche Eisenbahnstrecke eröffnet worden?
3. Aus welchem Jahrhundert sind die Stadtmauern?
4. Welcher berühmte Maler hat in Nürnberg gelebt?
5. Wo können junge Leute in Nürnberg übernachten?
6. Warum sind Hans und Walter in die Kaufhäuser gegangen?
7. Was haben sie am Abend getan?

---

¹ German ordinal numbers may be written as a numeral followed by a period:
vierzehnten.   ² **übernachten**   stay overnight.

☞ UNIT 30

A. UNITS OF SPEECH AND VOCABULARY

I. STUDY AND READ ALOUD.

Sie kosten vier Mark das Dutzend.	They cost four marks a dozen.
Es kostet eine Mark das Kilo.	It costs one mark a kilogram.
Das Kalbfleisch schmeckt mir.	I like the veal.
Wir machen einen Spaziergang.	We are taking a walk.
Ich setze mir den Hut auf.	I'm putting on my hat.
Ich freue mich auf meinen Geburtstag.	I'm looking forward to my birthday.
Sie freut sich über das Geschenk.	She's pleased with the gift.
Die Schreibmaschine gehört ihm.	The typewriter belongs to him.
Ich interessiere mich für alte Briefmarken.	I'm interested in old stamps.
Sie wohnen in der Goethestraße.	They live on Goethe Street.
einen Spaziergang machen	to take a walk
in der Goethestraße	on Goethe Street

die Birne, -, -n	the pear	**der Geburtstag,**		
die Briefmarke,	the (postage)	**-s, -e**		the birthday
-, -n	stamp	**das Geschenk,**		
das Dutzend, -s, -e	the dozen	**-s, -e**		the gift
der Fisch, -es, -e	the fish	**das Kalbfleisch, -es** the veal		

239

das Kilo, -s, -s	the kilogram	der Spaziergang,	
die Mark, -, -	the mark	-s, ⁼e	the walk
die Münze, -, -n	the coin	sich freuen	to look for-
der Nachtisch,		+ auf + *acc.*	ward (with
-es, -e	the dessert		pleasure) to
der Park, -s, -e	the park	sich freuen	to be pleased
der Pfirsich, -s, -e	the peach	+ über + *acc.*	with
das Rindfleisch, -es	the beef	gehören + *dat.*	to belong (to)
der Schinken, -s, -	the ham	sich interessieren	to be interested
die Schreib-		+ für + *acc.*	(in)
maschine, -, -n	the typewriter	schmecken + *dat.*	to taste (good to)

| sich auf-setzen | setzte sich . . . auf | aufgesetzt | to put on |

II. DRILL. EXPRESS ORALLY IN GERMAN. REPEAT UNTIL IT IS NO LONGER
NECESSARY TO REFER TO SECTION I.

a. 1. They cost four marks a dozen.   2. They cost five marks a dozen.
3. They cost six marks a dozen.   4. They cost three marks a dozen.

b. 1. It costs one mark a kilogram.   2. The pears cost one mark a
kilogram.   3. These pears cost one mark a kilogram.   4. The large
pears cost one mark a kilogram.   5. The large peaches cost one
mark a kilogram.   6. These peaches cost one mark a kilogram.
7. The peaches cost one mark a kilogram.

c. 1. I like the veal.   2. I like the beef.   3. I like the ham.   4. I like
the fish.   5. I like the dessert.   6. He likes the dessert.   7. He likes
the fish.   8. He likes the ham.   9. He likes the beef.   10. He likes
the veal.   11. She likes the veal.   12. She likes the beef.   13. We
like the ham.   14. We like the fish.   15. Do you like the dessert?

d. 1. We are taking a walk.   2. We are taking a walk in the park.
3. They are taking a walk in the park.   4. She's taking a walk in
the park.   5. I'm taking a walk in the park.

e. 1. I'm putting on my hat.   2. He's putting on his hat.   3. The man
is putting on his hat. 4. The woman is putting on her hat.
5. She's putting on her hat.

f. 1. I'm looking forward to my birthday.   2. The child is looking forward to his birthday. 3. The girl is looking forward to her birthday. 4. The boy is looking forward to his birthday.

g. 1. She's pleased with the gift. 2. He's pleased with the gift. 3. My brother is pleased with the gift. 4. My mother is pleased with the gift.

h. 1. The typewriter belongs to him. 2. The typewriter belongs to her. 3. The typewriter belongs to me. 4. The typewriter belongs to us. 5. Does the typewriter belong to you?

i. 1. I'm interested in old stamps. 2. We are interested in old stamps. 3. He's interested in old stamps. 4. He's interested in old coins. 5. She's interested in old coins. 6. Are you interested in old coins?

j. 1. They live on Goethe Street. 2. She lives on Goethe Street. 3. He lives on Goethe Street. 4. I live on Goethe Street. 5. Do you live on Goethe Street?

B. MODEL SENTENCES

I. STUDY UNTIL EACH SENTENCE CAN BE GIVEN CORRECTLY FROM THE ENGLISH.

254. **Der vor dem Hause sitzende Mann liest ein Buch.**
255. **Die Schüler haben die vom Lehrer geschriebenen Sätze gelernt.**
256. **Hamburg ist eine in der ganzen Welt bekannte Stadt.**
257. **Ohne „Auf Wiedersehen" zu sagen, hat er das Haus verlassen.**
258. **Anstatt seinen Freund zu besuchen, ist er ins Kino gegangen.**
259. **Die Schuhe kosten dreißig Mark das Paar.**
260. **Wollen Sie diesen Hut oder d e n Hut?**
261. **Wer ihn kennt, ist sein Freund.**
262. **Wer dieses Buch liest, dem gefällt es.**
263. **Was er kauft, ist teuer.**

254. The man sitting in front of the house is reading a book.
255. The pupils studied the sentences written by the teacher.
256. Hamburg is a city well known throughout the whole world.
257. He left the house without saying "Good-by."
258. He went to the movies instead of visiting his friend.
259. The shoes cost thirty marks a pair.
260. Do you want this hat or that hat?

261. Whoever knows him is his friend.
262. Whoever reads this book likes it.
263. Whatever he buys is expensive.

II. DRILL. EXPRESS ORALLY IN GERMAN.

a. 1. The man sitting in front of the house is reading a book. 2. The man sitting in front of the house is reading a story. 3. The man sitting in front of the house is reading a letter. 4. The boy sitting in front of the house is eating an apple. 5. The boy sitting in front of the house is eating a piece of cake.

b. 1. The pupils studied the sentences written by the teacher. 2. The pupils (*f.*) studied the sentences written by the teacher. 3. The children studied the sentences written by the teacher (*f.*). 4. The girls studied the sentences written by the teacher (*f.*).

c. 1. Hamburg is a city well known throughout the whole world. 2. Berlin is a city well known throughout the whole world. 3. Munich is a city well known throughout the whole world. 4. Vienna is a city well known throughout the whole world.

d. 1. He left the house without saying "Good-by." 2. She left the house without saying "Good-by." 3. She came into the living room without saying "Good morning." 4. They came into the building without saying "Good morning."

e. 1. He went to the movies instead of visiting his friend. 2. She went to the movies instead of visiting her sister. 3. They went to town instead of visiting their parents. 4. I went to town instead of visiting my parents.

f. 1. The shoes cost thirty marks a pair. 2. These shoes cost thirty marks a pair. 3. Her shoes cost forty marks a pair. 4. His shoes cost fifty marks a pair.

g. 1. Do you want this hat or that hat? 2. Does he want this hat or that hat? 3. Does she want this hat or that hat? 4. Does your brother want this hat or that hat?

h. 1. Whoever knows him is his friend. 2. Whoever sees him is his friend. 3. Whoever sees her is her friend. 4. Whoever knows her is her friend.

i. 1. Whoever reads this book likes it. 2. Whoever reads the book likes it. 3. Whoever reads your book likes it. 4. Whoever reads his book likes it.

j. 1. Whatever he buys is expensive. 2. Whatever he gets is expensive. 3. Whatever he learns is important. 4. Whatever he does is important.

C. GRAMMAR

1. A participle or a descriptive adjective modifying a noun may itself be preceded by modifying elements. The participle or adjective has strong or weak endings like any descriptive adjective preceding a noun.

   a. **Der vor dem Hause sitzende Mann liest ein Buch.**
   The man sitting in front of the house is reading a book.

   b. **Die Schüler haben die vom Lehrer geschriebenen Sätze gelernt.**
   The pupils studied the sentences written by the teacher.

   c. **Hamburg ist eine in der ganzen Welt bekannte Stadt.**
   Hamburg is a city well known throughout the whole world.

   These constructions are *not* normally used in conversation, but they are common in literature and in scientific writing. In conversation, such constructions are replaced by relative clauses. The sentences above could be reconstructed as follows:

   a. **Der Mann, der vor dem Hause sitzt, liest ein Buch.**

   b. **Die Schüler haben die Sätze gelernt, die der Lehrer geschrieben hat.**

   c. **Hamburg ist eine Stadt, die in der ganzen Welt bekannt ist.**

2. The prepositions **anstatt** (instead of), **ohne** (without), and **um** (in order) may be used with **zu** and an infinitive.

   a. **Ohne „Auf Wiedersehen" zu sagen, hat er das Haus verlassen.**
   He left the house without saying "Good-by."

   b. **Anstatt seinen Freund zu besuchen, ist er ins Kino gegangen.**
   He went to the movies instead of visiting his friend.

   c. **Ich gehe in die Schule, um Deutsch zu lernen.**
   I go to school in order to learn German.

3. Nouns denoting units of measure require the definite article when used distributively.

    a. **Es kostet eine Mark das Kilo.**

       It costs one mark a kilogram.

    b. **Sie kosten vier Mark das Dutzend.**

       They cost four marks a dozen.

    c. **Die Schuhe kosten dreißig Mark das Paar.**

       The shoes cost thirty marks a pair.

   Note that **Mark** is unchanged in the plural.

4. The definite article is frequently used with stress in the sense of "that."

                 Wollen Sie diesen Hut oder d e n Hut?

                 Do you want this hat or that hat?

   Note that stress is indicated in print by spacing the type.

5. **Wer** (who, whoever) and **was** (what, whatever, that which) are used as relative pronouns without antecedents. They refer back to no specific nouns, unlike **der** (who, which, that) and **welcher** (who, which, that), which always have antecedents (see pages 147-148).

    a. **Wer ihn kennt, ist sein Freund.**

       Whoever knows him is his friend.

    b. **Was er kauft, ist teuer.**

       Whatever he buys is expensive.

   Note: In the above sentences, **der** or **das** may be added for emphasis.

    a. **Wer ihn kennt, der ist sein Freund.**

    b. **Was er kauft, das ist teuer.**

6. When a different case form is required in each clause, the appropriate form of the demonstrative pronoun **der** (he, that one) or **das** (that) *must* be used in the main clause.

    a. **Wer dieses Buch liest, dem gefällt es.**

       Whoever reads this book likes it.

D. EXERCISES

WRITE THE FOLLOWING SENTENCES IN GERMAN AND BE ABLE TO EXPRESS THEM ORALLY IN CLASS.

1. Whoever lives in this city knows my uncle.
2. Do you like this house or that one?
3. The girl waiting on the corner got on the bus.
4. This cheese costs three marks a kilogram.

5. My brother went out of the room without closing the door.
6. Give me whatever you have.
7. This book belongs to me, and that book belongs to him.
8. My sister wants more money in order to take a trip to Germany.
9. My shoes usually cost sixty marks a pair.
10. Whoever eats this fish likes it.
11. That woman is older than this woman.
12. He gave me the letter without reading it.
13. Did you see the man standing on the corner?
14. The little child wants whatever he sees.
15. The pupil ran quickly in order to be home before one o'clock.
16. You can have either this chair or that chair.
17. The father paid for the cake ordered by his children.
18. Whatever he writes is interesting.
19. These gloves cost ten marks a pair.
20. That is a painting famous throughout the whole world.
21. He went to bed without eating supper.
22. Whoever was in the kitchen ate the whole cake.
23. The boy played with his friends instead of studying his lessons.
24. Whoever was here yesterday will be here again tomorrow.

E. READING AND SPEAKING

I. READ THE FOLLOWING ALOUD UNTIL YOU ARE THOROUGHLY FAMILIAR
WITH IT.

Göttingen und Hannover

Von Nürnberg fuhren Hans und Walter mit der Eisenbahn (by rail)
nach Göttingen, wo sie sich die berühmte Universität ansahen. Sie
erinnerten sich daran, daß der Dichter Heine vor fast 140 Jahren an
der Universität studiert hatte. Dann fuhren sie nach Hannover weiter,   5
das wegen seiner Gärten berühmt ist. Der große Garten mit Orangerie,
Theater und Wasserspielen (fountains) gefiel ihnen sehr.

Hans sagte: „Dieser Garten hat dem ehemaligen (former) Königs-
haus (royal house) Hannover gehört. Ich erinnere mich jetzt daran,
daß die englischen Könige von Hannover gekommen sind."   10
„Ja", sagte Walter. „Georg I. wurde im 18. Jahrhundert König
von England und es war sein Großenkel (great-grandson), Georg III.,

der 1776 den Krieg gegen die dreizehn amerikanischen Kolonien führte
(carried on)."

15   „Jetzt ist Hannover die Hauptstadt des Landes Niedersachsen", las
Hans aus dem Reiseführer vor (aloud).

Vom Garten fuhren Hans und Walter zu den Messegeländen (fair
grounds), wo die deutsche Industrie ihre Ausstellungen (exhibits) hat.
Dann fuhren sie den Maschsee, einen großen See im Park, entlang.
20 Sie wollten schwimmen gehen, aber es war zu kühl.

„Ich bin müde", sagte Hans, „und ich habe Hunger."

„Gehen wir zum Kröpckeplatz. Das Café Kröpcke soll sehr gut
sein", sagte Walter.

Nachdem sie zu Abend gegessen hatten, gingen Hans und Walter
25 ins Theater, wo ein Schauspiel (play) von Shakespeare aufgeführt
(presented) wurde. Dann machten sie einen kleinen Spaziergang, bevor
sie wieder zum Hotel gingen. Das Wetter war schön. Der Mond und
die Sterne schienen am Himmel.

Am Morgen standen sie sehr früh auf, um wieder nach Hamburg
30 zu fahren, wo der große Dampfer wartete, der sie nach den Vereinigten Staaten zurückbringen sollte.

II. ANSWER THE FOLLOWING QUESTIONS IN GERMAN.

1. Wohin sind Hans und Walter von Nürnberg gefahren?
2. Welcher deutsche Dichter hatte an der Universität Göttingen
   studiert?
3. Welche Stadt ist wegen ihrer Gärten berühmt?
4. Welche Könige sind von Hannover gekommen?
5. Wer hat den Krieg gegen die dreizehn amerikanischen Kolonien
   geführt?
6. Warum konnten Hans und Walter nicht schwimmen gehen?
7. Wo haben sie zu Abend gegessen?
8. Was taten sie, ehe sie wieder zum Hotel gingen?
9. Wohin sind sie am Morgen gefahren?
10. Was hat dort auf sie gewartet?

☛ APPENDIXES

APPENDIXES

APPENDIX A   PRONUNCIATION GUIDE

The best way to learn to pronounce any language properly is to imitate the pronunciation of a good speaker. The following guide is provided for reference when such a speaker is not available. The student must realize that English equivalents are only approximate. They are to be used only as starting points. Imitate your instructor's pronunciation as closely as you can.

1. VOWELS

All German vowels are usually short before double consonants and long otherwise. Double vowels and vowels followed by **h** are long.

Short Vowels

GERMAN SPELLING	APPROXIMATE ENGLISH EQUIVALENT	ILLUSTRATION
a	*a*rt	Mann
ä	b*e*d	hätte
e	b*e*t	Bett
i	p*i*n	bin
o	c*o*me	kommen
ö	No equivalent. Round lips for *o* as in c*o*me, and pronounce *e* as in b*e*d.	könnte

249

GERMAN SPELLING	APPROXIMATE ENGLISH EQUIVALENT	ILLUSTRATION
u	p*u*ll	Fluß
ü	No equivalent. Round lips for *u* as in p*u*ll, and pronounce *i* as in p*i*n.	Flüsse

Long Vowels

a	f*a*ther	Vater
ä	f*ai*r	Väter
e	th*ey*	Weg Tee geht
i	mach*i*ne	gib ihr
o	Like *o* in r*o*pe, but without glide into *u*.	so Boot Ohr
ö	No equivalent. Round lips for *o* as in r*o*pe, and pronounce *e* as in th*ey*.	Söhne
u	p*oo*l	Fuß
ü	No equivalent. Round lips for *oo* as in p*oo*l, and pronounce *i* as in mach*i*ne.	Füße

2. DIPHTHONGS.

au	b*ou*gh	Baum
ai	r*i*de	Mai

GERMAN SPELLING	APPROXIMATE ENGLISH EQUIVALENT	ILLUSTRATION
ei	r*i*de	mein
äu	b*oy*	Bäume
eu	b*oy*	Leute
ie[1]	bel*ie*ve	sie

3. CONSONANTS.

b beginning a syllable	*b*ad	Bett geben
b ending a syllable	li*p*	gab
d beginning a syllable	*d*o	da jeder
d ending a syllable	bel*t*	Geld
f	*f*ive	fünf
g beginning a syllable	*g*ive	geben Tage
g ending a syllable[2]	like ch (see below)	Tag Weg
h at beginning of word	*h*ave	haben
h other than above	*h*onor, a*h*	sehen sah
j	*y*es	ja
k	*k*ing	Katze

[1] Although written with two symbols, this is really only a single sound. The pronunciation of ie in sie is exactly the same as that of i in gib or ihr.
[2] This is the North German pronunciation. In South Germany, Austria, and Switzerland, it is pronounced like *k*.

GERMAN SPELLING	APPROXIMATE ENGLISH EQUIVALENT	ILLUSTRATION
l	*l*augh, *never* like *l* in ba*ll*	lachen soll
m	*m*an	Mann
n	*n*ame	Name
p	*p*ost	Post
r	No equivalent. Made by trilling tip of tongue against ridge of gum behind upper front teeth, or back of tongue against soft palate. At end of syllable, similar to *r* in New England or Southern U. S. speech.	reden durch hier
s at beginning of syllable	*z*ebra	so Gläser
s at end of syllable	thi*s*	Glas
t	*t*o	tat
v	*f*or	vor
v in words of Latin or French origin	No*v*ember	November
w	*v*ine	Wein
z	ca*ts*	zehn schwarz

4. CONSONANT COMBINATIONS.

ch after **a, o, u, au**	No equivalent. Like *h* in a*h*em when clearing one's throat.	lachen noch Buch

GERMAN SPELLING	APPROXIMATE ENGLISH EQUIVALENT	ILLUSTRATION
ch other than above	No equivalent. Like *h* in *h*ue.	lächeln ich möchte solch durch
ck	sti*ck*er	stecken
ng	si*ng*	singen
pf	cu*pf*ul	Apfel
sch	*sh*ave	schreiben
ß	*s*o	Fluß
th	*Th*omas	Theater
tz	ca*ts*	sitzen

Several letters occurring only in words of foreign origin not appearing in the vocabulary of this text have been omitted. They are:

c before **a, o, u, au**	*k*ing	Café
c before **ä, e, i**	ca*ts*	Cäsar
qu	Like *kv*	Quelle
x	fo*x*	Max
y	Like German **ü.**	Physiker

5. SYLLABICATION.

When it becomes necessary to break a word at the end of a line, single consonants usually go with the following syllable, for example: **a-ber, De-zem-ber.** Consonant combinations representing a single consonant sound stay together: **Ti-sche.** Exceptions are **ng** and **ck,** which are broken up into **n-g** and **k-k** respectively: **sin-gen, stek-ken.** Compound words are broken so as to keep their component parts intact: **ein-ander.**

6. PUNCTUATION.

All subordinate clauses, including relative clauses, and infinitive phrases
consisting of one or more words in addition to **zu** and the infinitive,
are set off by commas:

    a. **Ich werde meinen Onkel sehen, wenn er uns besucht.**

    b. **Die Mädchen, die hier waren, sind jetzt fortgegangen.**

    c. **Der Schüler lief schnell, um vor ein Uhr zu Hause zu sein.**

    d. **Er geht zur Schule, um Deutsch zu lernen.**

APPENDIX B   DECLENSIONS

1. DECLENSION OF NOUNS.

	SINGULAR	PLURAL
NOM.	der Lehrer	die Lehrer
GEN.	des Lehrers	der Lehrer
DAT.	dem Lehrer	den Lehrern
ACC.	den Lehrer	die Lehrer
NOM.	die Hand	die Hände
GEN.	der Hand	der Hände
DAT.	der Hand	den Händen
ACC.	die Hand	die Hände
NOM.	das Haus	die Häuser
GEN.	des Hauses	der Häuser
DAT.	dem Hause	den Häusern
ACC.	das Haus	die Häuser
NOM.	die Aufgabe	die Aufgaben
GEN.	der Aufgabe	der Aufgaben
DAT.	der Aufgabe	den Aufgaben
ACC.	die Aufgabe	die Aufgaben
NOM.	der Professor	die Professoren
GEN.	des Professors	der Professoren
DAT.	dem Professor	den Professoren
ACC.	den Professor	die Professoren

NOM.	der Student	die Studenten
GEN.	des Studenten	der Studenten
DAT.	dem Studenten	den Studenten
ACC.	den Studenten	die Studenten

NOM.	das Hotel	die Hotels
GEN.	des Hotels	der Hotels
DAT.	dem Hotel	den Hotels
ACC.	das Hotel	die Hotels

2. STRONG DECLENSION OF ADJECTIVES.

	SINGULAR	PLURAL
NOM.	guter Freund	gute Freunde
GEN.	guten[1] Freundes	guter Freunde
DAT.	gutem Freund(e)	guten Freunden
ACC.	guten Freund	gute Freunde

NOM.	gute Freundin	gute Freundinnen
GEN.	guter Freundin	guter Freundinnen
DAT.	guter Freundin	guten Freundinnen
ACC.	gute Freundin	gute Freundinnen

NOM.	gutes Kind	gute Kinder
GEN.	guten[1] Kindes	guter Kinder
DAT.	gutem Kind(e)	guten Kindern
ACC.	gutes Kind	gute Kinder

3. WEAK DECLENSION OF ADJECTIVES.

	SINGULAR	PLURAL
NOM.	der alte Mann	die alten Männer
GEN.	des alten Mannes	der alten Männer
DAT.	dem alten Mann(e)	den alten Männern
ACC.	den alten Mann	die alten Männer

NOM.	welche junge Frau?	welche jungen Frauen?
GEN.	welcher jungen Frau?	welcher jungen Frauen?
DAT.	welcher jungen Frau?	welchen jungen Frauen?
ACC.	welche junge Frau?	welche jungen Frauen?

[1] The en ending of the masculine genitive singular and the neuter genitive singular has not been discussed in this text, because it occurs rarely in conversational German.

NOM.	dieses neue Buch	diese neuen Bücher
GEN.	dieses neuen Buches	dieser neuen Bücher
DAT.	diesem neuen Buch(e)	diesen neuen Büchern
ACC.	dieses neue Buch	diese neuen Bücher

4. DECLENSION OF ADJECTIVES AFTER ein-WORDS.

	SINGULAR	PLURAL
NOM.	kein guter Mann	keine guten Männer
GEN.	keines guten Mannes	keiner guten Männer
DAT.	keinem guten Mann(e)	keinen guten Männern
ACC.	keinen guten Mann	keine guten Männer
NOM.	ihre junge Tochter	ihre jungen Töchter
GEN.	ihrer jungen Tochter	ihrer jungen Töchter
DAT.	ihrer jungen Tochter	ihren jungen Töchtern
ACC.	ihre junge Tochter	ihre jungen Töchter
NOM.	unser neues Buch	unsere neuen Bücher
GEN.	unseres neuen Buches	unserer neuen Bücher
DAT.	unserem neuen Buch(e)	unseren neuen Büchern
ACC.	unser neues Buch	unsere neuen Bücher

5. DECLENSION OF PERSONAL PRONOUNS.

SINGULAR

NOM.	ich	[du]	er	es	sie
GEN.	meiner[1]	[deiner[1]]	seiner[1]	seiner[1]	ihrer[1]
DAT.	mir	[dir]	ihm	ihm	ihr
ACC.	mich	[dich]	ihn	es	sie

PLURAL

NOM.	wir	[ihr]	sie	Sie
GEN.	unser[1]	[euer[1]]	ihrer[1]	Ihrer[1]
DAT.	uns	[euch]	ihnen	Ihnen
ACC.	uns	[euch]	sie	Sie

[1] The genitive forms of the personal pronouns are rarely used in modern German and have therefore not been discussed in this functional text.

APPENDIX C   VERBS

1. AUXILIARY VERBS.

INFINITIVE

haben to have	**sein** to be	**werden** to become

PAST PARTICIPLE

gehabt	gewesen	geworden

PRESENT INDICATIVE

ich habe	ich bin	ich werde
du hast	du bist	du wirst
er hat	er ist	er wird
wir haben	wir sind	wir werden
ihr habt	ihr seid	ihr werdet
sie haben	sie sind	sie werden
Sie haben	Sie sind	Sie werden

PAST INDICATIVE

ich hatte	ich war	ich wurde
du hattest	du warst	du wurdest
er hatte	er war	er wurde
wir hatten	wir waren	wir wurden
ihr hattet	ihr wart	ihr wurdet
sie hatten	sie waren	sie wurden
Sie hatten	Sie waren	Sie wurden

FUTURE INDICATIVE

ich werde haben	ich werde sein	ich werde werden
du wirst haben	du wirst sein	du wirst werden
er wird haben	er wird sein	er wird werden

wir werden haben	wir werden sein	wir werden werden
ihr werdet haben	ihr werdet sein	ihr werdet werden
sie werden haben	sie werden sein	sie werden werden
Sie werden haben	Sie werden sein	Sie werden werden

PRESENT PERFECT

ich habe gehabt	ich <u>bin</u> gewesen	ich <u>bin</u> geworden
du hast gehabt	du bist gewesen	du bist geworden
er hat gehabt	er ist gewesen	er ist geworden
wir haben gehabt	wir sind gewesen	wir sind geworden
ihr habt gehabt	ihr seid gewesen	ihr seid geworden
sie haben gehabt	sie sind gewesen	sie sind geworden
Sie haben gehabt	Sie sind gewesen	Sie sind geworden

PAST PERFECT

ich hatte gehabt	ich <u>war</u> gewesen	ich <u>war</u> geworden
du hattest gehabt	du warst gewesen	du warst geworden
er hatte gehabt	er war gewesen	er war geworden
wir hatten gehabt	wir waren gewesen	wir waren geworden
ihr hattet gehabt	ihr wart gewesen	ihr wart geworden
sie hatten gehabt	sie waren gewesen	sie waren geworden
Sie hatten gehabt	Sie waren gewesen	Sie waren geworden

FUTURE PERFECT

ich werde gehabt haben	ich werde gewesen <u>sein</u>
du wirst gehabt haben	du wirst gewesen sein
er wird gehabt haben	er wird gewesen sein
wir werden gehabt haben	wir werden gewesen sein
ihr werdet gehabt haben	ihr werdet gewesen sein
sie werden gehabt haben	sie werden gewesen sein
Sie werden gehabt haben	Sie werden gewesen sein

ich werde geworden <u>sein</u>
du wirst geworden sein
er wird geworden sein
wir werden geworden sein
ihr werdet geworden sein
sie werden geworden sein
Sie werden geworden sein

PRESENT SUBJUNCTIVE I

ich habe	ich sei	ich werde
du habest	du seist	du werdest
er habe	er sei	er werde

wir haben	wir seien	wir werden
ihr habet	ihr seiet	ihr werdet
sie haben	sie seien	sie werden
Sie haben	Sie seien	Sie werden

PRESENT SUBJUNCTIVE II

ich hätte	ich wäre	ich würde
du hättest	du wärest	du würdest
er hätte	er wäre	er würde
wir hätten	wir wären	wir würden
ihr hättet	ihr wäret	ihr würdet
sie hätten	sie wären	sie würden
Sie hätten	Sie wären	Sie würden

PAST SUBJUNCTIVE I

ich habe gehabt	ich sei gewesen	ich sei geworden
du habest gehabt	du seist gewesen	du seist geworden
er habe gehabt	er sei gewesen	er sei geworden
wir haben gehabt	wir seien gewesen	wir seien geworden
ihr habet gehabt	ihr seiet gewesen	ihr seiet geworden
sie haben gehabt	sie seien gewesen	sie seien geworden
Sie haben gehabt	Sie seien gewesen	Sie seien geworden

PAST SUBJUNCTIVE II

ich hätte gehabt	ich wäre gewesen	ich wäre geworden
du hättest gehabt	du wärest gewesen	du wärest geworden
er hätte gehabt	er wäre gewesen	er wäre geworden
wir hätten gehabt	wir wären gewesen	wir wären geworden
ihr hättet gehabt	ihr wäret gewesen	ihr wäret geworden
sie hätten gehabt	sie wären gewesen	sie wären geworden
Sie hätten gehabt	Sie wären gewesen	Sie wären geworden

FUTURE SUBJUNCTIVE

ich werde haben	ich werde sein	ich werde werden
du werdest haben	du werdest sein	du werdest werden
er werde haben	er werde sein	er werde werden
wir werden haben	wir werden sein	wir werden werden
ihr werdet haben	ihr werdet sein	ihr werdet werden
sie werden haben	sie werden sein	sie werden werden
Sie werden haben	Sie werden sein	Sie werden werden

CONDITIONAL

ich würde haben	ich würde sein	ich würde werden
du würdest haben	du würdest sein	du würdest werden
er würde haben	er würde sein	er würde werden
wir würden haben	wir würden sein	wir würden werden
ihr würdet haben	ihr würdet sein	ihr würdet werden
sie würden haben	sie würden sein	sie würden werden
Sie würden haben	Sie würden sein	Sie würden werden

FUTURE PERFECT SUBJUNCTIVE

ich werde gehabt haben ich werde gewesen <u>sein</u> ich werde geworden <u>sein</u>
etc. etc. etc.

CONDITIONAL PERFECT

ich würde gehabt haben   ich würde gewesen <u>sein</u>
etc.   etc.

ich würde geworden <u>sein</u>
etc.

IMPERATIVE

habe!	sei!	werde!
habt!	seid!	werdet!
haben Sie!	seien Sie!	werden Sie!

2. MODAL AUXILIARIES.

PRESENT INDICATIVE

dürfen	können	mögen
(may, to be permitted to)	(can, to be able to)	(to like to, to care to)
ich darf	ich kann	ich mag
du darfst	du kannst	du magst
er darf	er kann	er mag
wir dürfen	wir können	wir mögen
ihr dürft	ihr könnt	ihr mögt
sie dürfen	sie können	sie mögen
Sie dürfen	Sie können	Sie mögen

müssen	sollen	wollen
(must, to have to)	(to be to, to be supposed to)	(to want to)
ich muß	ich soll	ich will
du mußt	du sollst	du willst
er muß	er soll	er will

wir müssen	wir sollen	wir wollen
ihr müßt	ihr sollt	ihr wollt
sie müssen	sie sollen	sie wollen
Sie müssen	Sie sollen	Sie wollen

PAST INDICATIVE

ich durfte	ich konnte	ich mochte
du durftest	du konntest	du mochtest
er durfte	er konnte	er mochte
wir durften	wir konnten	wir mochten
ihr durftet	ihr konntet	ihr mochtet
sie durften	sie konnten	sie mochten
Sie durften	Sie konnten	Sie mochten

ich mußte	ich sollte	ich wollte
du mußtest	du solltest	du wolltest
er mußte	er sollte	er wollte
wir mußten	wir sollten	wir wollten
ihr mußtet	ihr solltet	ihr wolltet
sie mußten	sie sollten	sie wollten
Sie mußten	Sie sollten	Sie wollten

FUTURE INDICATIVE

ich werde dürfen (können, mögen, müssen, sollen, wollen) etc.

PRESENT PERFECT

ich habe gedurft (gekonnt, gemocht, gemußt, gesollt, gewollt) etc.

PAST PERFECT

ich hatte gedurft (gekonnt, gemocht, gemußt, gesollt, gewollt) etc.

FUTURE PERFECT

ich werde gedurft (gekonnt, gemocht, gemußt, gesollt, gewollt) haben
etc.

PRESENT SUBJUNCTIVE I

ich dürfe	ich könne	ich möge
du dürfest	du könnest	du mögest
er dürfe	er könne	er möge
wir dürfen	wir können	wir mögen
ihr dürfet	ihr könnet	ihr möget
sie dürfen	sie können	sie mögen
Sie dürfen	Sie können	Sie mögen

ich müsse	ich solle	ich wolle
du müssest	du sollest	du wollest
er müsse	er solle	er wolle
wir müssen	wir sollen	wir wollen
ihr müsset	ihr sollet	ihr wollet
sie müssen	sie sollen	sie wollen
Sie müssen	Sie sollen	Sie wollen

PRESENT SUBJUNCTIVE II

ich dürfte ich könnte ich möchte ich müßte ich sollte ich wollte etc.

PAST SUBJUNCTIVE I

ich habe gedurft (gekonnt, gemocht, gemußt, gesollt, gewollt)
du habest gedurft (gekonnt, gemocht, gemußt, gesollt, gewollt) etc.

PAST SUBJUNCTIVE II

ich hätte gedurft (gekonnt, gemocht, gemußt, gesollt, gewollt) etc.

FUTURE SUBJUNCTIVE

ich werde dürfen (können, mögen, müssen, sollen, wollen)
du werdest dürfen (können, mögen, müssen, sollen, wollen) etc.

CONDITIONAL

ich würde dürfen (können, mögen, müssen, sollen, wollen) etc.

FUTURE PERFECT SUBJUNCTIVE

ich werde gedurft (gekonnt, gemocht, gemußt, gesollt, gewollt) haben
du werdest gedurft (gekonnt, gemocht, gemußt, gesollt, gewollt) haben
etc.

CONDITIONAL PERFECT

ich würde gedurft (gekonnt, gemocht, gemußt, gesollt, gewollt) haben etc.

3. INFLECTION OF A WEAK AND A STRONG VERB.

Active

INFINITIVE

sagen to say   laufen to run

PRESENT PARTICIPLE

sagend   laufend

PAST PARTICIPLE

gesagt   gelaufen

PRESENT INDICATIVE

ich sage	ich laufe
du sagst	du läufst
er sagt	er läuft
wir sagen	wir laufen
ihr sagt	ihr lauft
sie sagen	sie laufen
Sie sagen	Sie laufen

PAST INDICATIVE

ich sagte	ich lief
du sagtest	du liefst
er sagte	er lief
wir sagten	wir liefen
ihr sagtet	ihr lieft
sie sagten	sie liefen
Sie sagten	Sie liefen

FUTURE INDICATIVE

ich werde sagen	ich werde laufen
du wirst sagen	du wirst laufen
er wird sagen	er wird laufen
wir werden sagen	wir werden laufen
ihr werdet sagen	ihr werdet laufen
sie werden sagen	sie werden laufen
Sie werden sagen	Sie werden laufen

PRESENT PERFECT

ich habe gesagt	ich bin gelaufen
du hast gesagt	du bist gelaufen
er hat gesagt	er ist gelaufen
wir haben gesagt	wir sind gelaufen
ihr habt gesagt	ihr seid gelaufen
sie haben gesagt	sie sind gelaufen
Sie haben gesagt	Sie sind gelaufen

PAST PERFECT

ich hatte gesagt	ich war gelaufen
du hattest gesagt	du warst gelaufen
er hatte gesagt	er war gelaufen

wir hatten gesagt	wir waren gelaufen
ihr hattet gesagt	ihr wart gelaufen
sie hatten gesagt	sie waren gelaufen
Sie hatten gesagt	Sie waren gelaufen

FUTURE PERFECT

ich werde gesagt haben	ich werde gelaufen sein
du wirst gesagt haben	du wirst gelaufen sein
er wird gesagt haben	er wird gelaufen sein
wir werden gesagt haben	wir werden gelaufen sein
ihr werdet gesagt haben	ihr werdet gelaufen sein
sie werden gesagt haben	sie werden gelaufen sein
Sie werden gesagt haben	Sie werden gelaufen sein

IMPERATIVE

sage!	laufe!
sagt!	lauft!
sagen Sie!	laufen Sie!

PRESENT SUBJUNCTIVE I

ich sage	ich laufe
du sagest	du laufest
er sage	er laufe
wir sagen	wir laufen
ihr saget	ihr laufet
sie sagen	sie laufen
Sie sagen	Sie laufen

PRESENT SUBJUNCTIVE II

ich sagte	ich liefe
du sagtest	du liefest
er sagte	er liefe
wir sagten	wir liefen
ihr sagtet	ihr liefet
sie sagten	sie liefen
Sie sagten	Sie liefen

PAST SUBJUNCTIVE I

ich habe gesagt	ich sei gelaufen
du habest gesagt	du seist gelaufen
er habe gesagt	er sei gelaufen

wir haben gesagt   wir seien gelaufen
ihr habet gesagt   ihr seiet gelaufen
sie haben gesagt   sie seien gelaufen
Sie haben gesagt   Sie seien gelaufen

PAST SUBJUNCTIVE II

ich hätte gesagt   ich wäre gelaufen
du hättest gesagt   du wärest gelaufen
er hätte gesagt   er wäre gelaufen
wir hätten gesagt   wir wären gelaufen
ihr hättet gesagt   ihr wäret gelaufen
sie hätten gesagt   sie wären gelaufen
Sie hätten gesagt   Sie wären gelaufen

FUTURE SUBJUNCTIVE

ich werde sagen   ich werde laufen
du werdest sagen   du werdest laufen
er werde sagen   er werde laufen
wir werden sagen   wir werden laufen
ihr werdet sagen   ihr werdet laufen
sie werden sagen   sie werden laufen
Sie werden sagen   Sie werden laufen

CONDITIONAL

ich würde sagen   ich würde laufen
du würdest sagen   du würdest laufen
er würde sagen   er würde laufen
wir würden sagen   wir würden laufen
ihr würdet sagen   ihr würdet laufen
sie würden sagen   sie würden laufen
Sie würden sagen   Sie würden laufen

FUTURE PERFECT SUBJUNCTIVE

ich werde gesagt haben   ich werde gelaufen sein
du werdest gesagt haben   du werdest gelaufen sein
er werde gesagt haben   er werde gelaufen sein
wir werden gesagt haben   wir werden gelaufen sein
ihr werdet gesagt haben   ihr werdet gelaufen sein
sie werden gesagt haben   sie werden gelaufen sein
Sie werden gesagt haben   Sie werden gelaufen sein

CONDITIONAL PERFECT

ich würde gesagt haben	ich würde gelaufen <u>sein</u>
du würdest gesagt haben	du würdest gelaufen sein
er würde gesagt haben	er würde gelaufen sein
wir würden gesagt haben	wir würden gelaufen sein
ihr würdet gesagt haben	ihr würdet gelaufen sein
sie würden gesagt haben	sie würden gelaufen sein
Sie würden gesagt haben	Sie würden gelaufen sein

Passive

INFINITIVE

geliebt werden   to be loved   gesehen werden   to be seen

PRESENT INDICATIVE

ich werde geliebt	ich werde gesehen
du wirst geliebt	du wirst gesehen
er wird geliebt	er wird gesehen
wir werden geliebt	wir werden gesehen
ihr werdet geliebt	ihr werdet gesehen
sie werden geliebt	sie werden gesehen
Sie werden geliebt	Sie werden gesehen

PAST INDICATIVE

ich wurde geliebt	ich wurde gesehen
du wurdest geliebt	du wurdest gesehen
er wurde geliebt	er wurde gesehen
wir wurden geliebt	wir wurden gesehen
ihr wurdet geliebt	ihr wurdet gesehen
sie wurden geliebt	sie wurden gesehen
Sie wurden geliebt	Sie wurden gesehen

FUTURE INDICATIVE

ich werde geliebt werden	ich werde gesehen werden
du wirst geliebt werden	du wirst gesehen werden
er wird geliebt werden	er wird gesehen werden
wir werden geliebt werden	wir werden gesehen werden
ihr werdet geliebt werden	ihr werdet gesehen werden
sie werden geliebt werden	sie werden gesehen werden
Sie werden geliebt werden	Sie werden gesehen werden

PRESENT PERFECT

ich **bin** geliebt worden	ich **bin** gesehen worden
du bist geliebt worden	du bist gesehen worden
er ist geliebt worden	er ist gesehen worden
wir sind geliebt worden	wir sind gesehen worden
ihr seid geliebt worden	ihr seid gesehen worden
sie sind geliebt worden	sie sind gesehen worden
Sie sind geliebt worden	Sie sind gesehen worden

PAST PERFECT

ich **war** geliebt **worden**	ich **war** gesehen **worden**
du warst geliebt worden	du warst gesehen worden
er war geliebt worden	er war gesehen worden
wir waren geliebt worden	wir waren gesehen worden
ihr wart geliebt worden	ihr wart gesehen worden
sie waren geliebt worden	sie waren gesehen worden
Sie waren geliebt worden	Sie waren gesehen worden

FUTURE PERFECT

ich werde geliebt **worden sein**	ich werde gesehen **worden sein**
du wirst geliebt worden sein	du wirst gesehen worden sein
er wird geliebt worden sein	er wird gesehen worden sein
wir werden geliebt worden sein	wir werden gesehen worden sein
ihr werdet geliebt worden sein	ihr werdet gesehen worden sein
sie werden geliebt worden sein	sie werden gesehen worden sein
Sie werden geliebt worden sein	Sie werden gesehen worden sein

PRESENT SUBJUNCTIVE I

ich werde geliebt	ich werde gesehen
du werdest geliebt	du werdest gesehen

etc.

PRESENT SUBJUNCTIVE II

ich würde geliebt	ich würde gesehen

etc.

PAST SUBJUNCTIVE I

ich sei geliebt worden	ich sei gesehen worden

etc.

PAST SUBJUNCTIVE II

ich wäre geliebt worden	ich wäre gesehen worden

etc.

FUTURE SUBJUNCTIVE

| ich werde geliebt werden | ich werde gesehen werden |
| du werdest geliebt werden | du werdest gesehen werden |

etc.

CONDITIONAL

| ich würde geliebt werden | ich würde gesehen werden |

etc.

FUTURE PERFECT SUBJUNCTIVE

| ich werde geliebt worden sein | ich werde gesehen worden sein |
| du werdest geliebt worden sein | du werdest gesehen worden sein |

etc.

CONDITIONAL PERFECT

| ich würde geliebt worden sein | ich würde gesehen worden sein |

etc.

4. IRREGULAR VERBS.

INFINITIVE	PAST	PAST PARTICIPLE	PRESENT 3RD SING.	PRESENT SUBJ. II
beginnen (begin)	begann	begonnen		
bekommen (receive)	bekam	bekommen		
beschreiben (describe)	beschrieb	beschrieben		
bestehen (consist)	bestand	bestanden		
biegen (turn)	bog	ist gebogen		
binden (tie)	band	gebunden		
bitten (ask)	bat	gebeten		
bleiben (stay)	blieb	ist geblieben		
brennen (burn)	brannte	gebrannt		brennte
bringen (bring)	brachte	gebracht		brächte
denken (think)	dachte	gedacht		dächte
dürfen (be permitted)	durfte	gedurft	darf	dürfte
empfehlen (recommend)	empfahl	empfohlen	empfiehlt	
entscheiden (decide)	entschied	entschieden		
essen (eat)	aß	gegessen	ißt	
fahren (drive)	fuhr	ist gefahren	fährt	
fallen (fall)	fiel	ist gefallen	fällt	
fangen (catch)	fing	gefangen	fängt	
finden (find)	fand	gefunden		
fließen (flow)	floß	ist geflossen		
geben (give)	gab	gegeben	gibt	
gefallen (please)	gefiel	gefallen	gefällt	
gehen (go)	ging	ist gegangen		
gelingen (succeed)	gelang	ist gelungen		
genießen (enjoy)	genoß	genossen		

gewinnen (win)	gewann	gewonnen		
haben (have)	hatte	gehabt	hat	hätte
halten (hold)	hielt	gehalten	hält	
heißen (be called)	hieß	geheißen		
helfen (help)	half	geholfen	hilft	
kennen (know)	kannte	gekannt		kennte
kommen (come)	kam	ist gekommen		
können (can)	konnte	gekonnt	kann	könnte
lassen (let)	ließ	gelassen	läßt	
laufen (run)	lief	ist gelaufen	läuft	
lesen (read)	las	gelesen	liest	
liegen (lie)	lag	gelegen		
mögen (like)	mochte	gemocht	mag	möchte
müssen (must)	mußte	gemußt	muß	müßte
nehmen (take)	nahm	genommen	nimmt	
nennen (name)	nannte	genannt		nennte
rennen (run)	rannte	ist gerannt		rennte
scheinen (shine; seem)	schien	geschienen		
schlafen (sleep)	schlief	geschlafen	schläft	
schlagen (strike)	schlug	geschlagen	schlägt	
schließen (close)	schloß	geschlossen		
schreiben (write)	schrieb	geschrieben		
schwimmen (swim)	schwamm	ist geschwommen		
sehen (see)	sah	gesehen	sieht	
sein (be)	war	ist gewesen	ist	
senden (send)	sandte	gesandt		sendete
singen (sing)	sang	gesungen		
sitzen (sit)	saß	gesessen		
sollen (be supposed to)	sollte	gesollt	soll	sollte
sprechen (speak)	sprach	gesprochen	spricht	
stehen (stand)	stand	gestanden		
tragen (carry)	trug	getragen	trägt	
treffen (meet)	traf	getroffen	trifft	
treten (step)	trat	ist getreten	tritt	
trinken (drink)	trank	getrunken		
tun (do)	tat	getan		täte
verbringen (spend)	verbrachte	verbracht		verbrächte
verlassen (leave)	verließ	verlassen	verläßt	
verlieren (lose)	verlor	verloren		
verstehen (understand)	verstand	verstanden		
wachsen (grow)	wuchs	ist gewachsen	wächst	
waschen (wash)	wusch	gewaschen	wäscht	
werden (become)	wurde	ist geworden	wird	
wissen (know)	wußte	gewußt	weiß	wüßte
wollen (want)	wollte	gewollt	will	wollte
zerreißen (tear to pieces)	zerriß	zerrissen		
ziehen (pull)	zog	gezogen		

☞ VOCABULARIES

ABBREVIATIONS

acc.	accusative	*gen.*	genitive
adj.	adjective	*impers.*	impersonal
adv.	adverb	*pl.*	plural
comp.	comparative	*prep.*	preposition
conj.	conjunction	*pron.*	pronoun
dat.	dative		

GERMAN-ENGLISH

Note: Unless the accent is indicated, words are accented on the first syllable. However, words with inseparable prefixes are accented on the root syllable. Verbs with separable prefixes are hyphenated.

der **Abend, -s, -e** evening; **am** — in the evening; **heute abend** this evening, tonight; **zu** — **essen** to eat supper

das **Abendessen, -s** supper; **vor dem** — before supper; **nach dem** — after supper

abends in the evening; P.M.

aber but

ab-fahren (fuhr . . . ab, ist abgefahren; fährt . . . ab) to leave, depart

der **Abschied, -s, -e** departure; **beim** — at parting

acht eight

der, die, das **achte** the eighth

achtzehn eighteen

achtzig eighty

alle (*pl.*) all

alles everything; — **Fremde** everything strange, everything foreign

als than; when, as

also therefore, consequently

alt old

(das) **Ame'rika, -s** America

der **Amerika'ner, -s, -** American

die **Amerika'nerin, -, -nen** American girl, American woman

amerika'nisch American

sich **amüsie'ren** to have a good time; **sich glänzend** — to have a splendid time

an (+ *dat. or acc.*) at, to, on

anderer, andere, anderes other, different

ändern to change

angenehm pleasant

an-kommen (kam . . . an, ist angekommen; kommt . . . an to arrive

an-machen to put on (*light*)

an-rufen (rief . . . an, angerufen; ruft . . . an) to call up, telephone

sich **an-sehen (sah sich . . . an, angesehen; sieht sich . . . an)** to look at

anstatt (+ *gen.*) instead of

die **Antwort, -, -en** answer

antworten to answer

an-ziehen (zog . . . an, angezogen; zieht . . . an) to dress, put on; **sich** — to get dressed

der **Anzug, -s, ⸗e** suit

der **Apfel, -s, ⸗** apple

die **Apothe'ke, -, -n** pharmacy, drugstore

der **April', -s** April

die **Arbeit, -, -en** work

273

arbeiten to work
sich ärgern (über + *acc*.) to be vexed (about), annoyed (at)
der **Arm, -s, -e** arm
arm poor
der **Arzt, -es, ̈e** physician, doctor
auch also, too
auf (+ *dat. or acc*.) on, to, in
die **Aufgabe, -, -n** lesson
auf-hören to stop; **er hat auf-gehört zu lesen** he stopped reading
auf-machen to open
sich **auf-setzen** to put on (*a hat*)
auf-stehen (stand . . . auf, ist aufgestanden; steht . . . auf) to get up, stand up
das **Auge, -s, -n** eye
der **August', -s** August
aus (+ *dat*.) from, out of
ausgezeichnet excellent
aus-sehen (sah . . . aus, ausgesehen; sieht . . . aus) to look, appear; **gut —** to look good
die **Aussicht, -, -en** view
aus-steigen (stieg . . . aus, ist ausgestiegen; steigt . . . aus) to get off
das **Auto, -s, -s** car
der **Autobus, -busses, -busse** bus

der **Bahnhof, -s, ̈e** railroad station
bald soon
bauen to build
der **Baum, -es, ̈e** tree
(das) **Bayern, -s** Bavaria
der **Beamte, -n, -n** official; **ein Beamter** an official
sich **beeilen** to hurry
bedeuten to mean, signify
die **Bedeutung, -, -en** meaning
begegnen (+ *dat*.) (ist) to meet (*by chance*)
beginnen (begann, begonnen) to begin, start
begrüßen to greet

bei (+ *dat*.) at the house of; **— ihr** at her house; **— dem Onkel** at the uncle('s house)
beide both
der **Bekannte, -n, -n** acquaintance; **ein Bekannter** an acquaintance
bekommen (bekam, bekommen) to get, receive
der **Berg, -es, -e** mountain
(das) **Berlin', -s** Berlin
berühmt (wegen + *gen*.) famous (for)
beschreiben (beschrieb, beschrieben) to describe
besitzen (besaß, besessen) to possess
Besuch: zu — visiting
das **Beste** the best (thing)
bestehen (aus + *dat*.) to consist (of)
bestellen to order
besuchen to visit
betrachten to look at, consider
Bett: zu — to bed
bevor (*conj*.) before
bezahlen to pay
biegen (bog, ist gebogen) to turn
das **Bier, -s, -e** beer
das **Bild, -es, -er** picture; **auf dem —** in the picture
billig cheap, inexpensive
binden (band, gebunden) to tie
die **Birne, -, -n** pear
bis until
bitte please, you are welcome
bitten (um + *acc*.) (bat, gebeten) to ask (for)
blau blue
bleiben (blieb, ist geblieben) to remain, stay
der **Bleistift, -s, -e** pencil
blicken (auf + *acc*.) to glance, look (at)
die **Blume, -, -n** flower
der **Boden, -s, -** ground, floor

brauchen to need
braun brown
brennen (brannte, gebrannt) to burn
der Brief, -es, -e letter
die Briefmarke, -, -n postage stamp
bringen (brachte, gebracht) to bring
das Brot, -es, -e bread, loaf
die Brücke, -, -n bridge
der Bruder, -s, = brother
das Buch, -es, =er book
das Bundeshaus parliament building
das Büro', -s, -s office
bürsten to brush

da (*adv.*) there; (*conj.*) because, since
dahin (to) there, thither
die Dame, -, -n lady
der Dampfer, -s, - steamer, ship
der Dank, -s thanks; Gott sei —! Thank God!
danke thanks, thank you
danken (+ *dat.*) to thank
dann then
das that; — sind those are
daß (*conj.*) that
denken (dachte, gedacht) to think; ich denke an ihn I'm thinking of him
das Denkmal, -s, =er monument
denn because, for
derselbe, dieselbe, dasselbe the same
deutsch German
Deutsch German (*language*)
der Deutsche, -n, -n German; ein Deutscher a German; die Deutsche, -n, -n German girl, German woman
(das) Deutschland, -s Germany; nach — to Germany
der Dezem'ber, -s December
der Dichter, -s, - poet
dienen (+ *dat.*) to serve

der Dienstag, -s Tuesday
dies this; — sind these are
dieser, diese, dieses this, that
doch nevertheless, after all, yet
der Dom, -s, -e cathedral
die Donau, - Danube
der Donnerstag, -s Thursday
das Dorf, -es, =er village
dort there
drei three
dreimal three times
dreizehn thirteen
dreißig thirty
der, die, das dritte the third
drittens in the third place
dunkel dark
durch (+ *acc.*) through
dürfen (durfte, gedurft; darf) may, to be permitted (to); nicht — must not
Durst haben to be thirsty
das Dutzend, -s, -e dozen

eben just
die Ecke, -, -n corner; an der — on the corner, at the corner; um die — around the corner
ehe (*conj.*) before
eigen own; mein eigenes Haus my own house
ein, eine, ein a, an, one
einan'der one another
einige some
einmal once, one time
ein-steigen (in + *acc.*) (stieg ... ein, ist eingestiegen) to get in, on
ein-treten (in + *acc.*) (trat ... ein, ist eingetreten; tritt ... ein) to enter
einundzwanzig twenty-one; der, die, das einundzwanzigste the twenty-first
der Einwohner, -s, - inhabitant
einzig single; ein einziges Mal a single time, only once

das **Eis, -es** ice, ice cream
elf eleven
die **Eltern** (*pl.*) parents
empfehlen (empfahl, empfohlen; empfiehlt) to recommend
das **Ende, -s, -n** end
(das) **England, -s** England
der **Engländer, -s, -** Englishman
die **Engländerin, -, -nen** Englishwoman
Englisch English (*language*)
englisch English
der **Enkel, -s, -** grandson, grandchild
entscheiden (entschied, entschieden) to decide
entweder . . . oder either . . . or
erfahren (erfuhr, erfahren; erfährt) to experience, find out
sich erinnern (an + *acc.*) to remember
erkennen (erkannte, erkannt) to recognize
erklären to explain
errichten (+ *dat.*) to erect (to, in honor of)
erst not until
der, die, das **erste** the first; **Heute ist der — Februar** Today is the first of February
erstens in the first place
erzählen to tell, narrate
das **Essen, -s** meal, food
essen (aß, gegessen; ißt) to eat; **zu Mittag —** to eat lunch (*or* dinner); **zu Abend —** to eat supper (*or* dinner)
das **Eßzimmer, -s, -** dining room
etwas something; **— Angenehmes** something pleasant
(das) **Euro'pa, -s** Europe

fahren (fuhr, ist gefahren; fährt) to drive, ride, go
die **Fahrkarte, -, -n** (railroad *or* ship) ticket

die **Fahrt, -, -en** ride
fallen (fiel, ist gefallen; fällt) to fall
die **Fami'lie, -, -n** family
fangen (fing, gefangen; fängt) to catch
fast almost
der **Februar, -s** February
der **Feind, -es, -e** enemy
das **Feld, -es, -er** field
das **Fenster, -s, -** window
das **Fest, -es, -e** festival
finden (fand, gefunden) to find
der **Fisch, -es, -e** fish
die **Flasche, -, -n** bottle
das **Fleisch, -es** meat
fließen (floß, ist geflossen) to flow
das **Flugzeug, -s, -e** airplane
der **Fluß, des Flusses, die Flüsse** river; **an den —** to the river; **am —** at the river
folgen (+ *dat.*) (**ist**) to follow
fort-gehen (ging . . . fort, ist fort-gegangen) to go away
die **Frage, -, -n** question; **Er stellt mir eine —** He's asking me a question
fragen to ask
(das) **Frankreich, -s** France
franzö'sisch French
der **Franzo'se, -n, -n** Frenchman
Frau Mrs.; **die Frau, -, -en** woman, wife
Fräulein Miss
die **Freiheit, -** freedom
der **Freitag, -s** Friday
fremd strange, foreign; **der Fremde, -n, -n** stranger; **ein Fremder** a stranger
die **Freude, -, -n** joy, pleasure; **Das macht mir —** That gives me pleasure
freuen: es freut mich I'm glad; **sich — (auf +** *acc.*) to look forward to; **sich — (über +** *acc.*) to be pleased with

der **Freund, -es, -e** friend
die **Freundin, -, -nen** girl friend
der **Friede, -ns** peace
früh early; **morgen** — tomorrow
morning
der **Frühling, -s, -e** spring; **im** — in
spring
das **Frühstück, -s** breakfast; **vor
dem** — before breakfast; **nach
dem** — after breakfast
führen to lead; **Dieser Weg
führt zum Bahnhof** This is the
way to the railroad station
die **Füllfeder, -, -n** fountain pen
fünf five
fünfzehn fifteen
fünfzig fifty
für (+ *acc.*) for
der **Fuß, -es, ⸗e** the foot

ganz entire, whole, all of;
— **Deutschland** all of Germany; **den ganzen Sommer** the
whole summer (long)
der **Garten, -s, ⸗** garden
der **Gast, -es, ⸗e** guest
der **Gasthof, -es, ⸗e** inn
das **Gebäude, -s, -** building
geben (gab, gegeben; gibt) to
give; **es gibt** (+ *acc.*) there is;
there are
geboren born; **Wo sind Sie** —?
Where were you born?; **Wo
wurde Goethe** —? Where was
Goethe born?
der **Geburtstag, -s, -e** birthday
gefallen (gefiel, gefallen; gefällt)
to please; **das Haus gefällt
mir** I like the house
gehen (ging, ist gegangen) to go;
Wie geht es Ihnen? How are
you?; **Es geht mir gut** I'm
fine, well
gehören (+ *dat.*) to belong to
gelb yellow

das **Geld, -es, -er** money
gelingen (*impers.*) (**gelang, ist
gelungen**) to succeed; **es gelingt mir** I succeed
das **Gemälde, -s, -** painting
das **Gemüse, -s, -** vegetable
genießen (genoß, genossen) to
enjoy
das **Gepäck, -s** baggage
gerne gladly; **er lernt** — he
likes to study
das **Geschäft, -s, -e** shop; business
der **Geschäftsmann, -s, Geschäftsleute** businessman
das **Geschenk, -s, -e** gift
die **Geschichte, -, -n** story, history
die **Geschwister** (*pl.*) brothers and
sisters
das **Gesetz, -es, -e** law
das **Gesicht, -es, -er** face
gestern yesterday
gesund healthy, in good health,
well
gewinnen (gewann, gewonnen) to
win
gewöhnlich usual
glänzend splendid; **sich** — **amüsieren** to have a splendid time
das **Glas, -es, -er** glass; **ein** — **Bier**
a glass of beer
der **Glaube, -ns** faith
glauben to believe
das **Glück, -s** (good) luck; — **haben**
to be lucky
glücklich happy; **Wir wünschen
Ihnen glückliche Reise** We
wish you a pleasant trip
der **Gott, -es, -er** God
das **Gras, -es, -er** grass
grau gray
groß big, large, tall
die **Großmutter, -, ⸗** grandmother
der **Großvater, -s, ⸗** grandfather
der **Grund, -es, -e** reason
grün green
gut good

das **Haar, -s, -e** hair
haben to have
der **Hafen, -s, =** harbor
halb half; **eine halbe Stunde** half an hour; **— neun (Uhr)** half past eight (o'clock)
halten (hielt, gehalten; hält) to hold; to stop
die **Hand, -, =e** hand; **die — reichen** to shake hands
der **Handschuh, -s, -e** glove
die **Hauptstadt, -, =e** capital (city)
das **Haus, -es, =er** house; **nach Hause** home(ward); **zu Hause** at home
das **Heft, -es, -e** notebook
(das) **Heidelberg, -s** Heidelberg
heiß hot
heißen (hieß, geheißen) to be called; **Wie — Sie?** What's your name?; **ich heiße** my name is
helfen (+ dat.) (half, geholfen; hilft) to help
hell bright, light (*in color*)
der **Herbst, -es, -e** autumn, fall
herein-kommen (kam . . . herein, ist hereingekommen) to come in
Herr Mr.; **der Herr, -n, -en** gentleman
heute today; **— morgen** this morning
das **Herz, -ens, -en** heart
hier here; **— Hans** this is Hans
der **Himmel, -s, -** sky; **am — in** the sky
hinaus-gehen (ging . . . hinaus, ist hinausgegangen) to go out
hinten behind, in back
hinter (+ dat. or acc.) behind
histo′risch historical
hoch high
hoffen to hope
holen to fetch, get

hören to hear, listen to; **er hört Radio** he's listening to the radio
die **Hose, -, -n** (pair of) trousers
das **Hotel′, -s, -s** hotel
hübsch pretty
hundert a hundred, one hundred
Hunger haben to be hungry
der **Hut, -es, =e** hat

immer always; **— besser** better and better; **— mehr** more and more
in (+ dat. or acc.) in, into, at, to
interessant′ interesting
interessie′ren to interest; **sich — (für + acc.)** to be interested (in)
(das) **Ita′lien, -s** Italy
der **Italie′ner, -s, -** Italian
italie′nisch Italian

ja yes
die **Jacke, -, -n** jacket
das **Jahr, -es, -e** year
das **Jahrhun′dert, -s, -e** century
der **Januar, -s** January; **im — in** January
je ever
je (+ comp.) . . . desto (+ comp.) the (+ comp.) . . . the (+ comp.); **Je langsamer er spricht, desto besser verstehe ich ihn** The slower he speaks, the better I understand him
jeder (pron.) everyone, everybody; **jeder, jede, jedes (adj.)** each, every
jedesmal every time
jemand someone, somebody
jetzt now
der **Juli, -s** July; **im — in** July
jung young
der **Junge, -n, -n** boy
der **Juni, -s** June; **im — in** June

der **Kaffee, -s** coffee
der **Kaiser, -s, -** emperor
das **Kalbfleisch, -es** veal
kalt cold
kämmen to comb; **sich die Haare** — to comb one's hair
die **Karte, -, -n** ticket
der **Käse, -s** cheese
die **Katze, -, -n** cat
kaufen to buy
das **Kaufhaus, -es, ⸗er** department store
kein, keine, kein no, not any
der **Kellner, -s, -** waiter
kennen (kannte, gekannt) to know (= *to be acquainted with*)
kennen-lernen to get acquainted, meet (*for the first time*)
das **Kilo, -s, -s** kilogram
das **Kind, -es, -er** child
das **Kino, -s, -s** movies, movie theater
die **Kirche, -, -n** church; **in die** — to church; **in der** — in church, at church; **nach der** — after church
das **Kleid, -es, -er** dress, (*pl.*) clothes
klein small, little
klingeln to ring; **es klingelt** the bell is ringing
klopfen to knock; **es klopft** someone is knocking (at the door)
der **Koffer, -s, -** trunk, bag
(das) **Köln, -s** Cologne
Kölner (of) Cologne
kommen (kam, ist gekommen) to come
der **König, -s, -e** king
können (konnte, gekonnt; kann) can, to be able to **Deutsch** — to know German
das **Konzert', -s, -e** concert
der **Kopf, -es, ⸗e** head

kosten to cost
krank sick
die **Krawat'te, -, -n** necktie
die **Küche, -, -n** kitchen
der **Kuchen, -s, -** cake
die **Kunst, -, ⸗e** art
kurz short
die **Kusine, -, -n** cousin (*f.*)
küssen to kiss

lächeln to smile
lachen to laugh
der **Laden, -s, ⸗** store
das **Land, -es, ⸗er** country; **aufs** — to the country; **auf dem** —e in the country
lang long
langsam slow
lassen (ließ, gelassen; läßt) to let; **ein Haus bauen** — to have a house built
laufen (lief, ist gelaufen; läuft) to run
laut loud
leben to live, be alive
legen to put, lay
lehren to teach
der **Lehrer, -s, -** teacher
die **Lehrerin, -, -nen** teacher (*f.*)
leicht light (*in weight*); easy
leid: es tut mir — I'm sorry
lernen to learn, study
lesen (las, ge'esen; liest) to read
die **Leute** (*pl.*) people (*in a crowd*)
das **Licht, -s, -er** light; **das** — **anmachen** to put on the light
lieben to love
lieber rather; — **spielen** to prefer to play
liebsten: am — most gladly; **am** — **spielen** to like best to play
liegen (lag, gelegen) to lie, be (situated)
links left; **nach** — to the left

machen to do, make
das **Mädchen, -s, -** girl
der **Mai, -s** May; **im —** in May
das **Mal, -s, -e** time, occasion; **ein einziges —** only once
der **Maler, -s, -** painter
man one, people; **— sagt** one says, people say, they say
manche some
mancher, manche, manches many a
manchmal sometimes
der **Mann, -es, ⸗er** man
die **Mannschaft, -, -en** team
die **Mark, -, -** mark (*German monetary unit, equivalent to approximately 25 U.S. cents*)
der **März, -es** March; **im —** in March
die **Maus, -, ⸗e** mouse
die **Medizin', -** medicine; **eine — von der Apotheke holen** to get medicine from the drugstore
mehr more; **immer —** more and more; **nicht —** no more, not any more, no longer
mehrere several
mein my
meinen to say, think
meisten most; **die — Leute** most people
der **Mensch, -en, -en** man, human being, person
die **Milch, -** milk
die **Million', -, -en** million; **eine — Einwohner** a million inhabitants; **zwei Millionen Einwohner** two million inhabitants
die **Minu'te, -, -n** minute
mit (+ *dat.*) with; **miteinan'der** with each other
mit-kommen (kam . . . mit, ist mitgekommen) to come along
Mittag: zu — essen to eat lunch (*or* dinner)

das **Mittagessen, -s** lunch, dinner; **nach dem —** after lunch (*or* dinner)
mitten (in + *dat.*) in the middle (of); **— in der Stadt** in the middle of town
der **Mittwoch, -s** Wednesday; **am —** on Wednesday
möchte would like to
mögen (mochte, gemocht; mag) to like, care (to)
möglich possible
der **Monat, -s, -e** month; **nächsten —** next month
der **Mond, -es, -e** moon
der **Montag, -s** Monday; **am —** on Monday
montags on Monday(s)
der **Morgen, -s, -** morning; **Guten —!** Good morning! **gestern morgen** yesterday morning; **heute morgen** this morning; **Freitag morgen** Friday morning
morgen tomorrow
morgens in the morning(s), A.M.
müde tired
(das) **München, -s** Munich
die **Münze, -, -n** coin
das **Muse'um, -s, Museen** museum
müssen (mußte, gemußt; muß) must, to have (to)
die **Mutter, -, ⸗** mother

nach (+ *dat.*) after, to; **— Hause** home(ward); **fünf Minuten — acht** five minutes after eight
der **Nachbar, -s, -n** neighbor
die **Nachbarin, -, -nen** neighbor (*f.*)
nachdem (*conj.*) after
der **Nachmittag, -s, -e** afternoon; **am —** in the afternoon; **gestern nachmittag** yesterday afternoon; **heute nachmittag** this afternoon; **morgen nachmittag** tomorrow afternoon;

Sonntag nachmittag Sunday
afternoon
nachmittags in the afternoon(s)
P.M.
nächster, nächste, nächstes next
die Nacht, -, =e night; in der — at
night
nachts at night
der Nachtisch, -es dessert
die Nähe, - vicinity; in der — des
Turms near the tower
sich nähern (+ *dat.*) to approach
der Name, -ns, -n name
die Natur', - nature
neben (+ *dat. or acc.*) next to,
near
der Neffe, -n, -n nephew
nehmen (nahm, genommen;
nimmt) to take
nein no
nennen (nannte, genannt) to
name
nett nice
neu new
neun nine
neunzehn nineteen
neunzig ninety
nicht not; — wahr? isn't it?
aren't they? don't I? *etc.*
die Nichte, -, -n niece
nichts nothing; — Schlechtes
nothing bad
nie never
niemand no one, nobody
noch still, yet; — ein another;
— nicht not yet
der Norden, -s north; von Süden
nach — from south to north
die Nordsee, - North Sea
der Novem'ber, -s November
nur only

ob whether
obgleich' although
oder or
der Offizier', -s, -e officer

oft often
ohne (+ *acc.*) without
das Ohr, -s, -en ear
der Okto'ber, -s October
der Onkel, -s, - uncle
der Osten, -s east; von — nach
Westen from east to west
(das) Österreich, -s Austria
die Ostsee, - Baltic Sea

das Paar, -s, -e pair; ein — Handschuhe a pair of gloves; ein
paar Worte a few words
packen to pack
das Paket', -s, -e package
das Papier', -s, -e paper
der Park, -s, -e park
das Pferd, -es, -e horse
der Pfirsich, -s, -e peach
der Platz, -es, =e square, place
plaudern to chat
die Post, - mail; post office; mit
der — by mail
das Postamt, -s, =er post office
der Präsident', -en, -en president
der Preis, -es, -e prize
der Profes'sor, -s, Professo'ren professor
punkt zwölf Uhr (at) twelve
o'clock sharp

das Radio, -s, -s radio; — hören to
listen to the radio
der Rat, -s advice, counsel
das Rathaus, -es, =er city hall
rauchen to smoke
die Rechnung, -, -en bill
recht haben to be right
rechts right; nach — to the right
reden to talk
die Reederei', -, -en steamship company
der Regen, -s rain
regnen to rain; es regnet it is
raining
reich rich

reichen to extend, hand
reif ripe
die **Reise, -, -n** trip; **eine — machen** to take a trip
das **Reisebüro, -s, -s** travel agency
der **Reiseführer, -s, -** guide book
reisen (ist) to travel
der **Reisende, -n, -n** traveler; **ein Reisender** a traveler
rennen (rannte, ist gerannt) to run
das **Restaurant′, -s, -s** restaurant
der **Rhein, -s** Rhine; **am —** at, on the Rhine; **an den —** to the Rhine
richtig right, correct
die **Richtung, -, -en** direction; **in dieser —** in this direction
das **Rindfleisch, -es** beef
der **Ring, -s, -e** ring
rot red

die **Sache, -, -n** thing
sagen to say
sammeln to collect
der **Samstag, -s** Saturday
der **Satz, -es, ⸗e** sentence
sauber clean
schade: es ist — it's a shame
der **Schaffner, -s, -** conductor
scheinen (schien, geschienen) to shine; to seem; **die Sonne scheint** the sun is shining; **es scheint richtig zu sein** it seems to be correct
schicken to send
das **Schiff, -s, -e** ship
der **Schinken, -s, -** ham
schlafen (schlief, geschlafen; schläft) to sleep
das **Schlafzimmer, -s, -** bedroom
schlagen (schlug, geschlagen; schlägt) to strike, beat
schlecht bad, evil
schließen (schloß, geschlossen) to close
schließlich finally
schlimm bad; **das Schlimmste** the worst (thing)
das **Schloß, Schlosses, Schlösser** castle
schmecken (+ *dat.*) to taste (good to)
der **Schnee, -s** snow
schnell quick, fast
schon already
schön beautiful, nice
schreiben (schrieb, geschrieben) to write
die **Schreibmaschine, -, -n** typewriter
der **Schuh, -s, -e** shoe
die **Schuld, -, -en** debt
die **Schule, -, -n** school; **in der —** at school; **in die —** to school; **nach der —** after school
der **Schüler, -s, -** pupil
die **Schülerin, -, -nen** pupil (*f.*)
schwach weak
schwarz black
schwäbisch Swabian
die **Schweiz, -** Switzerland; **in der —** in Switzerland; **in die —** to Switzerland
schwer heavy, difficult
die **Schwester, -, -n** sister
schwimmen (schwamm, ist geschwommen) to swim
sechs six
sechzehn sixteen
sechzig sixty
der **See, -s, -n** lake; **am —** at the lake; **an den —** to the lake
die **See, -** ocean, sea; **an der —** at the sea(shore); **an die —** to the sea(shore)
sehen (sah, gesehen; sieht) to see
sehr very
seit (+ *dat.*) since
die **Seite, -, -n** side; page; **auf dieser —** on this side; **auf der anderen —** on the other side
selbst self; even

selten seldom
senden (sandte, gesandt) to send
der Septem'ber, -s September
sich setzen to sit down; sich an den
    Tisch — to sit down at the
    table
    sich himself, herself, itself,
    yourself, yourselves, them-
    selves, oneself
    sieben seven
der, die, das siebte the seventh
    siebzehn seventeen
    siebzig seventy
    singen (sang, gesungen) to sing
    sitzen (saß, gesessen) to sit
    so ... wie as ... as
    sobald' as soon as
der Sohn, -es, ²e son
    solcher, solche, solches such
der Soldat', -en, -en the soldier
    sollen (sollte, gesollt; soll) to be
    (supposed) to
der Sommer, -s, - summer; im —
    in summer
    sondern but
der Sonnabend, -s Saturday
die Sonne, -, -n sun
der Sonntag, -s Sunday
    sowohl ... als auch both ... and
(das) Spanien, -s Spain
der Spanier, -s, - Spaniard
    spanisch Spanish
    spät late
der Spaziergang, -s, ²e walk; einen
    — machen to take a walk
die Speisekarte, -, -n menu
der Speisewagen, -s, - dining car
das Spiel, -s, -e game
    spielen to play
    sprechen (sprach, gesprochen;
    spricht) to speak, talk
der Staat, -es, -en state; die Ver-
    einigten Staaten United States
die Stadt, -, ²e town, city; in der —
    in town; in die — to town,
    downtown

    stark strong
    statt-finden (fand ... statt, statt-
    gefunden) to take place
    stecken to put, stick
    stehen (stand, gestanden) to
    stand
    stehen-bleiben (blieb ... stehen,
    ist stehengeblieben) to stop
    stellen to put; er stellt mir eine
    Frage he is asking me a
    question
    sterben (starb, ist gestorben;
    stirbt) to die
der Stern, -s, -e star
die Straße, -, -n street
die Straßenbahn, -, -en streetcar;
    mit der — by streetcar
das Stück, -s, -e piece; ein — Käse
    a piece of cheese
der Student', -en, -en student
die Studen'tin, -, -nen student (*f.*),
    coed
    studie'ren to study (*at a uni-
    versity*)
der Stuhl, -es, ²e chair
die Stunde, -, -n hour; class
der Sturm, -s, ²e storm
    suchen to look for, seek
der Süden, -s south; von — nach
    Norden from south to north

der Tag, -es, -e day; acht Tage a
    week
die Tante, -, -n aunt
die Tasche, -, -n pocket
die Tasse, -, -n cup; eine — Tee
    a cup of tea
    tausend a thousand, one thou-
    sand
der Tee, -s tea
der Teil, -s, -e part
    telefonie'ren to call up
    teuer expensive, dear
das Tier, -s, -e animal
der Tisch, -es, -e table
die Tochter, -, ² daughter

das **Tor, -s, -e** gate
töten to kill
tragen (trug, getragen; trägt) to carry, wear
treffen (traf, getroffen; trifft) to meet; to hit
trinken (trank, getrunken) to drink
tun (tat, getan) to do; **es tut mir leid** I'm sorry; **ihm tun die Augen weh** his eyes hurt
die **Tür, -, -en** door
der **Turm, -s, ⸗e** tower

über (+ *dat. or acc.*) above, over
überall everywhere
die **Uhr, -, -en** clock; watch; **ein —** one o'clock; **um zwei —** at two o'clock; **Wieviel — ist es?** What time is it?
um (+ *acc.*) around; **— zwei Uhr** at two o'clock; **— zu (+ *inf.*)** in order to
und and
die **Universität', -, -en** university
unrecht haben to be wrong
unter (+ *dat. or acc.*) under
sich **unterhal'ten (unterhielt sich, unterhalten; unterhält sich)** to converse, chat

der **Vater, -s, ⸗** father
verbringen (verbrachte, verbracht) to spend
die **Vereinigten Staaten (*pl.*)** United States
verkaufen to sell
der **Verkäufer, -s, -** salesman
die **Verkäuferin, -, -nen** salesgirl
verlassen (verließ, verlassen; verläßt) to leave (behind)
verlieren (verlor, verloren) to lose
verstehen (verstand, verstanden) to understand

versuchen to try
der **Verwandte, -n, -n** relative; **ein Verwandter** a relative
der **Vetter, -s, -n** cousin
viel much; **viele** many
vier four
der, die, das **vierte** the fourth
das **Viertel, -s, -** quarter; **— nach sechs** quarter after six; **— vor eins** quarter of one
vierzehn fourteen
vierzig forty
der **Vogel, -s, ⸗** bird
das **Volk, -es, ⸗er** people, nation
von (+ *dat.*) from, of
vor (+ *dat. or acc.*) in front of; **— einem Monat** a month ago; **zehn Minuten — eins** ten minutes of one
vorgestern (the) day before yesterday
vorig previous
der **Vormittag, -s, -e** morning; **am —** in the morning
vorne forward, up front

wachsen (wuchs, ist gewachsen; wächst) to grow
wählen to elect
wahr: nicht —? isn't it? aren't they? don't I? etc.
während (+ *gen.*) during; (*conj.*) while
der **Wald, -es, ⸗er** forest, woods
wann? when? at what time?
warm warm
warten (auf + *acc.*) to wait (*for*)
warum? why?
was? what?
was für (ein)? what kind of?
waschen (wusch, gewaschen; wäscht) to wash; **sich —** to get washed
das **Wasser, -s, -** water
weder . . . noch neither . . . nor
der **Weg, -s, -e** way, road

wegen (+ *gen.*) because of, on account of

weh: mir tut der Arm — my arm hurts

weil because, since

die **Weile,** - while; **eine** — a (little) while

der **Wein, -s, -e** wine

weinen to weep

weiß white

weit far

welcher? which?

wem? (to) whom?

wen? whom?

wenig little (*in number*)

wenige few

wenn when, whenever, if

wer? who?

werden (wurde, ist geworden; wird) to become, get

das **Werk, -es, -e** work (of art)

wessen? whose?

der **Westen, -s** west; **nach** — to (the) west

das **Wetter, -s** weather

wichtig important

wie as

wie? how?

wieder again

Wiederhören: Auf — Good-by

Wiedersehen: Auf — Good-by

(das) **Wien, -s** Vienna

wieviel? how much? **Der wievielte ist heute?** What day of the month is today?

der **Wind, -es, -e** wind

der **Winter, -s,** - winter

wissen (wußte, gewußt; weiß) to know

wo? where?

die **Woche, -, -n** week

wohin? where (to)? whither?

wohnen to dwell, live

das **Wohnzimmer, -s,** - living room

wollen (wollte, gewollt; will) to want (to)

das **Wort, -es** word; die **Worte** words (*in a phrase*); die **Wörter** words (*individually*)

wünschen to wish

der **Zahn, -s, =e** tooth

der **Zahnarzt, -es, =e** dentist

zehn ten

zeigen to show

die **Zeit, -, -en** time

zerreißen (zerriß, zerrissen) to tear to pieces

ziehen (zog, gezogen) to pull

die **Zigaret'te, -, -n** cigarette

das **Zimmer, -s,** - room

zu (*adv.*) too, excessively; — (+ *dat.*) to; **zum Vater** to the father('s house); **zur Mutter** to the mother('s house)

zuerst' first

der **Zug, -es, =e** train; **mit dem** — by train

zurück'-kommen (kam . . . zurück, ist zurückgekommen) to come back

zusam'men together

zuviel' too much

zwanzig twenty

der, die, das **zwanzigste** the twentieth

zwei two

zweimal twice, two times

der, die, das **zweite** the second

zweitens in the second place

zwischen (+ *dat. or acc.*) between, among

zwölf twelve

ENGLISH-GERMAN

a, an ein, eine, ein
able: be — to können (konnte, gekonnt; kann)
above über (+ *dat. or acc.*)
account: on — of wegen (+ *gen.*)
acquaintance der Bekannte, -n, -n;
an — ein Bekannter
acquainted: become — with kennenlernen
advice der Rat, -s
after (*conj.*) nachdem; (*prep.*) nach
(+ *dat.*); **five minutes — eight** fünf
Minuten nach acht; **— all** doch
afternoon der Nachmittag, -s, -e;
in the —(s) am Nachmittag,
nachmittags; **Sunday —** Sonntag
nachmittag; **this —** heute nachmittag; **tomorrow —** morgen nachmittag
again wieder
ago vor (+ *dat.*); **a month —** vor
einem Monat
airplane das Flugzeug, -s, -e
alive: to be — leben
all (*pl.*) alle; **— of Germany** ganz
Deutschland; **— summer long** den
ganzen Sommer
almost fast
already schon
also auch
although obgleich
always immer
A.M. morgens
America (das) Amerika, -s

American der Amerikaner, -s, -;
— girl, — woman die Amerikanerin, -, -nen; (*adj.*) amerikanisch
among zwischen (+ *dat. or acc.*)
and und
animal das Tier, -s, -e
annoyed: be — (at) sich ärgern (über
+ *acc.*)
another noch ein, noch eine, noch
ein
answer die Antwort, -, -en; **to —**
antworten
any: not — kein, keine, kein
appear aus-sehen (sah . . . aus, ausgesehen; sieht . . . aus)
apple der Apfel, -s, =
approach sich nähern (+ *dat.*)
April der April, -s; **in — im** April
arm der Arm, -s, -e
around um (+ *acc.*)
arrive an-kommen (kam . . . an, ist
angekommen)
art die Kunst, -, =e
as (= *when*) als; **— . . . — so . . . wie;**
— soon — sobald
ask fragen; **— for** bitten um (+ *acc.*)
(bat, gebeten)
at an (+ *dat.*), bei (+ *dat.*), in
(+ *dat.*), um (+ *acc.*), zu (+ *dat.*);
— the corner an der Ecke; **— the
lake** am See; **— the river** am Fluß;
— the Rhine am Rhein; **— the
sea(shore)** an der See; **— the window** am Fenster; **— her house** bei

ihr; — **Mrs. Meyer's (house)** bei
Frau Meyer; — **my house** bei mir;
— **the uncle's (house)** bei dem
Onkel; — **church** in der Kirche;
— **school** in der Schule; — **one
o'clock** um ein Uhr; — **one o'clock
sharp** punkt ein Uhr; — **what time?**
wann? um wieviel Uhr? — **home**
zu Hause; — **parting** beim Abschied
August der August, -s; **in** — im
August
aunt die Tante, -, -n
Austria (das) Österreich, -s
autumn der Herbst, -es, -e; **in** — im
Herbst

bad schlecht, schlimm
bag der Koffer, -s, -
baggage das Gepäck, -s
Baltic Sea die Ostsee, -
Bavaria (das) Bayern, -s
be sein (war, ist gewesen; ist); — **able**
können (konnte, gekonnt; kann);
— **fine: I'm fine** es geht mir gut;
— **glad: I'm glad** es freut mich;
— **lucky** Glück haben; — **permitted to** dürfen (durfte, gedurft;
darf) — **situated** liegen (lag, gelegen); — **sorry: I'm sorry** es tut
mir leid; — **supposed to** sollen
(sollte, gesollt; soll); — **vexed
(about), annoyed (at)** sich ärgern
(über + *acc.*); — **well: I'm well**
es geht mir gut; **How are you?** Wie
geht es Ihnen? **there is, there are**
es ist, es sind; es gibt
beat schlagen (schlug, geschlagen;
schlägt)
beautiful schön
because da, denn, weil; — **of** wegen
(+ *gen.*)
become werden (wurde, ist geworden;
wird); — **acquainted with** kennen-
lernen
bed: to — zu Bett

bedroom das Schlafzimmer, -s, -
beef das Rindfleisch, -es
beer das Bier, -s, -e
before (*conj.*) bevor, ehe; (*prep.*) vor
(+ *dat.*)
begin beginnen (begann, begonnen)
behind (= *in back*) hinten; (*prep.*)
hinter (+ *dat. or acc.*)
believe glauben
belong (to) gehören (+ *dat.*)
Berlin (das) Berlin, -s
best: the — (*thing*) das Beste
better besser; — **and** — immer
besser
between zwischen (+ *dat. or acc.*)
big groß
bill die Rechnung, -, -en
bird der Vogel, -s, =
birthday der Geburtstag, -s, -e
black schwarz
blue blau
book das Buch, -es, =er
born geboren; **Where were you** —?
Wo sind Sie geboren?; **Where was
Goethe** —? Wo wurde Goethe
geboren?
both beide; —... **and** sowohl ... als
auch
bottle die Flasche, -, -n; a — **of milk**
eine Flasche Milch
boy der Junge, -n, -n
bread das Brot, -es, -e
breakfast das Frühstück, -s; **after** —
nach dem Frühstück; **before** —
vor dem Frühstück
bridge die Brücke, -, -n
bright hell
bring bringen (brachte, gebracht)
brother der Bruder, -s, =; **brothers and
sisters** die Geschwister (*pl.*)
brown braun
brush bürsten
build bauen
building das Gebäude, -s, -
burn brennen (brannte, gebrannt)
bus der Autobus, -busses, -busse

business das Geschäft, -s, -e; businessman der Geschäftsmann, -s, Geschäftsleute
but aber, sondern
buy kaufen

cake der Kuchen, -s, -
call: to be called heißen (hieß, geheißen); — up an-rufen (rief ... an, angerufen)
can (= be able to) können (konnte, gekonnt; kann)
capital (city) die Hauptstadt, -, ≃e
car das Auto, -s, -s
care (to) mögen (mochte, gemocht; mag)
carry tragen (trug, getragen; trägt)
castle das Schloß, Schlosses, Schlösser
cat die Katze, -, -n
catch fangen (fing, gefangen; fängt)
cathedral der Dom, -s, -e
century das Jahrhundert, -s, -e
chair der Stuhl, -es, ≃e
change ändern
chat plaudern
cheap billig
cheese der Käse, -s
child das Kind, -es, -er
church die Kirche, -, -n; after — nach der Kirche; at —, in — in der Kirche; to — in die Kirche
cigarette die Zigarette, -, -n
city die Stadt, -, ≃e; — hall das Rathaus, -es, ≃er
class die Stunde, -, -n
clean sauber
clock die Uhr, -, -en
close schließen (schloß, geschlossen)
clothes die Kleider (pl.)
coed die Studentin, -, -nen
coffee der Kaffee, -s
coin die Münze, -, -n
cold kalt
collect sammeln
Cologne Köln, -s; of — Kölner

comb kämmen; — one's hair sich die Haare kämmen
come kommen (kam, ist gekommen); — back zurück-kommen (kam ... zurück, ist zurückgekommen); — in herein-kommen (kam ... herein, ist hereingekommen)
concert das Konzert, -s, -e
conductor der Schaffner, -s, -
consequently also
consider betrachten
consist (of) bestehen (aus + dat.) (bestand, bestanden)
corner die Ecke, -, -n; at, on the — an der Ecke; around the — um die Ecke
correct richtig
cost kosten
counsel der Rat, -s
country das Land, -es, ≃er; in the — auf dem Lande; to the — aufs Land
couple das Paar, -es, -e
cousin der Vetter, -s, -n; (f.) die Kusine, -, -n
cup die Tasse, -, -n; a — of tea eine Tasse Tee

dark dunkel
daughter die Tochter, -, ≃
day der Tag, -es, -e; — before yesterday vorgestern; What — of the month is today? Der wievielte ist heute?
dear teuer
debt die Schuld, -, -en
December der Dezember, -s; in — im Dezember
decide entscheiden (entschied, entschieden)
dentist der Zahnarzt, -es, ≃e
depart ab-fahren (fuhr ... ab, ist abgefahren; fährt ... ab)
department store das Kaufhaus, -es, ≃er
departure der Abschied, -s, -e

describe beschreiben (beschrieb, beschrieben)

dessert der Nachtisch, -es

die sterben (starb, ist gestorben; stirbt)

different anderer, andere, anderes

difficult schwer

dining car der Speisewagen, -s, -

dining room das Eßzimmer, -s, -

direction die Richtung, -, -en; in this — in dieser Richtung

do machen; tun (tat, getan)

doctor der Arzt, -es, ⸗e

door die Tür, -, -en

dozen das Dutzend, -s, -e

dress das Kleid, -es, -er

dress an-ziehen (zog . . . an, angezogen); to get dressed sich anziehen

drink trinken (trank, getrunken)

drive (= ride) fahren (fuhr, ist gefahren; fährt)

drugstore die Apotheke, -, -n

during während (+ gen.)

dwell wohnen

each jeder, jede, jedes

ear das Ohr, -s, -en

early früh

east der Osten, -s; from — to west von Osten nach Westen

easy leicht

eat essen (aß, gegessen, ißt); — lunch (or dinner) zu Mittag essen; — supper (or dinner) zu Abend essen

eight acht; the eighth der, die, das achte

eighteen achtzehn

eighty achtzig

either . . . or entweder . . . oder

elderly: an — man ein älterer Mann

elect wählen

eleven elf

end das Ende, -s, -n

enemy der Feind, -es, -e

England (das) England, -s

English (adj.) englisch; (the) — (language) (das) Englisch

Englishman der Engländer, -s, -

Englishwoman die Engländerin, -, -nen

enjoy genießen, genoß, genossen

enter ein-treten (in + acc.) (trat . . . ein, ist eingetreten; tritt . . . ein)

entire der, die, das ganze

erect (to, in honor of) errichten (+ dat.)

Europe (das) Europa, -s

even selbst

evening der Abend, -s, -e; in the — am Abend; in the —(s) abends; this — heute abend; tomorrow — morgen abend; Tuesday — Dienstag abend; yesterday — gestern abend

ever je

every jeder, jede, jedes; — time jedesmal; everybody, everyone jeder

everything alles; — strange, foreign alles Fremde

everywhere überall

evil schlecht

excessively zu

expensive teuer

experience erfahren (erfuhr, erfahren; erfährt)

explain erklären

extend reichen

eye das Auge, -s, -n

face das Gesicht, -s, -er

faith (= belief) der Glaube, -ns

fall (= autumn) der Herbst, -es, -e; in — im Herbst

fall fallen (fiel, ist gefallen; fällt)

family die Familie, -, -n

famous berühmt; — for berühmt wegen (+ gen.)

far weit

fast schnell

father der Vater, -s, ⸗

February der Februar, -s; **in —** im Februar
fetch holen
few wenige; **a —** ein paar
field das Feld, -es, -er
fifteen fünfzehn
fifty fünfzig
find finden (fand, gefunden); **— out** erfahren (erfuhr, erfahren; erfährt)
fine: I'm — es geht mir gut
first zuerst; **the —** der, die, das erste; **the — of February** der erste Februar; **in the — place** erstens
fish der Fisch, -es, -e
five fünf
floor der Boden, -s, -
flow fließen (floß, ist geflossen)
flower die Blume, -, -n
follow folgen (+ *dat.*) (ist)
food das Essen, -s
foot der Fuß, -es, ⸗e
for (*conj.*) denn; (*prep.*) für (+ *acc.*); **he has been here — a year** er ist (schon) seit einem Jahr hier
foreign fremd
forest der Wald, -es, ⸗er
forty vierzig
forward (*up front*) vorne
fountain pen die Füllfeder, -, -n
four vier; **fourth** der, die, das vierte
fourteen vierzehn
France (das) Frankreich, -s; **to —** nach Frankreich
freedom die Freiheit, -
French französisch; **in —** auf französisch
Frenchman der Franzose, -n, -n
Friday der Freitag, -s; **— morning** Freitag morgen
friend der Freund, -es, -e; **girl —** die Freundin, -, -nen
from von (+ *dat.*); (= *out of*) aus (+ *dat.*)
front: up — vorne; **in — of** vor (+ *dat.*)

game das Spiel, -s, -e
garden der Garten, -s, ⸗
gentleman der Herr, -n, -en
German (*adj.*) deutsch; **(the) — language** (das) Deutsch; **in —** auf deutsch; **a —** ein Deutscher; **the —** der Deutsche, -n, -n; **the — girl, woman** die Deutsche, -n, -n
Germany (das) Deutschland, -s; **to —** nach Deutschland
get (= *fetch*) holen; (= *receive*) bekommen (bekam, bekommen); (= *become*) werden (wurde, ist geworden; wird); **— in, on** einsteigen (stieg . . . ein, ist eingestiegen) (in + *acc.*); **— up** aufstehen (stand . . . auf, ist aufgestanden)
gift das Geschenk, -s, -e
girl das Mädchen, -s, -; **— friend** die Freundin, -, -nen
give geben (gab, gegeben; gibt); **it gives me pleasure** es macht mir Freude
glad: I'm — es freut mich
gladly gerne; **most —** am liebsten
glance (at) blicken (auf + *acc.*)
glass das Glas, -es, ⸗er; **a — of beer** ein Glas Bier; **two glasses of beer** zwei Glas Bier
glove der Handschuh, -s, -e
go gehen (ging, ist gegangen); (= *to travel*) fahren (fuhr, ist gefahren; fährt); **— away** fort-gehen (ging . . . fort, ist fortgegangen); **— out** hinaus-gehen (ging . . . hinaus, ist hinausgegangen)
God der Gott, -es, ⸗er
good gut; **Good-by** Auf Wiedersehen
grandchild der Enkel, -s, -
grandfather der Großvater, -s, ⸗
grandmother die Großmutter, -, ⸗
grandson der Enkel, -s, -
grass das Gras, -es, ⸗er
gray grau
green grün

greet begrüßen
ground der Boden, -s, -
grow wachsen (wuchs, ist gewachsen; wächst)
guest der Gast, -es, ⸗e

hair das Haar, -s, -e
half halb; — an hour eine halbe Stunde; it's — past eight (o'clock) es ist halb neun (Uhr)
ham der Schinken, -s, -
hand die Hand, -, ⸗e; She is shaking hands with him Sie reicht ihm die Hand
happy glücklich
harbor der Hafen, -s, ⸗
hat der Hut, -es, ⸗e
have haben (hatte, gehabt; hat); — to müssen (mußte, gemußt; muß); — a good time sich amüsieren; — a house built ein Haus bauen lassen
head der Kopf, -es, ⸗e
health: in good — gesund
healthy gesund
hear hören
heart das Herz, -ens, -en; a weak — ein schwaches Herz
heavy schwer
Heidelberg (das) Heidelberg, -s
help helfen (+ dat.) (half, geholfen; hilft)
here hier
high hoch, höher, am höchsten
hold halten (hielt, gehalten; hält)
home: at — zu Hause; —(ward) nach Hause
hope hoffen
horse das Pferd, -es, -e
hot heiß
hotel das Hotel, -s, -s
hour die Stunde, -, -n
house das Haus, -es, ⸗er; at the — of bei (+ dat.); at her — bei ihr; to her — zu ihr; to her mother's — zu ihrer Mutter

how? wie?; How are you? Wie geht es Ihnen? — much? wieviel?
human being der Mensch, -en, -en
hundred hundert
hungry: to be — Hunger haben
hurry sich beeilen
hurt: my arm hurts mir tut der Arm weh; his eyes hurt ihm tun die Augen weh

ice (cream) das Eis, -es
if wenn
important wichtig
in in (+ dat.), an (+ dat.), auf (+ dat.); — church in der Kirche; — July im Juli; — the room im Zimmer; — school in der Schule; — (the) spring im Frühling; — town in der Stadt; — the afternoon(s) am Nachmittag, nachmittags; — the evening(s) am Abend, abends; — the morning(s) am Vormittag, vormittags; — the sky am Himmel; — the country auf dem Lande; — the middle of town mitten in der Stadt
in order to um zu (+ inf.)
inexpensive billig
inhabitant der Einwohner, -s, -
instead of anstatt (+ gen.)
interest interessieren; be interested (in) sich interessieren (für + acc.)
interesting interessant
into in (+ acc.)
Italian der Italiener, -s, -; (adj.) italienisch
Italy (das) Italien, -s; to — nach Italien

jacket die Jacke, -, -n
January der Januar, -s; in — im Januar
joy die Freude, -, -n
July der Juli, -s; in — im Juli
June der Juni, -s; in — im Juni
just eben

kill töten
kilogram das Kilo, -s, -s
kind: what — of? was für (ein)?
king der König, -s, -e
kiss küssen
kitchen die Küche, -, -n
knock klopfen; someone is knocking
at the door es klopft
know (= be acquainted with) kennen
(kannte, gekannt); — (as a fact)
wissen (wußte, gewußt; weiß);
— German Deutsch können

lady die Dame, -, -n
lake der See, -s, -n; at the — am See;
to the — an den See
large groß
last vorig
late spät
laugh lachen
law das Gesetz, -es, -e
lay legen
lead führen
learn lernen
leave: take — of Abschied nehmen
von (+ dat.)
leave (= depart) abfahren (fuhr . . .
ab, ist abgefahren; fährt . . . ab);
— (behind) verlassen (verließ, verlassen; verläßt)
left: on the — links; to the — nach
links
lesson die Aufgabe, -, -n
let lassen (ließ, gelassen; läßt)
letter der Brief, -es, -e
lie (= be situated) liegen (lag, gelegen)
light (in color) hell; (in weight) leicht
light das Licht, -s, -er; put on the —
das Licht an-machen
like mögen (mochte, gemocht; mag);
I — the house das Haus gefällt mir;
I — the veal das Kalbfleisch
schmeckt mir; I — to study ich
lerne gerne; I — best to study ich
lerne am liebsten

listen (to) hören; — to the radio
Radio hören
little (= small) klein; (a) — wenig
live (= be alive) leben; (= reside)
wohnen
living room das Wohnzimmer, -s, -
long lang; no longer nicht mehr
look (= appear) aus-sehen (sah . . .
aus, ausgesehen; sieht . . . aus);
— good gut aus-sehen; — at sich
an-sehen (sah sich . . . an, angesehen; sieht sich . . . an), betrachten, blicken auf (+ acc.); — for
suchen; — forward (with pleasure)
to sich freuen auf (+ acc.)
lose verlieren (verlor, verloren)
loud laut
love lieben
luck: good — das Glück, -s
lucky: be — Glück haben
lunch das Mittagessen, -s; eat — zu
Mittag essen

mail die Post, -; by — mit der Post
make machen
man der Mann, -es, ⸗er; (= human
being) der Mensch, -en, -en
many viele; — a mancher, manche,
manches
March der März, -es; in — im März
mark die Mark, -, - (equivalent to
approximately 25 U.S. cents)
may dürfen (durfte, gedurft; darf)
May der Mai, -s; in — im Mai
meal das Essen, -s
mean bedeuten
meaning die Bedeutung, -, -en
meat das Fleisch, -es
medicine die Medizin, -; get — from
the drugstore eine Medizin von der
Apotheke holen
meet treffen (traf, getroffen; trifft);
— (by chance) begegnen (+ dat.)
(ist); — (for the first time) kennen-
lernen
menu die Speisekarte, -, -n

middle: in the — of mitten in (+ *dat.*)
milk die Milch, -; a bottle of — eine Flasche Milch
million die Million, -, -en; a — inhabitants eine Million Einwohner; two — inhabitants zwei Millionen Einwohner
minute die Minute, -, -n
Miss Fräulein
Monday der Montag, -s; on —(s) am Montag; montags
money das Geld, -es, -er
month der Monat, -s, -e; next — nächsten Monat
monument das Denkmal, -s, =er
moon der Mond, -es, -e
more mehr; — and — immer mehr; not any — nicht mehr; the — he sees, the — he wants je mehr er sieht, desto mehr will er
morning der Morgen, -s, -; der Vormittag, -s, -e; Friday — Freitag morgen; this — heute morgen; yesterday — gestern morgen; good — guten Morgen; in the —(s) am Vormittag; morgens
most die meisten
mother die Mutter, -, =
mountain der Berg, -es, -e
mouse die Maus, -, =e
movies, movie theater das Kino, -s, -s
Mr. Herr
Mrs. Frau
much viel
Munich (das) München, -s
museum das Museum, -s, Museen
must müssen (mußte, gemußt; muß)
my mein

name der Name, -ns, -n; my — is ich heiße; What is your —? Wie heißen Sie? to — nennen (nannte, genannt); they give their —s Sie nennen ihre Namen
narrate erzählen
nation (= *people*) das Volk, -s, =er

nature die Natur, -
near neben (+ *dat. or acc.*); — the tower in der Nähe des Turms
necktie die Krawatte, -, -n
need brauchen
neighbor der Nachbar, -s, -n; (*f.*) die Nachbarin, -, -nen
neither . . . nor weder . . . noch
nephew der Neffe, -n, -n
never nie
nevertheless doch
new neu
next nächster, nächste, nächstes; — month nächsten Monat; — to neben (+ *dat. or acc.*)
nice schön
niece die Nichte, -, -n
night die Nacht, -, =e; at — in der Nacht, nachts
nine neun
nineteen neunzehn
ninety neunzig
no nein; (*adj.*) kein, keine, kein; — one niemand
nobody niemand
north der Norden, -s; from — to south von Norden nach Süden
North Sea die Nordsee, -
not nicht; — until erst
notebook das Heft, -es, -e
nothing nichts; — bad nichts Schlechtes
November der November, -s; in — im November
now jetzt

ocean die See, -
o'clock: one — ein Uhr; at one — um ein Uhr; at twelve — sharp punkt zwölf Uhr
October der Oktober, -s; in — im Oktober
of von (+ *dat.*); five minutes — eight fünf Minuten vor acht; in the middle — mitten in (+ *dat.*)
officer der Offizier, -s, -e

official der Beamte, -n, -n; **an** — ein Beamter
often oft
old alt
on auf (+ *dat. or acc.*), an (+ *dat.*), in (+ *dat.*); — **this side** auf dieser Seite; — **the other side** auf der anderen Seite; — **the corner** an der Ecke; — **Monday(s)** am Montag, montags; — **the Rhine** am Rhein; — **the river** am Fluß; — **Goethe Street** in der Goethestraße
on account of wegen (+ *gen.*)
once einmal; **only** — ein einziges Mal
one ein, eine, ein; — **another** einander; — **says** man sagt
only nur
open auf-machen
or oder
order bestellen
order: in — **to** um zu (+ *inf.*)
other anderer, andere, anderes; **another** noch ein, noch eine, noch ein
out of aus (+ *dat.*)
over über (+ *dat. or acc.*)
own eigen; **my** — **house** mein eigenes Haus; **to** — besitzen (besaß, besessen)

pack packen
package das Paket, -s, -e
page die Seite, -, -n
painter der Maler, -s, -
painting das Gemälde, -s, -
pair das Paar, -s, -e; **a** — **of gloves** ein Paar Handschuhe
paper das Papier, -s, -e
parents die Eltern (*pl.*)
park der Park, -s, -e
part der Teil, -s, -e
parting: at — beim Abschied
pay bezahlen
peace der Friede, -ns
peach der Pfirsich, -s, -e
pear die Birne, -, -n

pencil der Bleistift, -s, -e
people (= *nation*) das Volk, -es, ⸗er; (= *you, one, they*) man; — **say** man sagt; — (*in a crowd*) die Leute (*pl.*); — (= *human beings*) die Menschen (*pl.*)
permit: be permitted to dürfen (durfte, gedurft; darf)
pharmacy die Apotheke, -, -n
physician der Arzt, -es, ⸗e
picture das Bild, -es, -er; **in the** — auf dem Bild
piece das Stück, -s, -e; **a** — **of cheese** ein Stück Käse
place der Platz, -es, ⸗e; **take** — statt-finden (fand . . . statt, stattgefunden)
play spielen
pleasant angenehm
please gefallen (+ *dat.*) (gefiel, gefallen; gefällt); (**if you**) **please** bitte; **be pleased (with)** sich freuen (über + *acc.*)
pleasure die Freude, -, -n; **that gives me** — das macht mir Freude, das freut mich
P.M. nachmittags, abends
pocket die Tasche, -, -n
poet der Dichter, -s, -
poor arm
possess besitzen (besaß, besessen)
possible möglich
post office die Post, -; das Postamt, -s, ⸗er
prefer: I prefer to play ich spiele lieber
president der Präsident, -en, -en
pretty hübsch
previous vorig
prize der Preis, -es, -e
professor der Professor, -s, -en
pull ziehen (zog, gezogen)
pupil der Schüler, -s, -; (*f.*) die Schülerin, -, -nen
put legen; (= *stick*) stecken; — **a question to him** ihm eine Frage

stellen; — **on** (*a hat*) auf-setzen;
— **on** (*other clothes*) an-ziehen (zog
... an, angezogen); — **on** (*a light*)
an-machen

quarter das Viertel, -s, -; — **of one**
Viertel vor eins; — **after six**
Viertel nach sechs
question die Frage, -, -n; **he asks me**
a — er stellt mir eine Frage
quick schnell

radio das Radio, -s, -s; **listen to the** —
Radio hören
railroad station der Bahnhof, -s, ⸗e
rain der Regen, -s
rain regnen; **it is raining** es regnet
rather lieber
read lesen (las, gelesen; liest)
reason der Grund, -es, ⸗e
receive bekommen (bekam, bekommen)
recognize erkennen (erkannte; erkannt)
recommend empfehlen (empfahl, empfohlen; empfiehlt)
red rot
relative der Verwandte, -n, -n; **a** —
ein Verwandter
remain bleiben (blieb, ist geblieben)
remember sich erinnern (an + *acc.*)
request bitten (um + *acc.*) (bat,
gebeten)
restaurant das Restaurant, -s, -s
Rhine der Rhein; **at the** — am Rhein;
to the — an den Rhein
rich reich
ride die Fahrt, -, -en
right: on the — rechts; **to the** — nach
rechts; **be** — recht haben
ring der Ring, -es, -e
ripe reif
river der Fluß, Flusses, Flüsse; **at**
the — am Fluß; **to the** — an den
Fluß
room das Zimmer, -s, -

run laufen (lief, ist gelaufen; läuft);
rennen (rannte, ist gerannt)

salesgirl die Verkäuferin, -, -nen
salesman der Verkäufer, -s, -
same derselbe, dieselbe, dasselbe
Saturday der Samstag, -s, -e; der
Sonnabend, -s, -e
say sagen
school die Schule, -, -n; **after** — nach
der Schule; **at** — in der Schule;
to — in die Schule
sea die See, -; **at the** —(shore) an der
See; **to the** —(shore) an die See
second der, die, das zweite; **in the** —
place zweitens
see sehen (sah, gesehen; sieht)
seek suchen
seem scheinen (schien, geschienen);
it seems to be right es scheint
richtig zu sein
seldom selten
sell verkaufen
send schicken; senden (sandte, gesandt)
sentence der Satz, -es, ⸗e
September der September, -s; **in** —
im September
serve dienen (+ *dat.*)
seven sieben; **seventeen** siebzehn
seventh der, die, das siebte
seventy siebzig
several mehrere
shake: She is shaking hands with him
Sie reicht ihm die Hand
shame: it's a — es ist schade
sharp: (at) twelve o'clock — punkt
zwölf Uhr
shine scheinen (schien, geschienen)
ship das Schiff, -s, -e; (= *steamer*)
der Dampfer, -s, -
shoe der Schuh, -s, -e
shop das Geschäft, -s, -e
short kurz
show zeigen
sick krank

side die Seite, -, -n; **on this** — auf dieser Seite; **on the other** — auf der anderen Seite
signify bedeuten
since (*conj.*) da, weil, denn; (*prep.*) seit (+ *dat.*)
sing singen (sang, gesungen)
single einzig; **one** — **time** ein einziges Mal
sister die Schwester, -, -n
sit sitzen (saß, gesessen); — **down** sich setzen; — **down at the table** sich an den Tisch setzen
six sechs
sixteen sechzehn
sixty sechzig
sky der Himmel, -s, -; **in the** — am Himmel
sleep schlafen (schlief, geschlafen; schläft)
slow langsam
small klein
smile lächeln
smoke rauchen
snow der Schnee, -s
soldier der Soldat, -en, -en
some einige, manche
somebody jemand
someone jemand; — **is knocking at the door** es klopft
something etwas; — **pleasant** etwas Angenehmes
sometimes manchmal
son der Sohn, -es, ꞊e
soon bald
sorry: I'm — es tut mir leid
south der Süden, -s; **from** — **to north** von Süden nach Norden
Spain (das) Spanien, -s; **to** — nach Spanien
Spaniard der Spanier, -s, -
Spanish spanisch
speak sprechen (sprach, gesprochen; spricht)
spend (*time, vacations*) verbringen (verbrachte, verbracht)

splendid glänzend; **to have a** — **time** sich glänzend amüsieren
spring der Frühling, -s, -e; **in** — im Frühling
square der Platz, -es, ꞊e
stamp die Briefmarke, -, -n
stand stehen (stand, gestanden); — **up** auf-stehen (stand . . . auf, ist aufgestanden)
star der Stern, -s, -e
start beginnen (begann, begonnen)
state der Staat, -es, -en; **United States** die Vereinigten Staaten
station: railroad — der Bahnhof, -s, ꞊e
stay bleiben (blieb, ist geblieben)
steamer der Dampfer, -s, -
stick stecken
still noch; (—) **another** noch ein
stop (= *stand still*) stehen-bleiben (blieb . . . stehen, ist stehengeblieben); (= *cease*) auf-hören
store der Laden, -s, ꞊; **department** — das Kaufhaus, -es, ꞊er
storm der Sturm, -s, ꞊e
story die Geschichte, -, -n
strange fremd
stranger der Fremde, -, -n; **a** — ein Fremder
street die Straße, -, -n; **on Goethe** — in der Goethestraße
streetcar die Straßenbahn, -, -en; **by** — mit der Straßenbahn
strike schlagen (schlug, geschlagen; schlägt)
strong stark
student der Student, -en, -en; (*f.*) die Studentin, -, -nen
study lernen; — (*at a university*) studieren
succeed gelingen (*impers.*) (gelang, ist gelungen); **I** — es gelingt mir
such solcher, solche, solches
suit der Anzug, -s, ꞊e
summer der Sommer, -s, -; **in** — im Sommer; **the whole** — (**long**) den ganzen Sommer

sun die Sonne, -, -n
Sunday der Sonntag, -s, -e
supper das Abendessen, -s; **after** —
nach dem Abendessen; **before** —
vor dem Abendessen; **eat** — zu
Abend essen
supposed: be — **to** sollen (sollte,
gesollt; soll)
swim schwimmen (schwamm, ist geschwommen)
Switzerland die Schweiz; **in** — in der
Schweiz; **to** — in die Schweiz

table der Tisch, -es, -e
take nehmen (nahm, genommen;
nimmt); — **place** statt-finden (fand
. . . statt, stattgefunden); — **a trip**
eine Reise machen; — **a walk**
einen Spaziergang machen
talk reden; sprechen (sprach, gesprochen; spricht)
tall groß
taste (good to) schmecken (+ *dat.*)
tea der Tee, -s
teach lehren
teacher der Lehrer, -s, -; (*f.*) die
Lehrerin, -, -nen
team die Mannschaft, -, -en
tear to pieces zerreißen (zerriß, zerrissen)
telephone an-rufen (rief . . . an, angerufen)
tell erzählen
ten zehn
than als
thank danken (+ *dat.*); — **God!**
Gott sei Dank!
thanks, thank you danke
that (*adj.*) dieser, diese, dieses; der,
die, das; (*pron.*) das; (*conj.*) daß
then dann
there da, dort; — (= *thither*) dahin;
— **is,** — **are** es ist, es sind; es gibt
therefore also
these: — **are** dies sind
thing die Sache, -, -n

think denken (dachte, gedacht); **I** —
of (about) him ich denke an
ihn
third der, die, das dritte; **in the** —
place drittens
thirsty: be — Durst haben
thirteen dreizehn
thirty dreißig
this (*adj.*) dieser, diese, dieses; (*pron.*)
dies; — **is the way to the station**
dieser Weg führt zum Bahnhof;
— **morning** heute morgen; — **afternoon** heute nachmittag; — **evening**
heute abend
those: — **are** das sind
thousand tausend
three drei; — **times** dreimal
through durch (+ *acc.*)
Thursday der Donnerstag, -s, -e
tie binden (band, gebunden)
tie die Krawatte, -, -n
time die Zeit, -, -en; (= *occasion*)
das Mal, -s, -e; **every** — jedesmal;
one — einmal; **two times** zweimal;
three times dreimal; **to have a good**
— sich amüsieren; **to have a
splendid** — sich glänzend amüsieren; **What** — **is it?** Wieviel Uhr
ist es? **At what** — ? Um wieviel
Uhr?
tired müde
to an (+ *acc.*), auf (+ *acc.*), in
(+ *acc.*), nach (+ *dat.*), zu (+
dat.); — **bed** zu Bett; — **church** in
die Kirche; — **Germany** nach
Deutschland; — **her house** zu ihr;
— **school** in die Schule; — **Switzerland** in die Schweiz; — **town** in die
Stadt; — **the country** aufs Land;
— **the lake** an den See; — **the left**
nach links; — **the mother('s house)**
zur Mutter; — **the post office** zum
Postamt; — **the Rhine** an den
Rhein; — **the right** nach rechts;
— **the river** an den Fluß; — **the
sea(shore)** an die See; — **the west**

nach Westen; — the window ans
Fenster
today heute
tomorrow morgen; — morning morgen früh
too (= *also*) auch; (= *excessively*) zu
tooth der Zahn, -s, ⸗e
tower der Turm, -s, ⸗e
town die Stadt, -, ⸗e; in — in der
Stadt; to —, downtown in die Stadt
train der Zug, -es, ⸗e; by — mit dem
Zug
travel reisen (ist)
traveler der Reisende, -n, -n; a —
ein Reisender
tree der Baum, -es, ⸗e
trip die Fahrt, -, -en; die Reise, -, -n;
to take a — eine Reise machen
trousers die Hose, -, -n
trunk der Koffer, -s, -
try versuchen
Tuesday der Dienstag, -s, -e
turn biegen (bog, ist gebogen)
twelve zwölf
twentieth der, die, das zwanzigste
twenty zwanzig
twenty-one einundzwanzig
twice zweimal
two zwei; — times zweimal
typewriter die Schreibmaschine, -, -n

uncle der Onkel, -s, -
under unter (+ *dat. or acc.*)
understand verstehen (verstand, verstanden)
United States die Vereinigten Staaten;
to the — nach den Vereinigten
Staaten
university die Universität, -, -en
until bis; not — erst
up front vorne
usual gewöhnlich

veal das Kalbfleisch, -es
vegetable das Gemüse, -s, -

very sehr
vex: to be vexed (about) sich ärgern
(über + *acc.*)
vicinity die Nähe, -
Vienna (das) Wien, -s
view die Aussicht, -, -en
village das Dorf, -es, ⸗er
visit besuchen
wait (for) warten (auf + *acc.*)
waiter der Kellner, -s, -
walk der Spaziergang, -s, ⸗e; to take
a — einen Spaziergang machen
want (to) wollen (wollte, gewollt;
will)
warm warm
wash waschen (wusch, gewaschen;
wäscht); to get washed sich waschen
watch die Uhr, -, -en
water das Wasser, -s, -
way der Weg, -s, -e; This is the — to
the railroad station Dieser Weg
führt zum Bahnhof
weak schwach
wear tragen (trug, getragen; trägt)
weather das Wetter, -s
Wednesday der Mittwoch, -s; on —
am Mittwoch
week die Woche, -, -n; a — acht Tage
weep weinen
well gut; I'm — es geht mir gut;
(= *healthy*) gesund
west der Westen, -s; to (the) — nach
Westen
what? was? — kind of? was für
(ein)?; What kind of reason does
he have? Was für einen Grund hat
er? What kind of reasons does she
have? Was für Gründe hat sie?
What time is it? Wieviel Uhr ist
es?
when (*conj.*) als, wenn; (= *whenever*)
wenn; (= *at what time?*) wann?
where wo; (= *whither*) wohin
whether ob

which? welcher, welche, welches?
while die Weile, -; a (little) — eine
Weile; (*conj.*) während
white weiß
who? wer?
whole ganz; the — summer (long) den
ganzen Sommer
whom? wen?; (to) — ? wem?
whose? wessen?
why warum
win gewinnen (gewann, gewonnen)
wind der Wind, -es, -e
window das Fenster, -s, -
wine der Wein, -s, -e
winter der Winter, -s, -; in — im
Winter
wish wünschen
with mit (+ *dat.*)
without ohne (+ *acc.*)

woman die Frau, -, -en
woods der Wald, -es, =er
word das Wort, -es, Wörter (*individually*), Worte (*in a phrase*)
work arbeiten
work die Arbeit, -, -en; — (of art)
das Werk, -s, -e
worst: the — thing das Schlimmste
write schreiben (schrieb, geschrieben)
wrong: to be — unrecht haben

year das Jahr, -es, -e
yellow gelb
yes ja
yesterday gestern; (the) day before —
vorgestern
yet (= *nevertheless*) doch; (= *still*)
noch
young jung

INDEX

aber 121
accusative 12
  after prepositions 13, 44-45, 73
  definite time 81
  direct object 12
  duration of time 81
  two accusatives 211
adjectives
  after **alles, etwas, nichts** 140
  comparison 51, 65, 74
  declension 256-257
  derived from names of cities 194
  der-words 28
  descriptive 50, 51, 57
  ein-words 36-37, 50
  indefinite numerical 157
  modified 243
  possessive 37
  strong endings 51, 157, 256, 257
  superlative 74
  used as nouns 139-140
  used as pronouns 50
  weak endings 57, 256-257
adverbs
  comparison 74
  form 57
  of time 29
  ordinal 164
  superlative 74
alles, adjectives after 140
als 122, 211
als (ob) 195, 211
an 13, 44
anstatt zu + *inf.* 243
antworten 58, 64, 89, 99
article, definite 4, 11, 20
  contracted with prepositions 44, 164
  declension 28
  referring to articles of clothing and
    parts of the body 66
  used as demonstrative adjective 244
  with abstract nouns 211
  with names of days, months, seasons
    81
  with nouns of relationship 66

article, indefinite 4-5, 12, 20
  declension 28
  omitted before predicate nouns of
    vocation 106
auxiliary verbs 11-12
  inflection 258-261
  modals 82, 89, 91, 106, 157, 261-263

brennen 202

capitalization 5
cardinal numbers, *see* numbers
cases, *see* nominative, genitive, dative,
  accusative
clauses
  main 5, 29, 51
  subordinate 121-123, 149, 185
commands
  familiar 106, 113-114
  first person 58
  formal 43
  indirect 176
  of verbs with separable prefixes 131
  sein 236
comparison
  of adjectives 51, 65, 74
  of adverbs 74
conditional 184
conditional perfect 185
conditions
  real 185
  omission of **wenn** 185
  unreal 185-186
conjunctions 121-123
consonants 251-253

da 122
da(r)-compounds 130-131, 236
das 91, 97, 123
daß 123, 227
dates 126, 228
dative 20-21
  after certain verbs 64
  after prepositions 21, 35, 44, 45, 88,
    164